Mississippi River Bridge, Vicksburg, Mississippi

Dunleith Mansion, Natchez, Mississippi

Fine Dining
Mississippi Style

by John M. Bailey

**Recipes from eighty-eight of the most outstanding chefs
at some of the finest restaurants
and bed and breakfast inns in Mississippi**

John M. Bailey

About the author:
    Native Mississippian
    Graduate of the University of Mississippi
    Favorite hobbies: Photography, cooking and collecting cookbooks
    Associate Member of the American Culinary Federation
    Member of the North Mississippi Chefs Association ACF
    Member of the American Southern Food Institute
    John has served as a food judge for the Mississippi Gulf Coast
        Chefs Association Seafood Classic.
    John and his wife Ann reside in Germantown, Tennessee

Copyright 1999 John M. Bailey

ISBN 0-942249-05-4
Library of Congress: 99-073785

First Printing June 1999

Cover photograph by John M. Bailey
Cover design by Herschel Wells

Published by
Toof Cookbook Division
STARR★TOOF
670 South Cooper Street
Memphis, Tennessee 38104
800-722-4772

Dedicated to my wonderful wife and best friend
Ann
a great cook in her own right

Introduction

In the fall of 1997, I knew that I would be retiring at the end of the year from a sales career with a major Fortune 500 corporation. I pondered as to what I could do that would be enjoyable and yet keep me active as I started my retirement. Being a native Mississippian, I started this "project" to showcase the many fine chefs in my home state. After canvassing the entire state the last ten months, I can assure you that fine dining is alive and well!

Fine dining exists from one end of the state to the other. The food was wonderful! The state of Mississippi has always referred to itself as the Hospitality State. The chefs were most cordial during my visits to their establishments and were very agreeable to share their recipes with me for the cookbook.

Mississippi, geographically, can be divided into 4 (or 5) distinctively different regions. I chose to go with 1) The Hill Country, 2) The Delta & River Country, 3) The Heartland and 4) The Coast. As you will soon see, most of the recipes described in this book are far from the "down home" food associated with most Southern states, and Mississippi in particular.

Many of the chefs interviewed had a very diverse background in culinary experiences and training. In fact, it would be difficult to classify their style of cooking strictly as "New South". These recipes have been tested over the years in restaurants throughout Mississippi. Now enjoy them in your kitchen. They are on the house, compliments of the chef.

John M. Bailey

Acknowledgments:

All photographs pages 6-16 courtesy of Mississippi Department of Tourism unless otherwise designated

I would like to thank the following people:

The Chefs of Mississippi for all of their great recipes!

Mississippi Department of Economic and Community Development Division of Tourism Development for their beautiful pictures and helpful information.

Bill Williams Jr. AIA for the use of his wonderful line art drawings.

Natchez Division of Tourism for their help.

Northwest Mississippi Chefs Association ACF and the Mississippi Gulf Coast Chapter ACF for all of their help and encouragement.

The Catfish Institute for all of their wonderful recipes.
C. F. Gollott & Son Seafood, Inc. for all of their great seafood recipes.

I would also like to thank the following for their help on this project:

W. Jett Wilson, attorney
Ed Neal, CPA
Allen Entezari

JMB

TABLE OF CONTENTS

Please note all recipes were written and contributed by the finest chefs, restaurants and bed and breakfast establishments in Mississippi. These recipes are not written for the inexperienced cook. If there are any questions about cooking terms, please refer to the extensive glossary beginning on page 169. Some minor editing was done for added clarity on each recipe.

John M. Bailey

Mississippi Beach, pristine white sand and swaying palm trees – PHOTO BY JOHN BAILEY

Ballet Mississippi

The magnolia flower, Mississippi's state flower and tree — PHOTO BY JOHN BAILEY

Ann Bailey admiring a beautiful magnolia tree at Natchez Trace Craft Center near Jackson
— PHOTO BY JOHN BAILEY

Father Ryan House at Biloxi– PHOTO BY JOHN BAILEY

Antebellum Home – COURTESY OF MONMOUTH PLANTATION

Spanish moss-draped oak trees – PHOTO BY JOHN BAILEY

Dunn's Falls, Meridian, where Stetson hats were first made – PHOTO BY JOHN BAILEY

Mimosa tree overlooking the bay at Ocean Springs – PHOTO BY JOHN BAILEY

Rowan Oak, William Faulkner's home in Oxford– PHOTO BY JOHN BAILEY

Ruins of Windsor, near Port Gibson

Catch the wind on the beautiful Mississippi Gulf Coast – PHOTO BY JOHN BAILEY

Spectacular sunsets and warm nights are waiting in Mississippi

One hundred fifty-year-old lighthouse at Biloxi – PHOTO BY JOHN BAILEY

Cypress swamp as seen from Natchez Trace Parkway– PHOTO BY JOHN BAILEY

Mississippi Delta region, the land of cotton

Mississippi Casinos offer Las Vegas style gaming – PHOTO COURTESY OF SILVER STAR CASINO

Hot air balloon racing over the Mississippi Delta catfish ponds

CORINTH Mississippi's Gateway City is steeped in history and splendor. Corinth is known for its grand antebellum homes, Civil War battlefields and splendid Northeast Mississippi museum. Woodall Mountain, the state's highest point, is nearby in Tishomingo county. The Natchez Trace Parkway, one of the nation's finest scenic byways, begins its trek through Mississippi near here.

TUPELO The birthplace of Elvis Presley is also home to museums, golf courses, parks, and historic landmarks. The city is a mecca for history buffs, shoppers, and rock & roll pilgrimages. Tupelo is also one of the largest furniture manufacturing centers in the country. The district office for the Natchez Trace Parkway is located here.

OXFORD A Southern Classic is home to William Faulkner's Rowan Oak. The University of Mississippi Museums and the Center for the Study of Southern Culture and Blues Archive are located nearby. Oxford has been voted by several national publications as "one of the top ten retirement cities" in the United States.

COLUMBUS has some of the South's most beautiful antebellum homes and quaint antique shops. A nationally recognized Pilgrimage is held here annually. Tennessee Williams was born here and his boyhood home has been preserved and used as the Visitor's Welcome Center. Mississippi University for Women is located here.

WEST Point is located in Mississippi's Prairie Belt area. The nearby Old Waverly Golf Club will host the 1999 Ladies Professional Golf Association's national tournament.

STARKVILLE is home to Mississippi State University. Visitors can enjoy an interesting tour of the McKay Enology Laboratory on the MSU campus where muscadine wine, juice and jelly are produced. Some of the best cheese found anywhere in the South is also made here.

KOSCIUSKO is located on the Natchez Trace Parkway. It was the childhood home of television personality and talk show host Oprah Winfrey. In the Spring of the year a Natchez Trace Festival is held. Each December, a Candlelight Tour of Historic Homes is held.

THE GENERALS' QUARTERS

Bed & Breakfast Inn
924 Fillmore Street
Corinth, MS 38834

Beautifully restored two-story Victorian structure built in 1872 with many of the original features still intact. It is located in the historic district of this old Civil War town. Grounds are beautifully landscaped with a lovely pond, magnolias, roses and azaleas. Shiloh National Military Park and Pickwick Lakes are located nearby.

Luke & Charlotte Doehner, Owners

THE GENERALS' QUARTERS HOUSE SALAD

1	head cleaned and cored iceberg lettuce	4	bunches cleaned scallions
1	head cleaned and cored romaine lettuce	¼	cup toasted pecan halves semi-crushed (can use walnuts)

Dressing:

½	ounce granulated sugar	6	ounces all vegetable oil
1	ounce salt	1	teaspoon crushed garlic
3	ounces cider vinegar		

Place ingredients into a carafe and stir briskly. Be sure to shake the carafe to blend the dressing just before pouring over the salad.

Dice the iceberg and romaine lettuce into bite size pieces (approximately 1 inch square) Place into large salad bowl. Top with chopped scallions and crushed pecans. Ladle dressing over the top just before serving.

Yield: 10 salads

This salad is served with every dinner at The Generals' Quarters.

THE GENERALS' QUARTERS BISCUITS

3	cups presifted flour	¾	teaspoon salt
4½	teaspoons baking powder	¾	cup premium shortening
¾	teaspoon cream of tartar	1	large egg
2½	tablespoons granulated sugar	1	cup buttermilk
		4	tablespoons melted butter

Preheat oven to 450 degrees. Lightly butter a 12 by 18-inch sheet pan.

Sift flour, baking powder, cream of tartar, sugar and salt together into a large mixing bowl. Cut in shortening using your hands until the shortening pieces are about the size of a dime. Do not overwork. Beat the egg lightly and slowly add buttermilk. Make a well in the middle of the dry mix. Pour the egg and buttermilk mixture into the center well. Using your hand blend the ingredients together. Do not overwork. Turn the dough onto a lightly floured table. Roll to a one-inch thickness. Cut with round biscuit cutter. Place cut biscuits onto butter baking tray.

Place in preheated oven on top rack. Reduce oven temperature to 350 degrees. Bake for 20 minutes. Brush tops of biscuits with melted butter and reduce oven temperature to 200 degrees. Finish baking for an additional 10 minutes.

Yield: 24 2½-inch biscuits

These biscuits are served with breakfast and country dinners at The Generals' Quarters.

THE GENERALS' QUARTERS
COUNTRY DINNER

Honey Roasted Chicken, Oven Roasted Potatoes
& Country Vegetables

HONEY ROASTED CHICKEN

10 8-ounce bone-in chicken breasts

Egg Wash:

1 cup of water	½ teaspoon paprika
4 large eggs	1½ teaspoon crushed garlic
1 teaspoon salt	¾ cup presifted flour
½ teaspoon coarse pepper	

Basting Mix:

4 ounces honey	1 ounce lemon juice
2 ounces melted butter	

Preheat oven to 375 degrees.

In a large mixing bowl, combine salt, pepper, paprika and flour. Gently mix together with a fork. In another bowl beat eggs and water until frothy. Add crushed garlic. Add dry ingredients to wet ingredients gradually. Mix with wire whip until smooth.

Clean chicken breasts thoroughly. Remove any excess fat. Place chicken breasts into egg wash mixture (about 3 at a time). Press chicken pieces into wash until coated. Remove from wash and gently shake breast to remove excess. Place on 12-inch by 18-inch baking pan. When all 10 pieces are done, place pan of chicken breasts into preheated oven on center rack. Bake for 30 minutes.

Blend together honey, melted butter and lemon juice into a small mixing bowl. Use basting brush to blend mixture.

Remove pan of chicken breasts from the oven. Generously baste with honey mixture. Replace pan back in oven for an additional 45 minutes. Chicken will be golden brown.

OVEN ROASTED POTATOES

8 10-ounce baking potatoes	½ tablespoon coarse black pepper
4 tablespoons all vegetable oil	1 tablespoon coarse thyme
1 tablespoon salt	

Preheat oven to 375 degrees.

Clean baking potatoes and cut into 1-inch square pieces. Place vegetable oil into large frying pan. Heat to approximately 300 degrees. Add raw cut potatoes. Cook for approximately 20 minutes while turning the potatoes to brown on all sides. Sprinkle dry ingredients over potatoes and stir to coat well. Turn browned potatoes into a 4-quart baking dish. Cover and bake for 30 minutes.

COUNTRY VEGETABLES

1 large onion, chopped	4 large carrots peeled and sliced ¼-inch
4 ounces butter	
4 large zucchini peeled and sliced ¼-inch	8 ounces shredded cheddar cheese Salt and lemon pepper
8 medium yellow squash peeled and sliced ¼-inch	

In an 8-quart saucepan, sauté the onions in butter until the onions are clear. Add zucchini, squash and carrots in layers. Lightly salt and lemon pepper the layers. Cook over medium heat until tender, approximately 15 minutes.

Top with cheddar cheese. Cover with lid to melt cheese. Serve immediately.

Serves 10.

This dinner is one that resembles a meal that may have been served in an inn during the early 1900's. It is still one of the favorites here at The Generals' Quarters Bed and Breakfast Inn.

SHERRIED SWEET POTATO PECAN PIE

2   9-inch deep dish pie crust shells

Sherried Sweet Potatoes:

2½	pounds yams, peeled and boiled till soft	2	ounces sherry
½	cup butter or margarine	½	cup packed brown sugar

In a large mixing bowl, combine all ingredients. Mix until smooth.

1½	cups sherried sweet potatoes	½	teaspoon salt
1	teaspoon cinnamon	1	teaspoon vanilla extract
½	cup sugar	1	cup crushed toasted pecans
4	large eggs		
½	cup honey		

Preheat oven to 350 degrees.

Combine sherried sweet potatoes, cinnamon and honey in a large mixing bowl. In a separate bowl, combine sugar and eggs until smooth, and then add salt, vanilla and pecans. Combine both mixtures by gradually adding egg mixture to sweet potatoes while gently stirring mixture.

Pour into pie crust and bake in preheated oven for 50 minutes. Bake on center rack. Test center with toothpick for doneness. Should be served slightly warm, topped with lightly sweetened whipped cream.

Yield: 2 pies

One of the favorite desserts at The Generals' Quarters.

VANELLI'S
1302 North Gloster
Tupelo, MS 38802

John "Yanni" Kapenekas
Bill Kapenekas
Proprietors

VANELLI'S GRECIAN SPAGHETTI

2	tablespoons mushrooms	2	tablespoons sliced bell pepper
¼	cup cauliflower	⅛	cup olive oil
¼	cup broccoli		Salt (to taste)
2	tablespoons sliced onions		Pepper (to taste)
8	ounces cooked spaghetti noodles		Parmesan cheese (to taste)
		1	clove chopped, fresh garlic

Place skillet on stove with olive oil. Let the oil get hot for approximately 1 minute. Add garlic. In small container mix mushrooms, cauliflower, broccoli, bell pepper and onions. Put contents in skillet, sauté until vegetables are heated completely, approximately 2 to 3 minutes. Add salt and pepper. Add spaghetti, cook approximately 1 more minute. Place on plate and top with Parmesan cheese, then garnish. It is optional, but if an order calls for Italian sausage or shrimp; you should sauté 1 Italian sausage cut into slices or 5 shrimp, then place on top.

Serves 1.

VANELLI'S GREEK SALAD

¼ head of lettuce, chopped
½ tomato, diced
¼ red onion, chopped
2 pepperoncini peppers

¼ cucumber wedges, sliced and peeled
½ bell pepper, sliced
⅛ pound feta cheese
2 Greek olives

2 ounces salad dressing oil (regular vegetable oil for light flavor or olive oil for heavier flavor)

Dash of lemon juice

Dash of salt
Dash of granulated garlic

Dash of oregano (fresh is best)

Combine all vegetable ingredients in 8-inch bowl (except Greek olives and pepperoncini peppers. Add herbs/spices and oil/lemon mixture and mix thoroughly. Place in bowl or small plate. Place the two peppers on side of salad and put a little feta cheese on top with olives on top of that.

Serves 2.

AUTHOR'S NOTE: Some Greek salads are served with a few peeled and deveined boiled shrimp placed on the salad.

FILET MIGNON WITH TIFFANY TOPPING

Tiffany Topping:
1 pound fresh crabmeat, shredded
½ pound fresh mushrooms, sliced

10 green onions, chopped, tops only
1 cup scampi butter (See recipe below)

Topping servings: 8

Sauté mushrooms and green onion tops in scampi butter. Add crabmeat, heat thoroughly and hold at a low temperature. Grill filets to desired doneness. Top with crabmeat topping.

SCAMPI BUTTER

¾ cup butter
4 cloves garlic, crushed
¼ cup dry white wine

2 tablespoons lobster base*
Lemon juice to taste

Melt butter. Add lobster base and stir until dissolved. Add crushed garlic and sauté. Add lemon juice and wine. Heat thoroughly.

Lobster base can be ordered from restaurant supply houses if not available at your supermarket.

ZEBRA CHEESECAKE

Winner of Taste of Tupelo Dessert Award 1996

Crust:

1½	cups graham cracker crumbs	3	tablespoons melted butter
		¼	cup sugar

Filling:

4	8-ounce packages cream cheese (softened)	1	cup heavy cream or whipping cream
1¼	cups sugar	2	teaspoons vanilla extract
3	tablespoons cornstarch	8	ounces white chocolate
¼	teaspoon salt	8	ounces semisweet chocolate squares
5	large eggs		
1	8-ounce container sour cream		

Glaze:

½	cup heavy whipping cream	4	ounces semisweet chocolate squares

Early in day or day ahead:

1) Preheat oven to 350 degrees F. Grease 9 by 3-inch springform pan. In bowl, mix graham cracker crumbs, sugar and melted butter; firmly press onto bottom of springform pan for crust. Bake crust 10 to 12 minutes. Remove crust from oven and let cool.

2) In large bowl, with mixer at medium speed, beat cream cheese until light and fluffy. In small bowl, mix sugar, cornstarch and salt; gradually beat into cream cheese until blended. With mixer at low speed, gradually beat in eggs, sour cream, vanilla and 1 cup of heavy cream until blended and smooth.

3) Divide batter evenly into two 4-to-8 measuring cups or other containers with pouring spout. In small saucepan over low heat, melt 8 squares semi-sweet chocolate. In another small saucepan over very low heat, melt white chocolate. Stir melted semisweet chocolate in batter in one measuring cup and stir melted white chocolate into batter in second measuring cup.

4) To create "zebra" design, pour half of dark batter into springform pan. Holding white batter about 2 feet above pan, pour about half of batter (pouring from this height will cause batter in center of cake to be pushed toward edge of pan, forming zebra or bull's-eye design). Repeat procedure 3 times, decreasing the amounts of batter each time and pouring from high above pan only into center, ending with white batter. (Top of cake should look like a series of concentric circles.)

5) Bake cheesecake 30 minutes. Turn oven control to 225 degrees F. and bake 1 hour and 45 minutes longer or until center is set. Turn off oven; let cheesecake remain in oven 1 hour. Remove cheesecake from oven. Run thin-bladed spatula of knife around edge of cheesecake to loosen from side of pan. Cool cake in pan on wire rack. Refrigerate cheesecake at least 6 hours or until well chilled.

One hour before serving:

6) Prepare glaze: In 1-quart sauce pan over medium heat, heat remaining 4 squares semisweet chocolate until melted and smooth. Cool glaze 10 minutes. Meanwhile, carefully remove cake from pan to cake plate: with spatula, spread glaze over top and side. Refrigerate 30 to 45 minutes until glaze is set. If you like, garnish with whipped cream, Maraschino cherries and mint.

Yield: 20 servings.

Elvis Presley's Boyhood Home
Tupelo, Mississippi

THE BOTTLETREE BAKERY

923 Van Buren
Oxford, MS 38655

Cynthia Gerlach
Owner

Ms. Gerlach, an Oregon native, came to The University of Mississippi to attend the Center for the Study of Southern Culture, where she earned two degrees with an emphasis on Southern folk art. In fact, folk art by Southern artists grace the walls of the bakery. Bottletree Bakery has been featured in Mississippi magazine.

NUTMEG CAKE

Cake:

1½	cups sugar	1	teaspoon baking powder
½	cup shortening		
	Zest of one orange, chopped fine	1	teaspoon baking soda
1	teaspoon vanilla	1	whole grated nutmeg
3	eggs		
2	cups all-purpose flour	1	teaspoon salt
		1	cup buttermilk

In a large bowl of electric mixer, combine sugar, shortening, zest and vanilla. Add eggs one at a time. Sift flour, baking powder, baking soda, nutmeg, salt, and add alternately with buttermilk until well mixed. Pour batter into two 9-inch greased and floured cake pans. Bake 25 minutes at 350 degrees. Cool slightly and remove from pans. Cool.

Frosting:

3	cups brown sugar	¾	cup half and half cream
½	cup butter		
	Pinch salt	1	teaspoon vanilla
		1	teaspoon bourbon

Combine sugar, butter, salt and cream to saucepan. Stir over low heat until dissolved. Bring to a boil, stirring often until it reaches 238 degrees. Remove from heat. Beat in electric mixer until cool and add bourbon and vanilla.

COFFEE PIE

Crust:

3	ounces cream cheese	½	cup butter
		1¼	cups flour

In food processor or bowl of electric mixer combine cream cheese and butter. Add flour all at once. Mix until dough is formed. Pat dough to thinly line 9-inch pie plate. Chill.

Filling:

1	tablespoon strong coffee	1	tablespoon apple cider vinegar
¼	cup butter, melted	3	eggs, lightly beaten
1	teaspoon vanilla	1	tablespoon flour
		1½	cups sugar

Combine coffee, butter, vanilla and vinegar. Set aside while beating eggs. Whisk flour and sugar together. Add butter mixture whisking to combine. Add eggs to mixture. Pour into cream cheese crust and bake at 350 degrees for 45 minutes.

Yield: 1 pie

BERRY PECAN MUFFINS

1	cup butter (room temperature)	3½	cups all-purpose flour
1	cup sugar	1½	cups whole wheat flour
1	cup powdered sugar	2	tablespoons baking powder
1	cup ground pecans		
2	tablespoons vanilla extract	½	teaspoon salt
4	eggs	1	cup fresh or frozen berries
2	cups buttermilk		

Cream butter, sugar and powdered sugar in food processor or electric mixer until light and fluffy. Add ground pecans and vanilla extract. Combine thoroughly. Add eggs, one at a time, mixing between each addition. Add buttermilk. In a separate large bowl, sift flours, baking powder and salt. Toss berries in flour mixture to coat lightly.

Make a well in center of flour and fruit. Add butter mixture. Stir just to combine. Fill every other cup in well-oiled muffin tin. Bake 20 minutes at 350 degrees.

Yield: approximately 18

DOWNTOWN GRILL

1115 Jackson Avenue
Oxford, MS 38655

Patty & William Lewis
Jackie & George Falls
Allison & Louis Brandt
Partners in Downtown Grill
Lee Cauthen, General Manager
Dixie D. Grimes, Chef

*The Downtown Grill opened February 1, 1989. It was the first upscale restaurant to open on Oxford's historic downtown square. The building was constructed in 1889 and is listed in the National Register of Historic Places. One of the restaurant's signature dishes, "Catfish Lafitte", has been featured in **Southern Living** magazine. This recipe has also received an award from the Catfish Institute. In 1992, the Downtown Grill won an award as "Best Neighborhood restaurant" from **Mississippi** magazine.*

FILET DIANE

1	8-ounce filet (butterflied into two 4-ounce pieces)	2	tablespoons dry sherry
1	ounce butter	1	teaspoon Worcestershire sauce
3	tablespoons minced shallot		
2	tablespoons minced parsley	2	teaspoons Dijon mustard
1	tablespoon brandy	1	tablespoon chives

1) Sauté filets in a skillet in hot butter. Remove and keep warm. Season lightly with salt and pepper.

2) Add shallots, parsley and chives, and sauté for about 1 minute.

3) Add brandy, sherry and Worcestershire sauce to skillet and simmer for about 1 minute.

4) Pour sauce over steak and serve immediately. Use large round plate and garnish with tomato wedge and parsley.

Serves 1.

CATFISH LAFITTE

1	(7 to 9-ounce) catfish fillet	½	ounce dry vermouth
	Egg wash (2 eggs per 1 cup milk, beaten) per quantity	½	cup heavy cream
		1	tablespoon chopped green onions
2	cups plain flour	1	wedge of lemon
	Raw, deveined shrimp (31 to 35 count) 3 each per fillet	1	ounce melted butter
½	teaspoon chopped garlic		Salt (2 teaspoons per 2 cups flour and dash)
6	(¼ x 3-inch) strips of ham		Cayenne pepper (1 teaspoon per 2 cups flour and dash)

1) Put flour into bowl for dredging and season with salt and cayenne pepper.

2) Dredge fillet in flour, then egg wash, and again in flour.

3) Drop fillet into fryer (360 degrees) and cook until catfish is floating and golden brown in color. (Approximately 5 to 6 minutes.)

4) After dropping catfish, sauté shrimp in buttered skillet until light pink on both sides. (Do not overcook.)

5) Add garlic, ham and vermouth.

6) Add heavy cream, ½ tablespoon green onions, and squeeze lemon wedge.

7) Dash with salt and cayenne pepper.

8) Continue to reduce cream for 1 to 2 minutes.

9) Entire process should approximately coincide with cooking of fish fillet. Remove fish from fryer and place on large plate.

10) Arrange shrimp in row onto fish and lace gaps with ham strips.

11) Spatula sauce onto fish and sprinkle remaining green onions onto fillet.

12) Garnish with lemon wedge and parsley sprig and serve.

Serves 1.

GRILLED CATFISH WITH BEURRE BLANC SAUCE

4	(7 to 9-ounce) catfish fillets		Salt and pepper to taste
1	whole purple onion (cut julienne style)	1	pound butter
1	cup olive oil	1	6-ounce beer
1	large green bell pepper	1½	ounces hot pepper sauce
1	cup yellow mustard	4	ounces white vinegar
		4	ounces white wine

In large bowl, mix purple onion, mustard, beer, green pepper, olive oil together. Place catfish in marinade and refrigerate overnight. The next day, place fish on baking sheet, cover the top with purple onions and bake in 350 degree oven for 20 minutes.

In separate bowl, cream butter (butter should be at room temperature) and add hot pepper sauce, salt and pepper, white wine and vinegar. This is your beurre blanc.

Place fish on center of large round plate, top with one scoop of beurre blanc. Best served with grilled asparagus and garlic mashed potatoes. Garnish with fresh parsley and lemon wedges.

Serves 4.

PATTY'S PECAN PIE

3	large eggs	¼	teaspoon vanilla
½	cup sugar with 2 tablespoons of flour added	2	tablespoons melted butter
⅛	teaspoon salt	1½	cups pecan halves, broken again in half
1½	cups light corn syrup	1	unbaked pie shell

Sprinkle broken pecan halves on bottom of pie shell.

Beat eggs with whisk or in mixer, but not to death. Add remaining ingredients in order as listed above.

Pour filling gently over pecans. Allow pecans to settle on top.

Bake at 325 degrees until golden brown and center is set.

Note: 3 recipes will make four pies, but you must still use 1½ cups of pecans per pie.

BARKSDALE-ISOM BED & BREAKFAST
(circa 1835)
1003 Jefferson Avenue
Oxford, MS 38655

Susan Barksdale Howorth, Proprietor
Nancy Nations, Chef

Mrs. Sarah Isom served as the gracious hostess to General Ulysses S. Grant during the Union occupation and the founding fathers of the University of Mississippi. From the Civil War to the Faulkner years to today, Isom Place continues to embody the unique traditions of graceful, Southern hospitality. William Faulkner used Isom Place as the fictional setting for his short story "A Rose for Emily." Barksdale-Isom is conveniently located in the heart of Oxford – a three-minute walk from historic Oxford Square.

B & I BLUEBERRY BREAD

½	cup (1 stick) butter, softened	2	cups all-purpose flour
1	cup granulated sugar	1	teaspoon baking powder
2	eggs	1	teaspoon baking soda
½	teaspoon pure vanilla extract	1	cup fresh blueberries
1	cup sour cream		

Preheat oven to 350 degrees. In a large bowl, cream the butter and sugar together. Beat in the eggs, vanilla and sour cream. Mix in the flour, baking powder and baking soda. Slowly fold in the blueberries.

Pour the batter into a greased 9 x 5-inch loaf pan and bake for one hour or until a tester comes out clean. Let cool on a wire rack.

Yield: 1 loaf

B & I CHEESE GRITS

2	teaspoons salt	4	bunches chopped green onions
2	14.5-ounce cans chicken broth	1	tablespoon chopped garlic
1½	cans water	1	tablespoon chopped basil
2	cups uncooked quick grits	2	cups chopped peppered ham
24	ounces sharp cheddar cheese		Hot pepper sauce to taste
½	cup butter, melted		Salt and pepper to taste
4	eggs, beaten		
½	cup milk		

Boil water and chicken broth. Add salt and grits, stirring slowly to prevent clumps and reduce heat to low, stirring occasionally for 2 to 3 minutes. Take off heat and add cheese, stirring until cheese is completely melted. Season with a dash of ground pepper and hot sauce. Add butter, eggs and milk – making sure each is thoroughly blended. Fold in onions, ham, garlic and basil.

Preheat oven to 350 degrees. Grits may be cooked in a 9 x 13 x 2-inch casserole or individual ramekins for one hour.

Serves 18.

Lyceum at University of Mississippi

CITY GROCERY

152 Courthouse Square Oxford, MS 38655

John Currence, Chef Owner

Both the restaurant and bar have been hailed coast-to-coast as one of the finest establishments in Mississippi in publications such as The New York Times, The Atlanta Journal/Constitution, The Los Angeles Times, The London Times, Southern Living, The Memphis Flyer, Seattle Daily, Esquire, USA Today, etc. Perhaps the finest flattery to be bestowed upon City Grocery was the invitation to cook at the James Beard Foundation in New York City in the summer of 1995. The spring of 1996 saw the filming of the "Great Chefs of the South" in the City Grocery kitchen and the City Grocery team returned to the James Beard House in the summer of 1997.

HOT SAUCE CHEESE STRAWS

2	cups extra sharp Vermont white cheddar, shredded	¾	teaspoon cayenne pepper
¾	pound butter, softened to room temperature	1½	tablespoons hot pepper sauce
2¼	teaspoons Kosher salt	1	teaspoon baking soda
		3	cups all-purpose flour

Whip butter with paddle attachment in mixer until smooth. Add cheese and blend well. Whip in salt, cayenne, hot pepper sauce and baking soda. Slowly add the flour until fully incorporated. Place dough in a cookie press and pipe out into desired shapes and sizes. Bake at 375 degrees on a cookie sheet until golden. These will keep very well for a couple of weeks in an airtight container.

Yield: Makes lots, but trust me you will eat them. J.C.

John Currence, City Grocery, Oxford, MS

CARAMELIZED VIDALIA ONION SOUP WITH HOT SAUCE CHEESE STRAWS

5	pounds Vidalia onions (sliced thin, root to stem)	3	stalks celery, small dice
4	tablespoons unsalted butter	1	tablespoon minced garlic
2	tablespoons brown sugar	1	tablespoon herbs de Provence
1½	teaspoons Kosher salt	2	cups sherry
1	tablespoon whole leaf thyme	¾	gallon chicken stock/water*
3	tablespoons pure olive oil	1	cup heavy cream Salt and pepper to taste

Heat butter in a large sauté pan and toss in onion, thyme, salt and brown sugar. Sauté over low/ medium heat, turning occasionally, until onion is deep golden brown. The trick is to leave them alone long enough, without turning, so they can caramelize, but not burn. When the onion has caramelized, deglaze pan with sherry and set aside. Heat oil in a small soup pot and sauté celery and garlic with the herbs de Provence, until tender. Add onion mix and bring back to a simmer. Add chicken stock/water, bring to a simmer over medium heat and allow it to reduce for 20 minutes. Remove from heat and allow to cool for five minutes then stir in cream. Purée in batches or force through a food mill and season with salt and white pepper to taste.

This soup is excellent served either hot or chilled.

If straight chicken stock is not available, a mixture of canned chicken broth and water of any reasonable proportion will suffice.

Yield: 1¼ gallons

RABBIT SPRING ROLLS

1	bunch scallion whites	2	tablespoons olive oil
1	tablespoon minced garlic	1½	tablespoons rice wine vinegar
½	head bok choy, julienned	3	tablespoons soy sauce
1	carrot, shredded	1½	cups rabbit skirt steak*
1	tablespoon minced ginger	1	egg, lightly beaten
1	teaspoon sesame oil	1½	teaspoons cornstarch

Tenderize rabbit (or other meat) with tenderizing hammer. Season with salt and black pepper and brown in sauté pan with olive oil. Remove from heat and cool. Julienne when cool, set aside. In a large sauté pan, heat sesame oil and olive oil. Season oil with garlic purée and scallion and sauté until tender. Add carrots and sauté again. Add egg and let sit briefly so that egg on pan will cook. Scrape pan and cook again until egg is all cooked. Add bok choy, soy and rice wine vinegar and wilt bok choy briefly. If liquid remains in bottom of pan, add 2 teaspoons water to cornstarch and add cornstarch slowly to mix and heat until liquid thickens. Remove from heat, cool and roll in eggroll skins according to directions on packet, seal with egg. Dip with Oriental Dipping Sauce (recipe to follow).

Substitute chicken, duck, pork, beef, shrimp or crab for rabbit if you prefer.

Yield: 8 to 10 rolls

ORIENTAL DIPPING SAUCE
(for Spring Rolls)

¼	cup Dijon mustard	½	tablespoon dry mustard
¼	cup honey		
¾	cup soy sauce	¼	tablespoon ginger powder
1	teaspoon sesame oil	2	tablespoons rice wine vinegar

Combine all above ingredients, except dry mustard and ginger in stainless bowl, and whisk together well. Slowly add the dry mustard and ginger, while whisking so that dry ingredients do not clump.

Yield: About 1½ cups.

PAN ROASTED POUSSIN STUFFED WITH DRIED BLACK MISSION FIG & ROSEMARY BREAD PUDDING

8	poussin (young hens – available at specialty markets)*	3	tablespoons dry sage
16	cups shredded stale French bread	1	tablespoon salt
12	whole eggs	3	tablespoons cracked black pepper
3	cups half and half	2	cups dried black mission figs, chopped
2	cups garlic cloves		
2	cups pure olive oil		
1	cup fresh rosemary leaves, chopped	¼	cup white truffle oil

Place garlic and olive oil in a shallow container and cover with foil and roast at 350 degrees for 45 minutes or until very tender. Let cool, remove garlic and reserve oil for cooking. Whisk together eggs and half and half in a bowl until well combined. You want to incorporate some air into the mixture here so that the pudding will soufflé during the cooking process. Pour this mixture over the bread and add the roasted garlic, rosemary, sage, figs, salt and pepper and blend together gently but fully. (This mixture should be very moist, but not runny unless squeezed.) Sprinkle the cavity of the birds with salt and black pepper and stuff with the bread pudding mixture. Heat large pan with some of the roasted garlic olive oil until hot and brown each bird on all sides, removing them to a baking pan. Place the pan in a 450 degree oven and bake for 12 to 15 minutes or until the juices from the leg run clear. Drizzle the tops of these with white truffle oil for service.

Goes very well with your mashed potato recipe and sautéed asparagus.

This works best with a boned bird. If poussin are not available, Cornish game hens work well as do quail. Just remember to adjust down the cooking time considerably.

Yield: 16 servings

ANTHONY'S
116 West Main Street
West Point, MS 39773

Carter Fraley
Owner

Chef Carter Fraley is a 1994 graduate of the University of Mississippi. He worked in an apprenticeship program at Oxford's City Grocery while enrolled at Ole Miss (1990-1994). Chef Carter worked for 2 years at Old Waverly Golf Club before opening Anthony's in 1996.

SEAFOOD STUFFED SMOKED PRIME RIB

Seasoning for the prime rib: 2 tablespoons dry oregano, 2 tablespoons dry thyme, 2 tablespoons fine cracked black pepper, 2 tablespoons granulated garlic and 2 tablespoons season salt. **Mix all together.**

Preparation of rib: Rub whole prime rib down with Worcestershire sauce and cover with the rub above. Smoke with charcoal and hickory wood 2 to 3 hours.

Seafood Stuffing:

6	cups beef stock	1½	cups 70 to 90 count peeled and deveined shrimp
2	cups sliced shiitake mushrooms		
2	cups sliced green onions	½	cup crawfish stock
1	cup crawfish tails	1	tablespoon Creole seasoning
1½	cups crab meat		

Cut 10 prime 12 to 14-ounce ribeye steaks. Heat up in boiling pot of beef stock or au jus. Serve steak with seafood stuffing ladled over the top of it. Make sure that the seafood is covered with plenty of beef stock to keep it moist.

Serves 10.

PORK TENDERLOIN

3	4-ounce Bryan pork tenderloins	1½	tablespoons white wine
½	teaspoon salt + ½ teaspoon black pepper + ½ teaspoon granulated garlic (mix together)	1½	tablespoons bourbon whiskey
		1½	teaspoons fresh chopped ginger
		1	teaspoon garlic, chopped
1	tablespoon toasted sesame oil	3	tablespoons heavy cream
2	tablespoons apple cider vinegar	2	tablespoons butter

Cut pork tenderloin into medallions and pound thin. Season with salt, pepper and garlic mixture and sauté with toasted sesame oil. After cooked, remove pork and add ginger, garlic, vinegar, whiskey and wine. Simmer over low heat until it is reduced by half. Add cream and butter until smooth. Pour over pork. Serve with garlic mashed potatoes and vegetable.

Serves 3.

GRILLED HALIBUT WITH SWEET GINGER SHRIMP SCAMPI

8	10-ounce halibut fillets	2	ounces white wine
2	tablespoons lemon pepper seasoning	2	tablespoons fresh ginger
1	tablespoon toasted sesame oil	1	tablespoon fresh garlic
5	butterflied shrimp (21 to 25 count)	1	tablespoon parsley
		2	tablespoons sugar
1	teaspoon salt and pepper	1	ounce heavy cream
		3	tablespoons butter

Grill halibut with oil and lemon pepper seasoning.

Sauté shrimp with oil, salt and pepper. Then add garlic and ginger. Deglaze with wine and reduce to half. Add cream and butter till smooth. Add parsley and pour over fish with the shrimp on top of fish.

Serves 8.

OLD WAVERLY GOLF CLUB

1802 Magnolia West Point, MS 39773

Home of the 1999 LPGA Tournament

David Schnell, Executive Chef

Chef David is a native of Austin, Texas. He began his culinary training under a 3 year apprenticeship program with the Petroleum Club of Houston. In 1989 he became Executive Sous Chef at the Capitol City Club in Atlanta. In 1992 he became Executive Sous Chef at the Capitol City Country Club in Atlanta. He returned to Texas in 1994 as Executive Sous Chef for the Houston Club and River Oaks Country Club. He joined Old Waverly in 1997.

NIÇOISE SALAD

2	cups mixed greens	3	ounces fresh herb vinaigrette
1	blanched baked red potato	1	4-ounce tuna fillet, seasoned with salt and pepper, herbs and char-grilled
1	hard boiled egg		
6	Kalamata olives, pitted and halved		
1	ounce green beans, marinated in herb vinaigrette		

Single serving.

JUMBO LUMP CRAB MEAT & SHRIMP COCKTAIL

3	16 to 20 count shrimp, skewered to keep straight, cooked in a court bouillon, P&D	1	leaf bibb lettuce
		1	ounce remoulade sauce
1	ounce jumbo lump crab	1	ounce red sauce

Yield: One serving

GRILLED CHICKEN CAESAR SALAD

1	8-ounce chicken breast, brushed with pesto and char-grilled to order
2	cups large diced romaine lettuce
3	ounces Caesar dressing
½	cup croutons
2	ounces Parmesan cheese

Toss the lettuce and dressing together and place into basket. Top with sliced chicken and garnish with croutons and cheese.

Serves 1.

FRENCH ONION SOUP

10	yellow onions, thinly sliced
1	tablespoon dry thyme
3	bay leaves
1	cup sherry wine
2	quarts chicken stock
2	quarts beef stock

Sauté the onions in whole butter until golden brown. Add herbs, wine and stock. Simmer for 20 minutes, skimming frequently.

Yield: One gallon

LOUISIANA CRAWFISH CAKES

4	pounds crawfish tail meat
2	each red and green peppers, small diced
1	onion, small diced
8	ounces Dijon mustard
4	ounces white wine
2	ounces Worcestershire sauce
4	ounces hot pepper sauce
8	eggs
	Bread crumbs as needed

Combine all ingredients and form into 2-ounce cakes. Bread in flour, eggs and bread crumbs. Deep fry to order.

Yield: 30 cakes

SHRIMP FRIED GRITS

2	pounds grits, cooked in a light chicken stock
1½	pounds smoked cheddar cheese, grated
1	pound shrimp pieces
1	cup cooked bacon, chopped fine
1	each red and green pepper, fine diced
2	tablespoons Cajun spice

While the grits are cooking, sauté the peppers and shrimp with the Cajun spice. To the finished grits, add the shrimp mix, bacon and cheese. Pour onto a sheet pan about 1-inch thick and put into cooler to chill. Cut with a circle cutter, bread with flour-eggs-bread crumbs, and deep fry to order.

Yield: 12 to 18

ROASTED LOBSTER TAIL

1	6-ounce lobster tail
3	16 to 20-count shrimp, char-grilled
1	teaspoon candied orange zest
	Salt and pepper

Remove tail from shell, season with salt, pepper and zest. Brush with butter and roast in oven. Remove shell and place on a bed of chow chow and ladle sauce on top.

Yield: 1 serving

VEGETABLE CHOW CHOW

5	pounds carrots, julienne
5	each red and green bell peppers, julienne
2	jicama, peeled and julienne
5	cups cider vinegar
5	cups sugar
1	tablespoon red pepper flakes
3	ounces fresh ginger, thinly sliced
4	ounces cilantro, chopped

Bring to a boil the vinegar, sugar, ginger and pepper flakes and strain over the vegetables. Add cilantro and toss together. Chill thoroughly.

Yield: 30 servings

CHILI VANILLA RUM SAUCE

1	cup white wine	1	fresh jalapeño,
2	shallots, minced		minced
½	vanilla bean, split	1	pinch saffron
	lengthwise	1	cup rum

Reduce shallots and wine by half. Add remaining ingredients and reduce to syrupy consistency.

Yield: 10 servings

POACHED CATFISH WITH LEMON & HERBS

1	6-ounce catfish fillet	1	teaspoon herbs de Provence
¼	cup white wine	1	cup fresh spinach
	Juice of ½ lemon		Fresh vegetables as needed

Place the catfish in a pie pan, season with salt and herbs, add wine, cover with plastic wrap and put into steamer for 6 minutes. Steam the spinach for 2 minutes and place in center of the plate. Place catfish on top of spinach and squeeze lemon juice on top. Surround with steamed mixed vegetables.

Serves 1.

VEGETARIAN PASTA

1½	cups angel hair pasta, cooked al dente	2	tablespoons olive oil
4	shiitake mushrooms, sliced	½	teaspoon roasted garlic
2	artichoke hearts, quartered	½	teaspoon herbs de Provence
½	each red and green bell pepper, cut julienne	3-4	slices each zucchini, squash, carrot, char-grilled
			Juice of 1 lemon

In a medium hot pan, add oil, garlic and herbs. Add peppers and sauté for 1 minute, then add mushrooms and artichokes. Sauté until al dente, then add pasta and toss until hot. Squeeze lemon and toss again, then plate and surround with grilled vegetables.

HALF ROTISSERIE DUCK

1	half duck, marinated, rotisserie cooked, skin from breast removed and reserved	4	ounces timbale wild rice pilaf
		5	shiitake mushrooms, sautéed in olive oil
2	ounces orange ginger vinaigrette (recipe below)	6	snow peas

Yield: One serving

Marinade:

1	cup red wine	1	tablespoon juniper berries
1	cup orange juice		
3	shallots, minced	1	ounce fresh thyme
6	cloves garlic, minced	3	bay leaves
2	stalks celery, small diced	2	ounces fresh ginger, thinly sliced
1	carrot, small diced	2	tablespoons whole black peppercorns

Combine all ingredients and marinate duck for 24 hours.

ORANGE GINGER VINAIGRETTE

2	cups duck fat drippings from rotisserie	2	tablespoons fresh cilantro, chopped
2	shallots, minced	2	tablespoons fresh ginger, minced
4	cloves garlic, minced	¼	teaspoon red pepper flakes
1	orange, zest and juice	1	cup cider vinegar
1	teaspoon orange compound		

Combine all ingredients except oil. Whisk in the oil to emulsify. Fine julienne the reserved duck skin, making sure it is very crispy and use for garnish.

CHAR-GRILLED ATLANTIC SALMON

1	6-ounce salmon fillet	4	ounces spinach soufflé (recipe below)
2	ounces whole grain mustard sauce (recipe below)	2	tourn'ed potatoes, steamed
¼	leek, julienned and deep fried	4	slices carrot, cut on a bias

Yield: One serving

WHOLE GRAIN MUSTARD SAUCE

6	shallots, sliced	3	quarts chix velouté
2	leeks, sliced	2	cups Creole mustard
2	cups sherry		
2	quarts heavy cream		

Combine shallots, leeks and sherry and reduce by half. Add cream and reduce to napé. Add velouté and simmer for 10 minutes. Strain and add mustard.

Yield: 1 gallon

SPINACH SOUFFLÉ

1	box chopped spinach	1	cup Swiss cheese, grated
12	eggs	1	tablespoon nutmeg
1	quart heavy cream		Salt and pepper to taste

Combine all ingredients, pour into timbale molds and bake in a water bath at 325 degrees until set. Reheat to order in steamer and unmold.

SMOKED PORK TENDERLOIN "MONTEGO BAY"

1	Waverly Reserve pork tenderloin	6	asparagus
1.5	ounces pineapple chutney (recipe below)	3	ounces duchess carrots, piped on plate
1	purple potato, steamed, sliced and grilled		

Season pork tender with jerk seasoning, smoke for 3 minutes in stove top smoker, sear on flat top and roast in oven until internal temperature is 145 degrees.

PINEAPPLE CHUTNEY

2	fresh pineapples, peeled and medium diced	2	shallots, minced
		1	cup pineapple juice
1	tablespoon fresh ginger, peeled and minced	½	cup cider vinegar
		½	cup sugar
		1	red bell pepper, fine diced
1	fresh jalapeño, minced		

Combine all ingredients, bring to a boil, and simmer until a syrupy consistency. Chill.

Yield: 10 orders

GRILLED SHRIMP BROCHETTES

6	16 to 20-count shrimp	4	mushrooms
½	red pepper, medium diced	1	cup cheese tortellini
½	green pepper, medium diced	3	ounces Asiago Cream Sauce
		5	asparagus

Build brochettes alternating mushroom, shrimp, pepper, shrimp, pepper, shrimp, mushroom. Combine equal parts of pesto and olive oil and season brochettes. Char-grill to order and serve on a bed of tortellini tossed with Asiago Cream Sauce and arrange asparagus accordingly.

IRON MIKE'S PORK CHOP

1	10-ounce pork chop	5	asparagus
2	ounces honey green peppercorn sauce	½	red and ½ green bell pepper, julienne
4	ounces herbed spaetzle (recipe below)		

HONEY GREEN PEPPERCORN SAUCE

3	shallots, fine diced	2	ounces brandy
3	cloves garlic, minced	6	ounces red wine
1	3-ounce can green peppercorns	1	cup honey
		¾	cup cider vinegar
		½	gallon demi-glaze

Sauté shallots and garlic. Add peppercorns, sauté for 2 minutes and flambé with brandy. Add wine, honey and vinegar and reduce to light syrup. Add demi-glaze and simmer for 10 minutes.

Yield: ½ gallon

HERBED SPATZLE

(for Iron Mike's Pork Chop recipe)

12	eggs	3	teaspoons salt
1½	cups milk	6	cups flour
3	tablespoons fresh basil, chopped	6	tablespoons olive oil
3	tablespoons fresh tarragon, chopped	2	cups fresh spinach, chiffonade
1	teaspoon nutmeg		

Combine eggs, milk, herbs, salt and nutmeg. Whisk together and add flour and oil. Cook in chicken stock by pushing through a colander. Cook to al dente. To serve, sauté in brown butter until light brown, then add spinach.

COLORADO LAMB CHOPS

2	double lamb chops, seasoned with salt and pepper, char-grilled	4	ounces Duchess carrots, piped on plate
2	ounces rosemary-thyme sauce (recipe below)	6	asparagus
1	purple potato, steamed, sliced and grilled	3	roasted garlic cloves Rosemary and thyme sprigs for garnish

Yield: One order

ROSEMARY-THYME SAUCE

1	onion, large diced	1	ounce fresh rosemary
2	celery stalks, large diced	3	cups red wine
2	carrots, large diced	1	tablespoon black peppercorns
6	cloves garlic, chopped	3	quarts lamb stock
1	ounce fresh thyme	2	quarts demi-glaze

Sauté mirepoix until brown, add herbs and wine and reduce by half. Add stock and reduce to napé. Strain.

Yield: 1 gallon

Waverly Plantation
West Point, Mississippi

CAFÉ PORTOBELLA'S
OLD STATEHOUSE HOTEL

217 East Main Street
Starkville, MS 39759

Johnny & Alice Wooten, Chef Owners

Portobella's won 2 menu awards as well as "Best of Show" from the Golden Triangle Advertising Federation.

VICHYSSOISE SOUP

2	cups potatoes	1	cup heavy whipping cream
1	cup leeks		
1	quart chicken broth	1	tablespoon pepper
		1	teaspoon chives

Dice potatoes and cut white part of leeks and bring broth to a boil and cook potatoes for 30 minutes or until potatoes are done. Cool for 15 minutes and purée all mixture. Add cream and top with chives.

Serves 12.

Recipe notes: This is a cold potato soup.

PESTO SAUCE

2	pounds basil	1	cup garlic
3	cups pine nuts	1	pound butter
3	cups Parmesan cheese, shredded	1	tablespoon garlic salt
2	tablespoons black pepper	2	cups olive oil

Mix all ingredients in a large bowl. Place in blender 3 cups at a time and purée until all has been combined.

Serves 20.

CORN & BLACK BEAN SALAD

2½	cups corn	2	tablespoons lime juice
2	cups black beans		
½	cup red onion	¼	cup coriander
⅓	cup red pepper	1	pinch salt
1	jalapeño pepper	3	drops hot pepper sauce
3	tablespoons olive oil		
		½	teaspoon cumin

Finely chop red onion, red pepper and jalapeño pepper. Combine all the ingredients in a large bowl. Toss well. Cover and refrigerate for 1 to 2 hours. Season with more salt and hot pepper sauce if necessary.

Serve chilled or at room temperature.

Serves 6.

Recipe notes: This is a light and lively summer salad. Perfect for parties.

TUSCAN-STYLE SPAGHETTI SAUCE

1	pound ground beef	1	cup mushrooms
1	medium onion	¼	cup red wine
½	carrot	1	pinch salt
⅛	cup garlic	1	pinch pepper
½	teaspoon thyme	2	tablespoons olive oil
½	teaspoon oregano		
1¾	pounds tomatoes	⅛	cup Parmesan cheese, grated
⅛	cup tomato paste		
¼	cup sun-dried tomatoes		

Brown ground beef in skillet at medium heat Once browned, add chopped onion, carrot, celery, garlic, thyme and oregano. Sauté about 10 minutes until tender. Add tomatoes, sun-dried tomatoes, tomato paste and red wine. Simmer for 15 minutes.

Coarsely chop mushrooms. In another sauté pan, sauté mushrooms for 8 to 10 minutes until tender but still firm. Add to spaghetti sauce and simmer for another 10 to 15 minutes.

Toss with penné pasta, Parmesan cheese and fresh cilantro. Serve immediately.

Serves 4.

Recipe notes: This is a hearty pasta dish that should be served in large rustic bowls and accompanied by a green salad with peasant bread.

PORTOBELLA'S LASAGNE

3	tablespoons olive oil	½	tablespoon salt
1½	medium onions	½	tablespoon oregano
¾	teaspoon crushed red pepper	¾	teaspoon basil
4½	cloves garlic	¾	cup cabernet sauvignon
1½	pounds lean ground beef	1½	eggs
¾	pound mushrooms	⅞	pound spinach, chopped
¾	pound tomato sauce	1½	cups ricotta cheese
2⅝	pounds tomatoes, canned	¾	cup Parmesan cheese, grated
½	pound tomato paste	¾	pound lasagne
		¾	pound mozzarella cheese

Preheat the oven to 350 degrees. In a large sauté pan, heat 1 tablespoon oil. Sauté finely chopped onion, red pepper flakes and minced garlic. Add ground beef and cook until brown. Add sliced mushrooms and sauté gently. Blend in tomato sauce, canned tomatoes with liquid, tomato paste, salt, oregano, basil and wine. Simmer about 15 minutes, breaking tomatoes into small pieces as the mixture cooks.

In a medium bowl, mix egg with spinach, ricotta cheese, Parmesan cheese and remaining 1 tablespoon oil.

To assembly, pour half of the meat sauce into a 9 x 13-inch pan and cover with a layer of lasagne noodles. Spread entire spinach mixture over lasagne noodles. Repeat, layering with remaining lasagne and meat sauce. Cover and bake at 350 degrees for 45 minutes. Remove the cover and arrange sliced mozzarella on top. Bake 15 minutes longer until cheese has melted.

Serves 12.

CHICKEN CURRY

4	chicken breast halves	4	tablespoons flour
4	tablespoons corn oil	2	pinches white pepper
4	tablespoons sugar	1	quart broccoli, chopped
4	tablespoons soy sauce	½	teaspoon salt
		1	cup coconut milk

Heat oil and curry powder in a wok. Cut the chicken into ¼-inch strips and stir fry along with the sugar, soy, salt and garlic.

In a medium saucepan over low heat, melt butter. Blend in flour, then add coconut milk in a steady stream. Cook and stir until thick and bubbly, about 5 minutes. Add chicken, broccoli and peanuts to the sauce and cook until heated through. Serve on steamed rice.

Serves 4.

Recipe notes: Broccoli gives this classic dish an interesting twist and if you like it spicy, increase the amount of curry.

MSU Chapel of Memories
Starkville, Mississippi

MICHAEL BOLAND'S RESTAURANT

205 5th Street North
Columbus, MS 39703

Michael Boland, Chef/Owner

Michael Boland is a graduate of the Johnson & Wales Culinary School in Charleston, South Carolina.

TOMATO BASIL SOUP

1	large yellow onion, diced	1	teaspoon dried basil
1	16-ounce can diced tomatoes, strained	1	teaspoon dried thyme
2	tablespoons olive oil	1	quart heavy cream
2	tablespoons garlic, chopped		Salt and pepper to taste
1	teaspoon dried oregano	1	cup white wine

Sauté onions and garlic in oil. Add tomatoes, herbs and wine. Simmer for 10 minutes. Add cream and simmer for 5 minutes.

Serves 4.

SMOKED BEEF TENDERLOIN

4	beef tenderloin filet mignon	Hickory chips

Following items for herb mixture:

1	tablespoon oregano	1	tablespoon salt
1	tablespoon basil	1	tablespoon pepper
1	tablespoon thyme		

In your grill, ignite hickory chips. Generously coat steaks with herb mixture. Let stand. When chips are ignited, place steaks on grill and cover. Turn off gas heat completely and let smoke bellow from covered grill for 5 minutes not letting steaks be touched by direct heat. Re-ignite grill and complete cooking.

Serves 4.

CRÈME BRÛLÉE

7	egg yolks	2	cups heavy cream
5	whole eggs	1½	cups sugar
1	quart half and half	1	tablespoon vanilla

Heat cream, half and half, sugar and vanilla in a saucepan until it boils. Whisk together eggs and egg yolks. Blend boiling cream mixture into eggs and then strain through a sieve. Pour strained mixture into individual soufflé cups, place in a warm water bath and bake at 250 degrees for 1 hour and 15 minutes. Remove cover and chill. When chilled, sprinkle lightly with granulated sugar and broil with a blowtorch or broiler until crispy and golden brown.

Tennessee Williams' Birthplace
Columbus, Mississippi

HARVEY'S RESTAURANTS

University Management Corporation

104½ 3rd Street South
Columbus, MS 39701 (General Office)
Starkville   Tupelo   Tuscaloosa

Bill Montgomery
Corporate Chef

TOMATO-BASIL VINAIGRETTE

¾	cup red wine vinegar	1	teaspoon Kosher salt
1½	cups pure olive oil	2	tablespoons sugar
½	cup prepared marinara	1	teaspoon ground black pepper
½	ounce fresh basil		

1) Place red wine vinegar into mixing bowl.

2) Add the sugar, Kosher salt and black pepper.

3) Slowly add the olive oil to the vinegar mixture, whisk the oil in briskly, incorporate the oil before adding more oil.

4) Slice the basil thin, add to the vinaigrette and whisk.

5) Add the cold prepared marinara and whisk well.

Yield: 6 3-ounce servings

A flavorful vinaigrette just made for Harvey's Spring Salad.

HARVEY'S SUMMER SALAD WITH TOMATO-BASIL VINAIGRETTE

1¼	pounds fresh zucchini	2	4¾-quart servings romaine lettuce, shredded (each)
1¼	pounds fresh yellow squash	1	chicken breast (per salad)
1½	pounds carrots	3	ounces Tomato Basil Vinaigrette (per salad)
1	red pepper (each)		

1) Wash all vegetables. Peel carrots and run through the mandoline using the 3 mm blade. Cut the zucchini and yellow squash in the same manner. Cut the red peppers in half and discard the stem and seeds. Cut into julienne strips, mix all of the vegetables together.

2) Wash the romaine lettuce and trim the top ½-inch off the top leaves. Shred the lettuce very fine.

To serve: Cook a 5-ounce hot chicken breast completely, reserve. Place 1 quart of shredded romaine lettuce into a mixing bowl, add 1 full cup of the matchstick vegetables to the lettuce, add the chicken breast, cut pencil-thin, toss to mix all ingredients. Add 3 ounces of the tomato-basil vinaigrette, toss to coat all ingredients with the vinaigrette. Place the salad mixture onto a plate. Place 3 tomato wedges at 11, 2 and 5 o'clock. Grate fresh ground black pepper around the outside of the plate.

Yield: 6 servings

Crisp summer vegetables and warm grilled chicken make for a healthy luncheon salad. Can be tossed with your favorite salad dressing.

CHICKEN PASTA POMODORO

6	pounds diced tomatoes	1	ounce garlic cloves
¾	cup pure Italian olive oil	2	teaspoons Kosher salt
1	ounce fresh basil	1	teaspoon ground black pepper

1) Wash and core the tomatoes, cut into halves, squeeze out the seeds of the tomatoes, dice in the tomato dicer, and reserve in a mixing bowl.

2) Place large sauté pans over high heat, once pan is very hot, add the olive oil, let the oil get hot.

3) Add the garlic and cook for 4 to 5 seconds.

4) Carefully add the diced tomatoes, cook over high heat for 2 minutes, stir constantly.

5) Remove from heat and place into a large stainless container.

6) Add fresh chopped basil, salt and black pepper.

7) Date, label and place at sauté station.

8) **To serve:** Grill a 5-ounce hot chicken breast completely and cut pencil-thin, reserve.

9) Place 4 ounces of pomodoro sauce into a sauté pan, add 1 7-ounce bag of portioned hot penné pasta.

10) Add ½-ounce of fresh Parmesan cheese and add the cut chicken breast. Toss well.

11) Place into a white pasta bowl, sprinkle with ½-ounce Parmesan cheese, garnish the outside edge of the plate with fresh chopped parsley.

Serves 9.

A simple and refreshing pasta for a hot Mississippi evening!

MISSISSIPPI DELTA CRAWFISH GRITS

18	ounces yellow cornmeal	¼	pound unsalted butter
½	gallon water	2	teaspoons ground black pepper
1½	ounce chicken base	1	tablespoon olive oil
1½	cups Parmesan cheese	1	pound crawfish meat
5	grilled tomatoes (each)		

1) Wash and core tomatoes. Place into a mixing bowl. Add salad oil, toss to coat with oil and put on grill. Place so tomatoes do not flame up over flames. The tomatoes are to be well charred all over. When grilled, place back into the mixing bowl and cool. When chilled, place on cutting board and coarsely chop making sure to reserve the juice. Reserve tomatoes.

2) Bring water to a boil, add chicken base. Slowly add the yellow cornmeal one cup at a time. Make sure you whisk well after each addition of cornmeal. Once half of the cornmeal is added, turn the heat to low. Continue to mix well. There should be no lumps.

3) Add the fresh grated Parmesan, mix well and add crawfish.

4) Add the cubed unsalted butter, mix well.

5) Add the reserved coarsely chopped grilled tomatoes, mix well.

6) **To serve:** Place 4 ounces of Parmesan mashed potatoes into center of special plate. Ladle 2 ounces of veal jus around potatoes, place spiced 7-ounce chicken breast on top of potato, ladle 2 ounces of crawfish sauce on chicken.

Serves 12.

A great accompaniment to chicken, veal and fresh fish. We usually serve with a pan jus or gravy.

WOODY'S RESTAURANTS

619 North Gloster Street
Tupelo, MS 38801

2420 Military Road
Columbus, MS 39701

Mike Kemmesat, Owner Chef

Woody's specializes in steaks, pasta, seafood and wild game. The Columbus restaurant has been open for 10 years and the Tupelo restaurant 5 years. **Epicurius** *(food critic) for the* **Clarion-Ledger** *newspaper in Jackson, Mississippi gave the Columbus restaurant a 3½ star rating out of 4!*

SEAFOOD GUMBO WITH OKRA

2	bunches celery	2½	pounds bay shrimp
6	green bell peppers	2	pounds crawfish tails
4	large onions		
	Shells from 10 pounds shrimp	2	bags of okra
	Brown roux made with 3 pounds 60-40 butter blend	½	cup cayenne pepper sauce
		¼	cup Worcestershire sauce
3	gallons shrimp stock	2	No. 10 cans diced tomatoes
8	ounces seafood base	2	pounds kielbasa sausage
1	cup Cajun seasoning		

Dice celery, peppers and onions. In a large pot brown the shrimp shells, add four gallons water and seafood base then reduce by one-third. Make a very dark brown roux, add to stock and reduce by at least one-third, strain and discard shells. Sauté celery, peppers, onions and sausage with Cajun seasoning and add to the stock. Add the seafood and okra to stock. Cook till shrimp is done. Add two scoops of ice. Let cool and remove grease.

Makes large batch.

LOBSTER NEWBURG

12	ounces cooked lobster (tail meat)	¼	teaspoon dry mustard
¼	cup butter		Dash cayenne pepper
¼	cup sliced green pepper		Salt and pepper
½	cup sliced mushrooms (shiitake or any other)	⅔	cup milk or half and half
2	tablespoons all-purpose flour	¼	cup white wine, optional
			Chopped parsley
			Paprika
			Parmesan cheese

In a medium skillet, sauté the green pepper and mushrooms in the butter for 5 minutes. Add to this mixture the flour, mustard, salt and pepper. Mix well. Add the milk or half and half and the wine, if desired. Cook and stir constantly until mixture thickens, about 15 minutes. If you desire a thicker sauce, take an extra tablespoon of flour and dissolve it in 2 tablespoons water. Add this mixture to the sauce. Cook and stir a few minutes.

Add the lobster (cut into ¼-inch thick rounds) and 1 tablespoon chopped parsley. Place mixture in an ovenproof casserole. Sprinkle with paprika and Parmesan cheese. Bake at 375 degrees for 10 minutes. Serve hot with white rice and a tossed green salad and semi-dry Chardonnay, if desired.

Serves 4.

BANANAS FOSTER
(at tableside)

In a portable burner with a copper pan, heat 2 tablespoons butter. Add 4 tablespoons brown sugar. Mix well until sugar starts to melt. Add bananas sliced in any manner. Stir. Away from flame, add 2 tablespoons of rum. Put back on flame and flambé until caramelized. Add 1 tablespoon of fresh lemon and a dash of nutmeg. Add 1 tablespoon of banana liqueur and 1 tablespoon Grand Marnier. Flambé once again. Serve hot over ice cream.

Serves 1.

WINONA COUNTRY CLUB

Country Club Road
Winona, MS 38967

**Elizabeth Hammond
Restaurant Manager**

COUNTRY CLUB RANCH DRESSING

1	cup buttermilk	1	teaspoon seasoned
1	cup sour cream		salt
1	cup mayonnaise	½	teaspoon garlic
1	teaspoon black		powder
	pepper	1	teaspoon dried
			parsley

Mix all ingredients thoroughly with whisk and chill. Store in refrigerator.

COUNTRY CLUB CHICKEN SPAGHETTI

1	pound package spaghetti	½	small bottle tomato ketchup
1	large hen or 2 small fryers, boiled and chopped into bite-sized pieces	1	small can tomato sauce
1	large onion, chopped	2	tablespoons Worcestershire sauce
1	large bell pepper, chopped		Salt and pepper to taste
2	stalks celery, chopped		Cayenne pepper to taste
2	tablespoons margarine	1	cup chicken broth
1	quart canned tomatoes	1	can small English peas, drained
		½	pound grated cheddar cheese

Sauté onions, green pepper and celery in margarine. Add mixture to chicken, and combine with tomatoes, ketchup, tomato sauce, Worcestershire sauce and seasonings and mix well. Add chicken broth, English peas and half the grated cheese; mix well. Pour into casserole dish and spread remainder of cheese on top. May be frozen at this point. Bake at 350 degrees for 30 to 45 minutes until bubbly.

Serves 10.

CAFÉ ON THE SQUARE

114 West Jefferson
Kosciusko, MS 39090

Rose Dorchuck, Chef Owner

Rose Dorchuck was born in Beaumont, Texas. She has been cooking all of her life, as she came from a family of nine children. Her mother passed down the art of wonderful cooking. She has traveled all over the United States with her parents and with her husband, Phillip. For her, joy is found at the stove. Her passion for cooking has led her to create many delicious recipes.

Please note: Café on the Square's Spicy Honey Dressing may be ordered by calling 601-289-5888.

SHRIMP ETOUFFÉE

2	pounds shrimp, peeled and deveined	1	cup chicken broth
1	bunch green onions, chopped	2	tablespoons cornstarch, dissolved in ½ cup cold water
1	onion, chopped	1	tablespoon Worcestershire sauce
½	bell pepper, chopped	1	teaspoon tomato paste
½	cup celery, chopped	1	cup raw rice, cooked as directed
2	tablespoons olive oil		
½	stick margarine		

Cook onions, green onions, bell pepper and celery in olive oil and margarine. Add shrimp, cook 10 minutes. Add chicken broth and thicken with cornstarch in water. Add Worcestershire sauce and tomato paste. Cook 5 minutes. Serve over cooked rice.

Serves 6.

WALNUT CHICKEN SALAD

3	cups diced, boiled chicken breast	4	large red apples, diced with peeling on
2	cups pineapple chunks	1	cup walnut pieces
3	ribs celery, chopped	1	12-ounce bottle Café on the Square Spicy Honey Dressing

Toss together and chill for 2 hours before serving. Yields 4 generous servings.

CHICKEN LASAGNA ROLL-UPS IN ALFREDO SAUCE

1	pound ground chicken (ground turkey can be used)	1½	cups shredded mozzarella cheese
2	tablespoons margarine	¼	cup Parmesan cheese
½	box frozen chopped spinach	2	cans evaporated milk
½	pound lasagna noodles	2	cans water
⅓	teaspoon basil	¾	teaspoon basil
⅓	teaspoon oregano	¾	cup Italian bread crumbs

Cook lasagna noodles. Drain and rinse till cool. Lay flat and separated.

Filling: Brown chicken in margarine with ⅓ teaspoon basil and oregano until done. Add spinach and cook until done. Add Italian bread crumbs and ½ cup mozzarella cheese. Stir and set aside to cool. Spread ½ to ¾ cup filling on lasagna noodle. Roll up like jelly roll. Put in baking dish, seam side down.

Sauce: ¾ cup margarine, melted. Add ⅓ cup flour, salt and pepper to taste, canned milk and water. Cook until thick and creamy. Turn off. Add Parmesan and ¾ teaspoon basil. Pour sauce over rolls in baking dish. Sprinkle with remaining mozzarella. Bake at 350 degrees until bubbly.

Serves 6 to 8.

VENISON ROLL-UPS

20	tenderloin or backstrap steaks, cut ½-inch thick	20	small strips of jalapeño pepper Italian salad dressing
10	slices uncooked bacon		Salt and pepper to taste

Pound tenderloin steaks with mallet. Put into shallow dish and cover with Italian dressing. Let marinate 2 to 4 hours. Place a strip of jalapeño on one end of the steak. Roll up jelly roll fashion. Wrap ½ strip bacon around roll and secure with toothpick. Repeat until all are done. Cook on grill, watching constantly and turning until bacon is done.

Serves 4.

COCONUT CREAM PIE

1	baked pie shell	4	egg yolks, beaten
1	cup sugar	1	cup coconut, divided
2	tablespoons cornstarch	2	tablespoons butter
¼	teaspoon salt	1	teaspoon vanilla
2	cups milk		

Combine sugar, cornstarch and salt in boiler. Combine milk and egg yolks. Gradually add to sugar mixture. Cook over medium heat, stirring until thick. Remove from heat. Add ⅔ cup coconut, butter and vanilla. Pour into pie shell. Cover with wax paper while making meringue. Sprinkle meringue with coconut. Bake at 350 degrees until golden brown.

Meringue:

4	egg whites	¼	cup sugar
½	teaspoon cream of tartar		

Beat together and spread on pie. Sprinkle with remaining coconut.

IRISH CREAM CHEESECAKE

Crust:

2   cups chocolate (with white filling) cookie crumbs

¼   cup sugar
6   tablespoons butter, melted

Filling:

36   ounces cream cheese
1⅔   cups sugar
5   eggs
1½   cups Irish cream liqueur

1   tablespoon vanilla
1   cup semi-sweet chocolate chips

Topping:

1   cup whipping cream
2   tablespoons sugar

½   cup semi-sweet chocolate chips, melted

Chocolate Curls:

2   cups semi-sweet chocolate chips

Preheat oven to 350 degrees.

Crust: Combine chocolate crumbs and sugar in bowl; add melted margarine. Mix well and press into bottom of a 9-inch springform pan. Bake 7 to 10 minutes.

Filling: Beat cream cheese until smooth, add sugar and eggs, beating until fluffy. Add liqueur and vanilla, mix well. Sprinkle chocolate chips over crust. Spoon filling over chips. Bake 1 hour and 20 minutes or until center is set. Cool completely in pan.

Topping: Beat cream and sugar in a large chilled bowl until stiff. Continue to beat while adding melted chocolate. Spread mixture over cheesecake.

For Chocolate Curls: Melt chocolate in a small saucepan over low heat. Pour onto a baking sheet. Let stand at room temperature until set, but not firm. To make curls, pull a thin knife or cheese plane across surface of chocolate (curls will break if chocolate is too firm). Re-melt and cool as necessary to form desired number of curls. Arrange on cake. Refrigerate until ready to serve.

Serves 16 or more.

THE REDBUD INN

121 North Wells Street Kosciusko, MS 39090

Maggie Garrett, Chef Owner

As the home of Samuel Anderson Jackson and his new bride, Lillie, Kosciusko's Jackson-Niles House, circa 1884, enjoyed distinction as one of this city's finest examples of Queen Anne architecture. The Jackson-Niles House became the home of the Red Bud Inn ten years ago.

REDBUD'S CHEESE RING

1   pound sharp cheddar cheese, grated
¾   cup mayonnaise
1   clove garlic, pressed through a garlic press
5   slices bacon, cooked crisp and chopped

1   cup chopped pecans
1   tablespoon grated onion
½   teaspoon hot pepper sauce
1   cup strawberry preserves

Combine all ingredients except the preserves and mix well. Press into a ring-shaped mold which is lined with plastic wrap (this makes unmolding easier). Refrigerate for at least several hours.

When ready to serve, unmold on a platter and fill the center with the preserves or top with preserves. Serve with your favorite crackers. Delicious!

Serves a crowd.

SUMMERTIME SHRIMP SALAD

½	cup mayonnaise		chopped pimiento
1	tablespoon fresh parsley	½	teaspoon lemon juice
1	tablespoon finely chopped capers	1	green onion top, snipped
1	teaspoon dry mustard	1	clove garlic, crushed
1	teaspoon horseradish	2	cups shrimp, boiled, peeled and deveined
1	tablespoon		

Mix first 5 ingredients in a medium bowl. Add pimiento, lemon juice, onion and garlic; mix gently. Gently stir in shrimp. Refrigerate at least an hour before serving.

Yield: 2½ cups

SHRIMP RAMEKINS

1	cup mayonnaise	⅛	teaspoon thyme
⅓	cup chili sauce	1	teaspoon minced parsley
¼	teaspoon curry powder	⅛	teaspoon celery salt
¼	teaspoon dry mustard	1	cup chopped onion
4	drops hot pepper sauce	1	cup chopped celery
⅛	teaspoon garlic salt	1	teaspoon lemon juice
½	teaspoon horseradish	4	dozen shrimp, cooked, cleaned and peeled
½	teaspoon Worcestershire sauce		Parmesan cheese
1	teaspoon lemon-pepper seasoning		

Mix all ingredients except shrimp and cheese. Put shrimp in buttered baking shells or ramekins. Spread sauce over shrimp and sprinkle with Parmesan cheese. Bake in 350 degree oven until hot and bubbly, about 20 minutes.

Serves 4 to 6.

CHICKEN REDBUD

4	large chicken breasts, boned and halved	2	small cans mushrooms, stems and pieces
1	stick butter	½-1	cup white wine
1	onion, finely chopped		Flour to thicken sauce
1	clove garlic	½	pint heavy cream or half and half
1	can bouillon or consommé		Salt and red pepper to taste

Melt butter. Brown chicken in butter. Remove to baking pan. Cook onion and garlic in butter until tender, add flour, bouillon, white wine and mushrooms. Simmer slowly until well heated. Add cream or milk, stirring until smooth. Season with salt and red pepper. Pour over chicken and bake at 350 degrees for about 30 minutes. Serve with rice. Sauce with chicken may be frozen.

Serves 4.

CHOCOLATE CHIP PECAN PIE

1	cup sugar	1	cup pecans, chopped
4	eggs		
1	cup white corn syrup	½	cup chocolate chips
1	teaspoon vanilla	1	10-inch pie shell
1	stick butter		

Combine sugar, eggs, syrup, vanilla and mix well. Melt butter; add to mixture. Add pecans and chocolate chips, stirring until well mixed. Pour into 10-inch pie shell. (See pie crust recipe below.) Bake at 350 degrees for 50 minutes or until set.

MAGGIE'S PIE CRUST

2	cups flour	1	teaspoon salt
¾	cup shortening	⅓	cup cold water

Cut shortening into flour. Add just enough water to make dough stick together. Makes two 9-inch or 10-inch crusts.

DESOTO County is one of Memphis' largest suburbs and the fastest growing county in Mississippi. Hernando is the county seat. The Spanish explorer Hernando DeSoto first saw the Mississippi River from the river banks near here.

TUNICA County bills itself as "The South's Casino Capitol" and America's third largest gaming destination. It boasts ten world-class casinos, over six thousand hotel rooms and forty new restaurants.

CLARKSDALE is proud of its musical heritage. The famous Delta Blues Museum is worth a visit and houses thousands of books, records, tapes, photos and exhibits. The playwright, Tennessee Williams, lived here during his youth. Coahoma County also has casino gaming located on the Mississippi River.

CLEVELAND is the home of Delta State University. It has unique shopping districts, historic blues sites, four-star dining, performing arts and entertainment. It is the largest city in Bolivar County. Nearby Sunflower, Mississippi was the boyhood home of the former *New York Times* Food Editor, Craig Claiborne.

GREENVILLE and Washington County calls itself "The Most Southern Place on Earth." It is also the birthplace of Muppets creator Jim Henson. *Kermit the Frog* was named for a childhood friend of Henson's in nearby Leland.

INDIANOLA is the birthplace of musical legend B. B. King. While cotton and soybean cultivation is the backbone of farming in the rich Delta soil, farm-raised catfish has made an impact on the economy of Sunflower County. Some of the best pecans in the Mississippi Valley are harvested here.

BELZONI is home to the national Catfish Institute. Catfish has gone from a traditional Southern delicacy to the fifth most popular fish in America. Approximately 95 percent of the nation's farm-raised catfish are raised in Mississippi, Arkansas, Alabama and Louisiana.

GREENWOOD boasts the second largest cotton exchange in the United States. Historic downtown Greenwood has "Cotton Row" where buyers and sellers of cotton have maintained offices since the late 1800s. Florewood River Plantation is an authentic recreation of an 1850s plantation.

GRENADA is home to the largest freshwater body of water in the state, Grenada Lake. This 36,000-acre lake is popular with boating enthusiasts and provides some of the best fishing in the area. Nearby Tallahatchie County is home to the distinguished motion picture actor, Morgan Freeman.

VICKSBURG is referred to as "The Gibraltar of the South" because of the long siege that occurred here during the Civil War. It is also home to the Vicksburg National Military Park. The Civil War battlefield has been preserved here. Vicksburg is home to the Biedenharn Museum of *Coca-Cola* Memorabilia – a restored 1890 building where *Coca-Cola* was first bottled anywhere in the world in 1894. Vicksburg is known for its beautifully restored antebellum homes.

PORT GIBSON was described by General Grant as "too beautiful to burn." It is home to the Grand Gulf Military Monument Park. The "Ruins of Windsor" are located nearby on Rodney Road and was a movie location for *Raintree County* starring Elizabeth Taylor. Port Gibson is also known for its beautiful churches.

NATCHEZ is the oldest civilized settlement on the Mississippi River – older by two years than New Orleans. The city flourished before the Civil War with the exportation of cotton by steamboat – cotton grown on plantations in Mississippi and across the river in the rich Louisiana lowlands. Enormous fortunes were made from the land and the river. Cotton was king, money was plentiful and men spent it – particularly on dazzling mansions filled with the finest furnishings money could buy. Historic Natchez has pilgrimages in the spring and fall which attract thousands of tourists from all over the world. Natchez is included in Hugh Bayless's book as one of "The 100 Best Towns in America."

BONNE TERRE COUNTRY INN & CAFÉ

4715 Church Road West
Nesbit, Mississippi 38651

Max Bonnin, Owner

Bonne Terre is located on 100 beautifully manicured acres of rolling land in Nesbit, Mississippi. The Inn has 12 rooms and a 2-room suite. It also features a riding stable as well as two clear spring-fed lakes. Bonne Terre was featured in the September 1998 issue of Southern Living magazine. Bonne Terre has been featured twice on the Mid-South Gardens television show.

Tim Loving, Executive Chef

Chef Loving is a native of Germantown, Tennessee. He graduated from Germantown High School in 1986. He attended Denison University in Granville, Ohio and is a 1993 graduate of the Culinary Institute of America in Hyde Park, New York. He worked as a chef at Savanna's in Long Island and The Farmhouse in East Hampton before returning to the South to become the Executive Chef at Bonne Terre.

SOUTHERN PECAN TART WITH VANILLA CHANTILLY & BOURBON CARAMEL SAUCE

Pastry Dough:

8	ounces butter	3	eggs
9	ounces sugar	18	ounces flour

Cream butter and sugar until smooth in a mixer. Add eggs and mix. Add flour slowly and allow to incorporate until mixed. Wrap in plastic and allow to chill at least 3 hours for best results. Lightly grease an 8 to 10-inch tart mold. Flour counter surface and roll out enough dough to line the mold. (Chef Loving prefers a thin tart crust, about ¼-inch thick.) Gently place into mold being sure crust is snug against all edges. Pre-bake crust in 350 degree oven until light golden. Add pecan pieces to fill the bottom of the crust or to desired amount and fill with tart batter. (Recipe below.)

Batter:

5	ounces brown sugar	6	eggs
18	ounces light corn syrup	1½	ounces melted butter

Mix all ingredients in a mixing bowl with a whisk until smooth. Pour into tart. Make sure that the pecans are even throughout the tart. Bake at 350 degrees for about 45 minutes or until the middle of the tart is just set. Allow to cool for at least 20 minutes before slicing.

VANILLA CHANTILLY

1	cup heavy cream	¼	teaspoon vanilla extract
1	tablespoon powdered sugar		

Whip cream until medium peaks and add powdered sugar and extract and whip to just under stiff peaks. Once your tart is cooled, this is a great substitution for ice cream.

CARAMEL SAUCE

1	cup sugar	1	tablespoon butter
1	cup heavy cream	½	tablespoon bourbon

Cook sugar in heavy saucepan until caramel in color. Add butter and stir into caramel with wooden spoon. Add milk and bourbon and reduce heat to simmer and slowly cook until sugar melts into cream, stirring occasionally. Reduce to the desired consistency and allow to cool about 15 minutes before serving.

WILD MUSHROOM & GOAT CHEESE STRUDEL

2 ounces olive oil	1 cup red port
½ cup minced shallots	Fresh chopped thyme, rosemary and sage
2 tablespoons minced garlic	1 cup heavy cream
2 stalks minced celery	Salt and pepper to taste
¼ pound minced prosciutto	1 cup grated Parmesan cheese
¾ pound shiitake mushrooms	½ cup grated goat cheese
¾ pound white mushrooms	1 egg, beaten
¾ pound crimini mushrooms (or portobello)	1 cup bread crumbs
½ cup brandy	¼ pound melted butter
	Phyllo dough

Sweat first four ingredients in oil and add mushrooms. Sauté until dry. When the pan is dry, add brandy and port and reduce this liquid to a syrup consistency. Add cream and reduce until thick. Add herbs and mix, then allow the mixture to cool. When cool add egg, cheeses and bread crumbs. Season with salt and pepper. Lay out on a phyllo sheet and brush with melted butter over entire sheet. Lay a second sheet of phyllo over the first sheet and brush the top completely with butter. Repeat step 2 more times for a total of four sheets of phyllo, but do not butter the top of the last sheet. Place mushroom mixture across one end of the rectangle and gently roll up the phyllo into a strudel. Brush entire strudel with melted butter and place on a greased baking sheet and bake at 400 degrees for 10 minutes and then reduce oven to 300 degrees and bake to an internal temperature of 170 degrees.

Serves 6 to 8.

STEVE WALSNOVICH
Executive Chef

Chef Walsnovich is a native of Pittsburg, Pennsylvania. He served as a chef in a Pittsburg Italian restaurant 1978-1986. He is a 1992 graduate of the Pennsylvania Institute of Culinary Arts. He has served as the Executive Sous Chef at the Crescent Club and as Executive Chef at the River Terrace restaurant in Memphis. He has appeared on the Taste of the Nation television show. Chef Steve is a former executive chef at Bonne Terre.

MUFFULETTA SALAD WITH PASTA

1 cup sliced green olives	½ teaspoon red pepper flakes
1 cup sliced black olives	1 cup salami, julienne
2 ribs celery, cut on bias	½ cup red onion, julienne
½ cup red wine vinegar	½ cup roasted red pepper, julienne
1 tablespoon garlic, chopped	½ cup roasted yellow pepper, julienne
Salt and pepper to taste	3 cups farfalle (butterfly-shaped) pasta, cooked
1 tablespoon whole grain mustard	1 cup pepperjack cheese, cooked

Combine all ingredients (above) and marinate overnight.

10 cups cut romaine lettuce	20 slices English cucumber
30 slices Roma tomatoes	

Place 1 cup of cut romaine lettuce on desired salad plate. Top with marinated mixture. Garnish with sliced tomato and cucumbers.

Serves 10.

PAN-SEARED LAMB MEDALLIONS WITH ROGHAN JOSH SAUCE

(Appetizer)

24	2-ounce lamb medallions	2	teaspoons ground cloves
	Olive oil	2	tablespoons black pepper
	Montreal seasoning	2	onions, small diced
	Roghan Josh sauce (recipe below)	2	teaspoons coriander
2	tablespoons ginger, minced	4	teaspoons cumin
2	tablespoons garlic, minced	3	tablespoons paprika
¼	cup water	2	cinnamon sticks
2	tablespoons cardamom	2	cups beef consommé
4	bay leaves	1	cup sour cream

1) Combine lamb, olive oil and Montreal seasoning and reserve.

Steps 2 through 5 make roghan josh sauce:
2) Combine ginger, garlic and water and purée.

3) Sauté cardamom, bay leaves, cloves, black pepper and onion until soft.

4) Add ginger paste, coriander, cumin, paprika, cinnamon and beef consommé (simmer 15 minutes).

5) Temper in sour cream and reserve in steam well.

6) Sauté lamb medallions.

7) Add 2 ounces (per serving) of roghan josh sauce into skillet and bring to simmer.

8) Place on plate and garnish.

Serves 24.

STUFFED CHICKEN BREASTS WITH HERBS & CUCUMBER

10	6-ounce chicken breasts, skin on	Chives for garnish
2	each cucumbers, skinned and seeded	

For the stuffing:

1	ounce shallots, chopped finely	2	cups sour cream
2	ounces butter	2	cups bread crumbs
1½	pounds dark chicken meat, skinned and boned	¼	cup mixed herbs, chopped finely
2	each egg whites		Salt and pepper to taste

For the sauce:

3	ounces shallots, chopped finely	3	cups chicken stock
½	cup butter	½	cup mushrooms, chopped finely
1	cup white wine	2	cups heavy cream

Make the stuffing: Sweat the shallot in the butter until soft, then let cool. Grind the meat in a food processor. Add the shallot and egg white and grind again until very smooth. Put the mixture in a bowl; set over an ice bath, and stir in the sour cream and bread crumbs. Add the herbs and season.

Stuffing the chicken: Cut a pocket into the chicken breast and stuff with stuffing. Season the breast with salt and pepper.

Prepare the sauce: Cook the shallots and mushrooms in the butter until soft. Add the chicken stock and heavy cream and reduce to consistency. Season if necessary. Finish with whole butter.

Prepare the cucumber: Cut the cucumber in half lengthwise. Cut into large bias pieces. Blanch briefly in boiling water. Cool in ice bath and reserve.

Cooking the stuffed chicken: Brush melted butter onto chicken breast. Roast in the oven at 350 degrees until done.

The finished plate: Quickly sauté the cucumber slices. Place chicken on plate and spoon sauce over top. Garnish with snipped chives and cucumber slices.

Serves 10.

WHITE CHOCOLATE PEANUT CRÈME BRÛLÉE

2	quarts heavy cream	½	cup sugar
1	vanilla bean	¼	cup brandy
½	pound white chocolate, chopped	½	cup peanuts, chopped fine
½	cup sugar	24	small peanut butter cookies for garnish
1	zest of lemon		
20	egg yolks		

1) Place heavy cream in pot.

2) Split vanilla bean and add to cream.

3) Bring to boil and add chocolate, ½ cup sugar and zest.

4) Remove from heat.

5) Whip egg yolks and ½ cup sugar in stainless steel bowl.

6) Slowly add hot milk.

7) Add brandy.

8) Ladle 6 ounces into cups.

9) Place cups in roasting pan and fill with water (¾ full).

10) Place in 350 degree oven on bake.

11) Cook 10 minutes.

12) Sprinkle chopped peanuts on top of brûlée until covered completely.

13) Continue baking until done, approximately 15 minutes.

14) Remove from oven and cool.

15) Top with whipped cream, strawberries and cookies.

Serves 12.

ANDY BOUCHARD
Former Chef
Bonne Terre Country Inn & Café
Nesbit, Mississippi

ROASTED SALMON WITH SAFFRON LEEK SAUCE

4	6-ounce portions of salmon

For sauce:

2	ounces butter	3	cups heavy cream
1	ounce flour		A pinch of saffron
1	leek (only the white part)		Salt and pepper to taste
2	shallots		
16	ounces cooked rice (wild rice or Basmati rice) Oil to pan sear the salmon		Seasoning for salmon Salt, pepper and garlic

Sauce: Melt butter in a pot. Add shallots and leeks and sauté. Add flour and after butter and flour combine, add the heavy cream. Stir constantly until sauce thickens. Season with salt and pepper. Add saffron and simmer on low heat for 10 minutes.

Salmon: Have a very hot pot on the stove. Wash salmon. Dry the salmon and season with salt, pepper and garlic. Add olive oil in the pan and lay the salmon carefully in the pan skin side up. Turn the salmon after 2 to 3 minutes and put it in the oven for about 5 minutes at 400 degrees F. Have rice cooked and place in the middle of the plate. Put the salmon on top and add two spoons of sauce on top.

Serves 4.

PAN-SEARED MAHI-MAHI WITH RED WINE REDUCTION & BELL PEPPER SALSA

4   6-ounce portions of fresh Mahi-Mahi fish

RED WINE REDUCTION

1	cup orange juice	Olive oil to sear
4	cups red wine	fish
	(burgundy)	Fish seasoning:
1	cinnamon stick	Salt, pepper and
¼	cup sugar	garlic
	Salt and pepper to	
	taste	

BELL PEPPER SALSA

2	red + 2 green +	Olive oil
	2 yellow bell	(2 spoons)
	peppers	
1	fresh pineapple	
	Salt, vinegar,	
	pepper, sugar and	
	cayenne pepper to	
	taste	

Red Wine Reduction: Pour orange juice and red wine into a pot. Add sugar, salt, pepper and cinnamon stick. Reduce ingredients until it becomes a thick syrup. Take off stove and cool down.

Bell Pepper Salsa: Cut red, yellow and green peppers into small cubes. Cut the pineapple the same way. Add ingredients into a bowl and mix. Add salt, pepper, sugar, vinegar and cayenne pepper.

Mahi-Mahi: Season fish with salt, pepper and garlic and place in a hot pan with the olive oil. Sear on one side and put in preheated oven for 6 to 8 minutes.

Final preparation: Add the oil to the salsa. Place the salsa in the middle of the plate. Place the Mahi-Mahi on top. Sprinkle the red wine reduction over the fish.

Serves 4.

J. W. MILLER'S STEAKHOUSE

333 Lester Street Hernando, MS 38632

Paige & J. W. Miller, Proprietors

Paige and J. W. are both graduates of the University of Mississippi. They opened their beautiful new restaurant on the historic downtown square in the fall of 1997.

JUMBO SHRIMP WITH SCAMPINELLI SAUCE

6	16 to 20-count peeled and deveined jumbo shrimp per serving (tail on)	Scampinelli sauce (recipe below)

Sauté shrimp in skillet over medium heat until shrimp turns pink. Do not overcook. Pour Scampinelli sauce over cooked shrimp in dish. Serve with lots of bread.

SCAMPINELLI SAUCE

⅓	cup sweet mustard	1	clove garlic,
3	tablespoons Dijon		minced
	mustard	¼	teaspoon salt
1	tablespoon tomato	¼	teaspoon white
	paste		pepper
1	tablespoon hot	2	cups mayonnaise
	pepper sauce	¼	cup seeded tomato

Blend in processor sweet and Dijon mustard, tomato paste, pepper sauce, garlic, salt and white pepper. Stir in mayonnaise and chopped tomato. Sauce is also great as dipping sauce.

Serves 6.

SHRIMP REMOULADE

Sauce:
6	egg yolks, boiled and mashed	3	tablespoons horseradish
4	cloves garlic, chopped	2	tablespoons Worcestershire sauce
3	tablespoons spicy mustard	4	tablespoons vinegar
4	tablespoons prepared mustard (This is a dry spice!)	4	tablespoons chopped parsley
4	cups mayonnaise		Dash hot pepper sauce
1	tablespoon paprika		Salt and pepper to taste

Blend in blender and store in refrigerator. Serve over bed of shredded lettuce topped with 3 jumbo boiled, peeled and deveined shrimp. Place dressing on top of shrimp. Garnish salad with a quartered boiled egg and tomato wedge.

Serves 12.

TURKEY REUBEN WITH 1000 ISLAND DRESSING

Two pieces of turkey grilled on flat top.

Top with grilled sauerkraut and 2 slices of Swiss cheese, melted.

A small ladle of 1000 Island dressing (recipe below) on toasted rye bread.

1000 ISLAND DRESSING

8	hard boiled eggs	½	cup water
1	cup ketchup		Salt and pepper to taste
2	quarts mayonnaise		
2	cups sweet relish	⅛	cup olive oil

Beat until blended well in large mixer.

Makes about 1 gallon.

PECAN PIE

9	eggs	1	box light brown sugar
3	cups white corn syrup	6	ounces melted butter
1	tablespoon vanilla extract	5	cups pecans
½	cup all-purpose flour	3	deep-dish pie shells

Beat eggs lightly then add vanilla, flour, brown sugar, corn syrup and butter. Mix on low speed until blended well. Prick unbaked pie shells with fork. Pour mixture into 3 pie shells evenly. Spread pecans on top of each pie evenly. Pat into mixture slightly. Bake at 350 degrees for 55 minutes.

Yield: 3 pies (18 slices total)

CHEF MILES MCMATH
Hernando, MS 38632

Chef McMath is a graduate of the Sullivan Culinary Academy in Louisville, Kentucky. He has been a chef since 1992. Miles is a former vice-president of the North Mississippi Chapter of the American Culinary Federation. Chef McMath is a former chef for Grand Casinos in Tunica, Mississippi.

MEDALLIONS OF VENISON WITH GORGONZOLA BUTTER SAUCE

1	whole small white tail backstrap (2 pounds)	1	teaspoon minced shallots
1	cup olive oil	¼	cup dry white wine
1	tablespoon black peppercorns	¼	cup heavy cream
1	tablespoon chopped garlic	2	tablespoons crumbled Gorgonzola cheese
3	tablespoons lemon juice	½	cup cold butter
		½	teaspoon white pepper

Place the game in a glass or enameled container. Make a marinade from the oil, peppercorn, garlic and lemon juice and pour over meat. Let it marinade for one hour. Meanwhile, prepare a charcoal fire or preheat a gas grill or broiler. To make the sauce, combine the shallots, wine and cream in a saucepan over moderate heat and reduce to half of original volume. Lower the heat and add the crumbled cheese. Stir until melted. Cut the cold butter in four pieces and add to the sauce a piece at a time, stirring all the while. Season with white pepper. Set aside in warm place but not over direct heat as it could cause sauce to separate. Put meat close to the heat source to allow olive oil to flare up and create a hot fire. (Be careful!) Keep turning meat to allow to char without overcooking the middle. Remove venison from heat when it is rare or no more than medium rare. Slice and arrange on individual plates. Top with sauce and serve.

Serves 4.

MALLARD DUCK WITH FIG PRESERVES

1	5-pound mallard	3	tablespoons white vinegar
¼	cup clarified butter		
½	cup dry white wine	1½	tablespoons fig preserves
1¼	cup duck stock		
2	large sugar cubes		Juice of ½ lemon

Dress and truss the duck and place in a braising pot with 2 tablespoons of clarified butter. Braise until the bird is medium rare. Remove duck and deglaze the pot with white wine. Reduce by a quarter and add duck stock. Remove the trussing strings from the duck. Meanwhile, prepare a caramel with the sugar cubes. Crush them and melt with 1 teaspoon of the stock mixture. Reduce the mixture if needed and pass the sauce through a fine sieve. Drain the figs well and add the juice and the lemon to the sauce in a small saucepan. Heat the figs and the remaining butter. Adjust the seasoning of the sauce. Arrange the duck on a platter with the sauce and figs around it. Serve with Dauphine potatoes and asparagus tips.

Serves 6.

MESCLUN GREENS WITH WALNUT CRUSTED GOAT CHEESE, BOSC PEARS & A PORT WINE VINAIGRETTE

1	ounce mesclun greens (field greens)	2	tablespoons port wine
¼	cup walnut pieces, coarsely chopped	2	ounces salad oil
3	ounces goat cheese	1	ounce apple cider vinegar
1	Bosc pear, cored and cut into 12 pieces lengthwise	1	teaspoon Dijon mustard
1	tablespoon unsalted butter	1	tablespoon honey
			Salt and pepper to taste

Preheat a medium-size sauté pan on medium heat. Cut goat cheese in half and form into about a 1½-inch patty. Press walnut pieces into goat cheese. Add butter to sauté pan and sear on both sides quickly (about one minute on each side) and remove. Toss greens with pears and vinaigrette and place on salad plate. Top with warm goat cheese and serve.

Serves 2.

Vinaigrette: Whisk port wine, vinegar and mustard together. Slowly drizzle in oil. Whisk in honey and add salt and pepper to taste.

GRILLED MISSISSIPPI QUAIL WITH FRIED SWEET POTATOES, WILTED GREENS & A BACON DEMI-GLACE

2	Mississippi farm-raised quail (deboned)	½	cup demi-glace or brown sauce
1	sweet potato	¼	cup unsalted butter
1	ounce mesclun salad greens		Salt and pepper to taste
¼	cup fried bacon cut in 1-inch pieces	1	tablespoon olive oil
		4	cups canola oil

Preheat grill on high. Preheat oven to 350 degrees. Rub quail with olive oil. Season with salt and pepper and set aside. Cut sweet potato into matchsticks (shoestrings) and submerge in water and set aside. Heat 4 cups of oil in cast iron skillet or deep fryer at 350 degrees. Place quail on the grill and sear on both sides at high temperature for about 2 minutes. Reduce heat to low and cook for approximately 8 minutes or until the internal temperature reaches 165 degrees. (If using charcoal grill, remove quail from direct heat and cook approximately 12 to 15 minutes.)

Meanwhile, place the potatoes in the 350 degree fat until crispy. Remove and drain on towel. Season with salt and pepper. Place mesclun greens on a sheet pan and go into a 350 degree oven for about 2 minutes or until just wilted. Remove greens and set aside. Place demi-glace in saucepan and on medium heat reduce by one-half. Season with salt and pepper, add butter and bacon and remove from heat and stir slowly until just blended. Place greens on a platter and top the greens with the quail. Pour the sauce over the quail and garnish with the fried sweet potatoes.

Serves 1.

MICHEL LENY
Senatobia, MS 38668

Chef Owner

*Chef Leny is a native of Brussels, Belgium. He became interested in cooking at an early age. His father was a chef at one of the big hotels in Brussels and at Maxim's in Paris. Chef Leny co-founded **Bonne Terre Country Inn & Café** in Nesbit, Mississippi. He is the owner of **Café Society** in Memphis, Tennessee.*

ITALIAN BREAD WITH SAINT ANDRE CHEESE & BOSC PEARS

5	cups water	4	slices of Italian paysanne bread (peasant bread)
2	tablespoons lemon juice	4	slices Saint Andre cheese (or brie)
2	tablespoons sugar		
1	vanilla bean		
2	bosc pears (or any pear)		

In saucepan, incorporate water, lemon juice, sugar and vanilla bean. Bring to a boil. Simmer for 30 minutes. Poach the pears in the sauce. Let the pears cool off in the liquid. Remaining sauce can be reduced to a syrupy consistency and spooned over the dish.

To serve: Slice of Saint Andre cheese over lightly toasted bread and topped with half a pear.

Serves 4.

GRAND CASINO RESORTS

13615 Old Highway 61 North Robinsonville, MS 38664

Ashley Wheeler
Chef & Production Manager

Chef Ashley is a native of Pontiac, Michigan. He has a Culinary Arts degree from Craft Community College in Lavonia, Illinois. He has been active with the American Culinary Federation since 1978. In 1980, he received the Bronze Medal at the Great Lakes Culinary Salon. Chef Ashley was certified as a C.W.C. in 1991. In 1994, he received his Hospitality Management degree. Prior to joining Grand Casinos, Chef Ashley was kitchen manager for Sheraton, Tunica.

SALMON NEVERNAIS

8	ounces salmon fillet	1	ounce white wine
1	zucchini, peeled	1	pinch salt
1	carrot, peeled	1	pinch white pepper
1	teaspoon chopped garlic	1	ounce olive oil
1	ounce fish fumet (optional)	2	ounces double cream
		1	tablespoon chopped parsley

Heat pan, season fish with salt and pepper. Sauté fish one minute on both sides, set aside. Heat pan, add wine, garlic, fish fumet, double cream and vegetables. Bring to a boil, remove the vegetables to plate. Put parsley in sauce. Boil sauce ½ minute, pour sauce next to vegetables, place salmon on top of sauce.

Serves 1.

FISH STOCK*

1	pound fish bones	1	tablespoon salt
1	carrot	1	teaspoon white pepper
2	stalks celery		
1	large onion	4	cups water
1	bunch parsley stems		

Put all ingredients in stock pot. Bring to a boil, set to simmer for one hour. Strain.

*For beef or chicken stock, substitute beef or chicken bones for the fish.

TOMATO FLORENTINE SOUP

½	cup green onions, chopped	2	regular cans chopped tomatoes
1	cup leeks, diced	2	ounces olive oil
¾	pound spinach, chopped	½	gallon hot chicken stock
1	tablespoon garlic, chopped		Salt and pepper to taste
½	tablespoon Italian seasoning	¼	teaspoon Parmesan cheese

Sauté leeks, green onions and garlic in olive oil, but do not brown. Add remaining ingredients except Parmesan cheese, bring to boil and set to simmer for about 20 minutes. Remove from stove and hold for service. Garnish with Parmesan cheese just before serving.

Yield: 12 8-ounce portions

CHICKEN WITH RICE SOUP

⅓	pound onions, diced	¾	gallon hot chicken stock
¼	pound celery, diced	¾	pound cooked rice
¼	pound carrots, diced	⅓	ounce parsley, chopped
	Salt and white pepper to taste	¾	pound chicken meat, cooked, diced

Add vegetables to hot chicken stock and simmer until tender. Add diced chicken meat, rice and salt and pepper. Simmer 5 minutes. Hold for service and sprinkle parsley over just before serving.

Yield: 12 portions

GRAND CASINO

13615 Old Highway 61 North Robinsonville, MS 38664

Moulay Elabdellaoui
Chef

Chef Moulay is a native of Morocco. He graduated from culinary schools in Morocco and France. He has been employed as a chef at the Oak Hurst Country Club in Greensboro, North Carolina and as banquet chef and executive sous chef at Fitzgerald's Casino in Tunica.

SPICY SPINACH DIP

2	tablespoons olive oil	1	pound cream cheese (at room temperature)
1	pound frozen spinach	1	tablespoon paprika
2	tablespoons cumin	1	tablespoon hot pepper sauce
2	teaspoons salt		
1	cup chopped onions	2	tablespoons chopped cilantro
1	cup diced tomatoes	2	tablespoons chopped garlic
½	cup chopped jalapeños		

In sauté pan: Heat the oil for 1 minute over medium heat. Add onions, tomato, garlic, jalapeños and all the spices. Cook until the onions are soft. Add the spinach and cook for 5 minutes. Add cream cheese and mix well.

Serve with flour tortillas or fried flour tortillas.

Serves 4.

LAMB LOIN MARINATED IN RED WINE

3	lamb loins	2	tablespoons black and red peppercorns (coarsely ground)
2	cups or more (if needed) dry red wine		
3	tablespoons juniper berries, coarsely ground	½	cup beef stock or 1 tablespoon beef base mixed with ½ cup hot water
1	tablespoon dried red pepper flakes	3	tablespoons chopped fresh garlic
6	bay leaves, crumbled		

Combine the wine, juniper berries, pepper flakes, garlic, black and red peppercorns, and bay leaves in a shallow non-aluminum container and add the lamb. Make sure the lamb is covered with red wine. Cover and refrigerate for 2 days.

Heat the grill. Remove the lamb from the marinade (reserve the marinade). Lightly sprinkle with salt and pepper, and grill to desired temperature. Meanwhile, strain the marinade into a saucepan and boil over high heat until reduced to 1 cup. Add the stock and simmer for 3 more minutes. Slice the lamb ½-inch thick and arrange 4 pieces on each plate. Spoon the sauce over the top and serve with your desired vegetables or starch.

Serves 6.

MOROCCAN STYLE GRILLED STUFFED VEAL CHOPS WITH RED ONIONS & RED WINE

6	veal chops	½	cup sliced almonds, toasted and coarsely chopped
6	tablespoons unsalted butter		
¼	cup chopped onions (for the stuffing)	¼	cup chopped cilantro
3	cloves garlic, minced	¼	cup chopped Kalamata olives
1	cup fresh bread crumbs		Salt and pepper to taste

FOR THE SAUCE
(RED ONION & RED WINE)

1	cup unsalted butter	3	tablespoons sugar
6	large red onions sliced ¼-inch thick		Salt and pepper to taste
3	cups full-bodied red wine (Zinfandel)		

Melt ½ cup butter in large heavy sauté pan over medium heat. Add the onions and cook until tender (about 15 minutes). Add 2 cups wine and continue cooking until the onions are very tender. Sweeten to taste with sugar and season with salt and pepper. Set aside.

For the stuffing: Heat 2 tablespoons butter in a small sauté pan. Add the onions and cook until done (about 6 minutes). Add the garlic and cook about 3 minutes. Remove from the heat and mix with the remaining butter, bread crumbs, almonds, cilantro and olives. Season to taste with salt and pepper. The stuffing should hold together when squeezed. If it is too dry, add 1 to 2 more tablespoons of butter.

Heat the grill. Stuff each chop with 2 tablespoons of the filling and brush with the oil. Sprinkle with salt and pepper and grill to a desired temperature.

When the chops are done, serve in plate and put the red onion and red wine sauce over the chops.

Serves 6.

BALLY'S SALOON & GAMBLING HALL

1450 Ballys Boulevard Robinsonville, MS 38664

**Randy Carmody, Executive Chef
Delta Steak House**

Chef Randy Carmody is a native of Manitowoc, Wisconsin. He served an apprenticeship under Executive Chef Richard Cater in Phoenix, Arizona. He graduated from Mesa Culinary School in Mesa, Arizona in 1981. He has worked as a chef in the casino industry since 1984, in Laughlin and Las Vegas, Nevada, prior to joining Bally's in Tunica in 1996.

MISSISSIPPI GULF CRAB CAKES

(Appetizer)

½	cup clarified butter	12	ounces mayonnaise
1	cup onion (¼ diced)	4	ounces Creole mustard
½	red pepper (¼ diced)	1	pound fresh bread crumbs
	Salt and cracked black pepper to taste	4	whole eggs
4	pounds jumbo lump crab meat (picked for shells)	½	cup fresh chopped parsley

Sauté onion and pepper in butter. Cool and mix gently with crab meat. Whip eggs, mustard, salt, pepper, parsley and bread crumbs into mayonnaise. Gently fold appariel mix into crab meat. Portion into 4-ounce crab cakes. Chill product. Bread cakes using standard breading procedure.

Serve with 2 ounces of tomato mustard coulis and 1 ounce remoulade.

Yield: 16 crab cakes

BLACKENED PORK MEDALLIONS

4 2-ounce pork tenderloin medallions
1 ounce blackened seasoning
6 ounces lemon-pepper linguini
2 ounces Cajun hollandaise sauce (recipe follows)

Season pork with blackened seasoning. Blacken in cast iron skillet until internal temperature reaches 160 degrees. Place medallions over cooked linguini and top with Cajun Hollandaise sauce.

Serves 1.

RED SNAPPER BOURBON STREET

2 4-ounce red snapper fillets
3 ounces (60 to 70-count) shrimp
2 ounces jumbo lump crab
1 ounce clarified butter
2 ounces lime Hollandaise sauce (recipe follows)

Broil snapper until done. Place on center of plate. In one ounce of butter, sauté shrimp and crab. Top snapper with mixture. Top with lime Hollandaise sauce.

Serves 1.

HOLLANDAISE SAUCE

(Basic)

12 egg yolks
24 ounces clarified butter
2½ lemons, juiced
Salt and hot pepper sauce to taste

Whisk egg yolks in double boiler until fluffed. Whisking continuously, gradually add clarified butter. Add lemon juice, salt and hot pepper sauce to taste.

LIME HOLLANDAISE SAUCE:

4 ounces basic Hollandaise sauce, blend in juice of 1 lime.

CAJUN HOLLANDAISE SAUCE:

4 ounces basic Hollandaise sauce, blend in 1 tablespoon of Cajun seasoning.

TIM MILLS

Executive Chef

Chef Mills is a native of Jackson, Tennessee. His apprenticeship was under Frans Hendriks with the Holiday Corporation from 1982-1988. He is a 1986 graduate of the Culinary Institute of America in Hyde Park, New York. Chef Mills worked for the Sheraton Washington from 1988-1989. He prepared banquet dinners for President Reagan while at the Sheraton. He also prepared dinners for President George Bush's Inaugural Ball. Tim is the former executive chef for Fitzgerald's Casino & Hotel in Tunica, Mississippi.

POTATO LEEK SOUP WITH SORREL & CRÈME FRAÎCHE

1¼ pounds potatoes, diced
1¾ gallons chicken stock
¼ pound leeks, julienne
1 ounce sorrel, chopped
2 cups blonde roux
1½ pints cream
Salt and pepper to taste

1) Sweat leeks in two tablespoons of butter.
2) Add chicken stock – bring to boil.
3) Add potatoes.
4) Add roux – bring to boil.
5) Add cream.
6) Season with salt and pepper.

Yield: 2 gallons

SNAKE BITES

(Appetizer)

12	16 to 20-count shrimp (3 shrimp per serving)	8	ounces garlic aioli (garlic mayonnaise)
12	jalapeño peppers (3 per serving)	4	cilantro sprigs
4	fried tortilla shells		Snake Bite breading (as needed)
12	ounces julienne vegetable mix (recipe follows)		

1) Fry breaded shrimp until golden brown.

2) Place julienne vegetable mix on plate spreading them evenly.

3) Place tortilla shell with garlic aioli at top of plate.

4) Stand up 3 fried shrimp in center of plate. One shrimp should point towards the left, one straight and one to the right.

Serves 4.

JULIENNE VEGETABLES FOR SNAKEBITES

2	cups red bell pepper, julienne	2	cups carrots, chopped
2	cups zucchini, julienne	5	limes (juice)
2	cups squash, julienne	½	cup cilantro

1) With a mandoline, julienne the outer skin of the zucchini and squash (set aside).

2) Proceed to julienne carrots after peeled (set aside).

3) Remove the seeds and pith from bell peppers and julienne manually with knife (set aside).

4) Place all vegetables in a mixing bowl and toss with cilantro and lime juice.

Yield: 1 batch

SNAKE BITE BREADING

4	ounces cornstarch slurry	1½	cups flour
2½	cups yellow cornmeal	2	eggs (for wash)
			Water (as needed)

1) Place peeled and deveined shrimp in slurry: then flour, egg wash and cornmeal.

2) Place on sheet pan with parchment.

GARLIC CILANTRO AIOLI

16	ounces mayonnaise	1	(each) lime (juice)
2	ounces garlic, chopped		Salt and white pepper to taste
1	ounce cilantro, chopped		

1) Combine all ingredients in a mixing bowl.

2) Mix thoroughly and season with salt and pepper.

MACADAMIAN GROUPER WITH LOBSTER RATATOUILLE

4	8-ounce grouper fillets	4	teaspoons vegetable oil
1	cup Macadamian Breading (crushed macadamia nuts)	2	cups Lobster Ratatouille (recipe below)
	Salt and pepper to taste	4	(each) dill sprigs

1) Rub grouper with oil – season with salt and pepper.

2) Roll grouper in breading. Bake at 425 degrees until golden brown.

3) Place grouper diagonally in center of plate.

4) Spoon ratatouille across grouper from one end of plate to the other.

5) Garnish with dill.

Serves 4.

LOBSTER RATATOUILLE

½	pound lobster meat, diced small	⅓	cup red bell pepper, diced small
⅓	cup zucchini, diced small	⅛	cup basil, chopped
⅓	cup squash, diced small	1	teaspoon garlic, chopped
⅓	cup red onion, diced small		Salt and pepper to taste

1) Sauté lobster until thoroughly cooked.

2) Add garlic, squash, zucchini, onion and pepper – sweat.

3) Stir in basil, season with salt and pepper.

4) All vegetables should be al dente – don't overcook.

Serves 2.

COLD POACHED, GRILLED SHRIMP COCKTAIL WITH MARINATED ANGEL HAIR VEGETABLES

12	10-count shrimp (10 per pound) 3 per serving	2	ounces roasted garlic vinaigrette (recipe below)
1	cup angel hair vegetables (recipe below)	4	ounces infused dill oil (recipe below)
		4	sprigs dill
		4	yellow tear drop tomatoes (halves)

1) In a mixing bowl, place angel hair vegetables. 2) Ladle in vinaigrette and toss gently. 3) Place angel hair in center of plate. 4) Place shrimp on plate at 12 o'clock, 4 o'clock and 8 o'clock – tails pointing out. 5) Squeeze infused dill oil in between each shrimp. 6) Garnish with sprig of dill and criss-crossed yellow tear drop tomato.

Serves 4.

COLD POACHING BOUILLON FOR GRILLED SHRIMP COCKTAIL

3	each lemon juice, fresh	¼	each Bermuda onion, sliced thin
3	each lime juice, fresh	½	tablespoon cracked black pepper
1	cup white wine (Chardonnay)	½	tablespoon salt
¼	cup fresh whole dill	1	each bay leaf
		1	to 1½ cups cold fish stock

1) In a mixing bowl, combine the juice of lemons, limes and wine. 2) Add to that, the salt, pepper, dill and onions. 3) Depending on the pungency of the lemons and limes, add fish stock (to create an equal balance). 4) Add bay leaf and stir.

Yield: Almost ½ gallon

COOKING SHRIMP FOR GRILLED SHRIMP COCKTAIL

10   count shrimp and cold poaching bouillon

1) Peel, devein and butterfly shrimp. 2) Loop tail through back side opening of shrimp and pull all the way through. 3) Place shrimp in bouillon for 30 minutes, then remove to drain. 4) On a clean broiler, mark shrimp on each side, thoroughly cooking. 5) Set aside in sheet pan to cool (place inside cooler).

INFUSED DILL OIL FOR GRILLED SHRIMP COCKTAIL

¼	cup dill, de-stemmed	1	cup olive oil

1) Wash and remove stems from dill – pat dry with towel. 2) Add dill and half of oil to Cuisinart – purée. 3) Add remaining oil to purée and mix. 4) Pour oil into squeeze bottle and store.

Yield: 1¼ cups

PAN ROASTED GARLIC VINAIGRETTE FOR GRILLED SHRIMP COCKTAIL

½	pint rice wine vinegar	¼	cup Dijon mustard
1½	pints olive oil		Salt and ground black pepper to taste
½	cup pan roasted chopped garlic		

1) In a sauté pan, lightly brown garlic – set aside. 2) In a mixing bowl, combine vinegar and oil – stir. 3) Add roasted garlic and Dijon mustard. Mix well. 4) Season with salt and pepper to taste. Mix well.

Yield: 1¼ quarts

ANGEL HAIR VEGETABLES FOR GRILLED SHRIMP COCKTAIL

1½	cups yellow squash	1½	cups daikon (large radish)
1½	cups carrots	½	cup chives, chopped fine
¾	cup red bell peppers		

1) With a mandoline, prepare angel hair vegetables with proper adjustment on mandoline. 2) Remove just the yellow skin of the squash – set aside. 3) Peel daikon and proceed with mandoline – set aside. 4) Peel carrots, proceed with mandoline – set aside. 5) Remove seeds, pith and majority of the meat from bell pepper, manually with a knife cut into angel hair – set aside. 6) Cut chives fine – set aside. Mix 2 through 6 thoroughly.

Yield: Small batch

HERB CRUSTED DUCK

1	7-ounce Muscovy duck breast	1	tablespoon fried leeks
1	tablespoon fine herbs (see recipe)	1	(each) grilled zucchini batonnet
⅛	ounce sliced foie gras	1	(each) grilled squash batonnet
3	ounces 5-grain medley (recipe below)	3	ounces sauce foie gras (see recipe)

1) In a sauté pan, place duck breast skin side down – render fat. 2) Encrust meat side of duck and sear (cook to desired temperature). 3) Place duck on cutting board and slice breast ¾ of the way through. 4) Place 5 grain in middle of plate – fan duck breast skin side up. 5) Place pan-seared foie gras atop duck breast. 6) Place fried leeks atop foie gras. 7) Criss-cross squash and zucchini at 12 o'clock on plate. 8) Ladle sauce around plate and on duck.
Serves 1.

FINE HERBS

1	ounce chervil, chopped	1	ounce parsley, chopped
1	ounce chives, chopped	1	ounce tarragon, chopped

Chop all of the above herbs and combine. Yield: 4 ounces

SAUCE FOIE GRAS

4	quarts veal stock	Salt to taste
1½	ounces foie gras	White pepper to
2	cups brown roux	taste
1	pint heavy cream	

1) Bring veal stock to a simmer. 2) Add roux. 3) Add foie gras and stir until smooth. 4) Add cream and stir. 5) Season with salt and pepper. Yield: 1⅛ gallons

FIVE GRAIN MEDLEY

4	ounces couscous, cooked	3	ounces pink lentils, cooked
4	ounces barley, cooked	1	tablespoon garlic, cooked
4	ounces brown rice, cooked	½	cup chives, chopped
4	ounces wild rice, cooked	½	cup clarified butter
			Salt and pepper to taste

1) Over moderate heat, add all grains. 2) Add garlic and chives. 3) Add butter and heat to 140 degrees. 4) Season with salt and pepper. Yield: One batch

SMOKED QUAIL WITH LINGONBERRY & VIDALIA ONION RELISH

2½	(each) 4-ounce European semi-boneless quail	4	ounces L & V onion relish (recipe below)
3	ounces sundried tomato polenta (recipe below)	1	sprig rosemary

1) Place polenta in center of plate. 2) Split quail in halves and arrange on plate with legs toward center. 3) Place L & V relish at 10 o'clock, 3 o'clock and 7 o'clock on plate. 4) Garnish with rosemary.
Serves 1.

SUNDRIED TOMATO POLENTA

1	cup yellow cornmeal	¼	cup sundried tomato (julienne)
6	cups chicken stock		Salt and white pepper to taste

1) Bring stock to a boil. 2) Add sundried tomatoes and season with salt and pepper. 3) While stirring, slowly add cornmeal. 4) Cook on low heat – constantly stirring. 5) Polenta is done when you can have the spoon stand straight up in it.
Yield: 1 batch

LINGONBERRY & VIDALIA ONION RELISH

1	cup sweet potato, small dice	1	cup lingonberries
1	cup green bell pepper, small dice	1	tablespoon basil (chiffonade)
1	cup Vidalia onion, small dice		Salt and pepper to taste

1) Dice sweet potatoes and deep fry – set aside to cool. 2) Sauté and sweat onions and peppers – set aside to cool. 3) In a mixing bowl, add potatoes, onions and peppers. 4) Fold in lingonberries and basil. 5) Season with salt and pepper.

Yield: Small batch

HOLLYWOOD CASINO
Robinsonville, MS 38664

Roland Schnider, Executive Chef

Chef Schnider is a native of Switzerland. He has lived in the United States since 1980. Prior to coming to this country, he served his culinary apprenticeship with various hotels in Switzerland. According to Chef Roland, the highlight of his career was an opportunity he had to prepare a State Dinner for Queen Elizabeth and Prince Phillip on their official state visit to Lucerne.

Chef Schnider, prior to joining Hollywood Casino, was in the restaurant business in Memphis and Germantown, Tennessee for twelve years. One year he won first prize in the Seafood competition for the Shelby County Chefs Association and placed second in the State/National competition.

PAN-SEARED STRIPED BASS & CRABCAKE WITH CORN RELISH & ROASTED RED PEPPER BEURRE BLANC

PAN-SEARED STRIPED BASS

10   3-ounce portions of striped bass

½	tablespoon chopped cilantro	1	teaspoon Worcestershire sauce
½	tablespoon chopped basil	1	tablespoon olive oil
½	teaspoon mustard seed		Salt to taste
½	teaspoon cracked peppercorns		

Mix cilantro, basil, mustard seed, peppercorns, Worcestershire sauce, olive oil and salt. Baste fish, sear and bake until fork tender. Serves 10.

CRAB CAKES

10	ounces jumbo lump crabmeat	1	teaspoon brown mustard
6	ounces scallops, patted dry	½	teaspoon Cajun seasoning
1	egg white	½	teaspoon Worcestershire sauce
¼	cup heavy cream		
1	teaspoon chopped chives		

Mix all of the above (crab cake) ingredients together to form 10 crab cakes.

CORN RELISH

1	cup roasted corn kernels	2	tablespoons white vinegar
1	tablespoon finely diced peppers	2	tablespoons olive oil
1	teaspoon chopped cilantro		Salt and pepper to taste
2	cloves garlic		

Mix all of the above ingredients to make relish. Serves 10.

ROASTED RED PEPPER BEURRE BLANC
(to use with Crab Cakes)

½	cup cider vinegar	Shallots, chopped
½	cup cream	Thyme
½	pound butter	
½	cup puréed roasted red peppers	

Garnish: 5 each corn tortillas, julienne

VEAL JOSEF

Veal scaloppini per person	Crabmeat stuffing (see recipe)
Seasoned salt	Hollandaise sauce (see recipe)
Butter	Bread crumbs

Season veal and sauté in melted butter for 2 minutes per side. Place veal on a baking pan and top with crab meat stuffing. Spoon Hollandaise over top and sprinkle with bread crumbs. Place under broiler until lightly browned. Serve immediately.

Serves 1.

CRABMEAT STUFFING

4	tablespoons butter	2	tablespoons sherry
1	large yellow onion, chopped	2	teaspoons lemon juice
1	pound button mushrooms, sliced	2	teaspoons Worcestershire sauce
6	green onions, chopped	2	teaspoons seasoned salt
1	14-ounce can diced tomatoes	¾	cup heavy cream
½	cup white wine	1	pound crabmeat

Sauté yellow onion and mushrooms in butter until softened. Add green onion and tomato. Sauté 5 to 10 minutes. Add white wine, sherry, lemon juice, Worcestershire sauce and seasoned salt. Simmer until liquid is reduced by half. Add heavy cream and simmer 5 to 10 more minutes. Remove from heat. Gently stir in crabmeat. Set aside to cool slightly.

HOLLANDAISE SAUCE

1	stick unsalted butter		Pinch cayenne pepper
3	egg yolks		Salt, white pepper to taste
2	tablespoons fresh lemon juice		

Melt butter in saucepan and set aside to cool to room temperature. Fill bottom of a double boiler with water and bring to a boil. Lower heat until water just simmers. In insert to a double boiler, mix egg yolks and lemon juice together. Place over bottom of double boiler. Whisk eggs until smooth and slightly thickened. Gradually whisk in butter in a slow, steady stream. Add cayenne pepper, salt and white pepper. Continue whisking until sauce thickens. Serve immediately.

ROAST GARLIC VINAIGRETTE

½	cup roasted garlic	½	quart balsamic vinegar
½	cup Dijon mustard	1	tablespoon seasonings
1	quart vegetable oil		

Mix garlic, Dijon, vinegar and seasoning in the mixer with the whip. Slowly add in all the oil.

Approximately ½ gallon

HOT BACON DRESSING

1	pound bacon, cut into ½-inch pieces	1	cup Dijon mustard
		½	cup water
1½	cups red wine vinegar	¾	cup brown sugar
		½	cup heavy cream

Brown bacon until very crisp. Remove bacon from pan and reserve. Add vinegar to bacon drippings in pan and bring to a boil. Add Dijon mustard and return to a boil. Add water and return to a boil. Add brown sugar and return to a boil. Add cream and return to a boil. Cook 3 to 4 minutes. Add bacon, cool slightly and serve.

ROCKEFELLER STUFFING

2	10 to 12-ounce boxes spinach, thawed	2	each yellow onions, chopped
1	head celery	½	cup wine
10	slices bacon		Bread crumbs
1	cup chopped parsley		Seasonings

Sauté bacon, spinach, celery, onion, wine and parsley. Chop everything in food processor until very fine. Fold in bread crumbs and seasonings.

BRIAN SCHACK

Executive Chef

Chef Brian is a native of Houston, Texas. He served his apprenticeship at the Fairmont Hotel in Chicago and the Ritz Carlton in Houston. Brian graduated from the Culinary Institute of America (CIA) in 1991. He was the Executive Chef at a private country club in the Pocono Mountains in 1992. Brian was a chef for L.B.'s Steakhouse, Grand Casino Gulfport and the Grand Indian management properties in Minnesota until early 1998. Until recently, he was the Executive Chef at Sam's Town. He is currently employed as a chef for Beau Rivage in Biloxi.

OYSTER & LOBSTER STRUDEL WITH WILD MUSHROOMS WITH 3 PEPPER RELISH & SWEET CAJUN BUTTER SAUCE

STRUDEL FILLING

2	ounces lobster tail, diced	1	tablespoon butter
2	medium-sized oysters, shucked and cleaned	1	egg white
		½	teaspoon cayenne
		½	teaspoon curry powder
1	medium-sized mushroom, small diced	½	teaspoon fresh chopped dill
3	ounces heavy cream	1	5-inch square phyllo dough
1	ounce everclear grain alcohol		Pinch of salt and white pepper

1) In a hot sauté pan, add butter.

2) Quickly add lobster, oysters and mushroom.

3) Lightly brown ingredients and then pour off excess butter and liquid.

4) Deglaze pan with everclear.

5) Add heavy cream, reduce until cream is thick and glazes ingredients.

6) Remove pan from heat and add spices.

7) Stir egg white and cool mixture in refrigerator.

8) Lightly butter phyllo on one side.

9) Place cooled ingredients corner to corner across buttered phyllo.

10) Fold two corners in and roll as though rolling an eggroll.

11) Brush outside of strudel with butter and sprinkle with kosher salt and sesame seeds.

12) Place strudel on a small cookie tray lined with parchment paper and bake in a 350 degree oven for about 5 minutes or until golden brown.

3 PEPPER RELISH

2	tablespoons small diced pimiento	1	tablespoon balsamic vinegar
2	tablespoons small diced yellow pepper	1	teaspoon finely chopped parsley
1	teaspoons small diced jalapeño pepper	1	teaspoon finely chopped dill
1	teaspoon gold tequila		Pinch of kosher salt and fresh cracked pepper

Mix all ingredients together and let stand refrigerated for 2 hours.

SWEET CAJUN BUTTER SAUCE

2	ounces semillion or sauvignon blanc	1	pound whole butter, cut into small chips
1	tablespoon honey		Juice of 1 lemon
1	teaspoon blackened spice		

1) In a medium-sized sauté pan, reduce wine, honey, lemon juice and spice over medium-high heat.

2) Quickly whip butter chips into reduction over low heat moving sauté pan on and off stove top to avoid breaking the sauce. Sauce should be lightly thick and creamy.

Plate Assembly:

1) Spoon relish in a small mound in the center of a plate.

2) Drizzle butter sauce around relish.

3) Place hot strudel on top of relish.

4) Garnish with fresh dill and julienne chives.

Serves 1.

SMOKED PORK TENDERLOIN WITH BBQ BOURBON DEMI-GLACE, WILTED COLLARD GREENS & CUMIN SPICED SWEET POTATO CHIPS

SMOKED PORK TENDERLOIN

1	pork tenderloin	1	tablespoon paprika
1	teaspoon cayenne	1	tablespoon chili
1	teaspoon cumin		powder
1	teaspoon salt	2	tablespoons sugar
1	teaspoon ground thyme		

1) Mix spices and rub into cleaned pork tenderloin.

2) Smoke pork over hickory wood using medium-high heat (about 250 degrees) until pork reaches an internal temperature of 140 to 150 degrees.

BBQ BOURBON DEMI-GLACE

1	teaspoon minced shallots	1	cup demi-glace or brown sauce
2	ounces Jim Beam	1	tablespoon whole butter
2	tablespoons of favorite BBQ sauce		

1) Add shallots to a hot sauté pan.

2) Quickly deglaze with Jim Beam and add BBQ sauce

3) Add demi-glace.

4) Reduce lightly and finish sauce by stirring in whole butter.

WILTED COLLARD GREENS

1	cup collard greens, cleaned and cut into 1-inch strips	1	tablespoon butter
		1	teaspoon sesame oil
1	tablespoon chopped bacon		Salt and pepper to taste

1) Blanch collard greens in boiling water for 1 minute until tender and deep green.

2) In a hot sauté pan, add bacon. Cook until just crispy and add blanched collards, sesame oil and butter.

3) Sauté until hot. Add salt and pepper to taste.

CUMIN SPICED SWEET POTATO CHIPS

1	tablespoon cumin	1	sweet potato, peeled
1	tablespoon kosher salt		

1) Mix cumin and salt.

2) Slice sweet potato on a slicer so that chips are paper thin.

3) Deep fry sweet potato chips until light and crispy.

4) Season with cumin and salt mixture.

Plate Assembly:

1) Place a 4-inch ring mold in the center of a warm plate.

2) Press collards into the bottom of the ring mold.

3) Thin slice warm pork loin on a bias.

4) Layer pork over collards in ring mold.

5) Remove ring gently and ladle sauce around pork and collards.

6) Center four sweet potato chips around pork and collards.

Serves 1.

SHERATON CASINO & HOTEL

1107 Casino Center Drive
Robinsonville, MS 38664

Greg Andrews
Executive Chef &
Food & Beverage Manager

Chef Greg is a 1987 graduate of the apprenticeship program sponsored by the ACF and the Westin Hotel chain. He has worked for Westin in Dallas, Hawaii and Orlando. Chef Greg has worked as a Sous Chef in the Memphis area with the Peabody and Adams Mark Hotel restaurant groups. He has been with Sheraton since July 1994.

RENO'S AT THE SHERATON

FROZEN SANGRIA SOUFFLÉ

12	egg yolks	6	egg whites,
½	cup sugar		whipped
1	cup sangria	3	cups cream,
4	gelatin leaves		whipped

Put gelatin sheets into lukewarm water. Whip egg yolks, sugar and sangria together with wire whip in stainless bowl. Cook in double boiler, whipping constantly until ribbon stage. Squeeze excess water from gelatin leaves, mix in well, remove from heat. Let cool to room temperature, whipping constantly. Fold whites and cream together, fold into yolk mixture. Put plexiform around ramekins, fill to top with mixture, freeze. Remove from freezer 2 to 3 minutes before service, remove sleeve, swirl with raspberry sauce, top with dollop of whipped cream. Place ramekin on dessert plate.

Serves 6.

ANCHO-DUSTED JUMBO SEA SCALLOPS WITH AZTECAN SAUCE

6	sea scallops	4	ounces rice pilaf
2	ounces cornmeal	3	ounces vegetable
1	tablespoon ancho powder		du jour
3	ounces Aztecan sauce (recipe below)		

Dry anchos in moderate oven, place in blender with cornmeal and grind. Dust scallops in meal and sauté in olive oil. Place timbale of rice in center of plate, place Aztecan sauce around rice and place scallops on sauce. Garnish with fresh cilantro.

Serves 1.

AZTECAN SAUCE

8	jalapeño peppers, chopped	1	quart orange juice
5	red bell peppers, chopped	1	quart chicken stock
8	tomatoes, seeded and chopped	1	bunch cilantro, chopped
6	onions, medium diced	2	ounces chipotle, seeded, chopped
1	cup garlic, minced	4	ounces brown sugar

Sauté onion, garlic and peppers in salad oil until onion turns clear. Add tomatoes and cilantro. Sauté lightly. Add orange juice, stock and brown sugar. Simmer 45 minutes and add chipotle during last 15 minutes. Purée, strain and adjust seasoning.

Makes 1 gallon

LOBSTER RELLENO
(Stuffed Lobster)

8	ounces lobster meat	2	teaspoons lobster base
2	ounces jack cheese, shredded	4	Anaheim chilies
2	tablespoons yellow onion, diced	4	eggs
		1	cup flour
8	ounces béchamel sauce	2	cups cornmeal

Fry chilies at 350 degrees until skin blisters. Place in hotel pan and cover with plastic and allow chilies to sweat. When cool, peel and cut slit down side of chilies, remove seeds and ribs.

NOTE: Do not overcook chilies, flesh should remain firm. Heating hotel pan in oven increases steaming effect. Do not remove stems.

Sauté lobster meat and onions until onions turn clear. Add lobster base and béchamel, bring to simmer then cool. Add cheese to cooled mixture and fill chilies. Place in freezer to firm up. Dredge stuffed chilies in flour. Remove excess flour, dip in egg wash and coat with cornmeal. Repeat breading process. Use wet hand, dry hand method for breading. (One hand touches only the wet ingredients, the other touches only dry ingredients.) Store frozen. NOTE: Before freezing, overlap slit and place cut side down on sheet pan.

Serves 4.

SALSA VERDE

4	each tomatillos	½	tablespoon rice wine vinegar
1	each yellow onion, large dice	½	cup chicken stock
1	each medium jalapeño, seeded and chopped	1	teaspoon garlic, minced
1	tablespoon brown sugar		Salt and white pepper to taste

Roast tomatillos in 350 degree oven until browned. Cool and peel. Sauté onion, jalapeño and garlic until onion turns clear. Add tomatillos, stock and cilantro. Simmer for 5 minutes. Add vinegar and sugar, simmer 2 to 3 minutes, purée and adjust seasonings. Servings: 4+

Service: Fry – from frozen in 350 degree fryer until golden brown and heated through. NOTE: Use caution when cutting chilies; trapped juices may spray.

HEMMINGS RESTAURANT AT THE SHERATON

CRAB CAKES

1	pound jumbo lump crab meat	3	ounces bread crumbs
2	each shallots, diced	¾	cup mayonnaise
2	tablespoons red and green peppers, diced	½	teaspoon Cajun seasoning
1	tablespoon chopped garlic		Cayenne pepper to taste
½	tablespoon chopped parsley		Salt to taste

Crab Cakes: Pick through crab meat to remove excess shells. Combine all ingredients and form into 8 patties. Heat a heavy skillet and coat with olive oil or clarified butter. Sauté cakes over medium heat and turn when golden brown on one side. Turn cakes over with a spatula and finish browning other side over medium heat. Make sure cakes are heated through before serving. Serve on a pool of Wasabi Butter Sauce.

Serves 4.

WASABI BUTTER SAUCE

2	tablespoons minced shallots	12	ounces softened unsalted butter – cut in pieces
½	cup white wine		
3	tablespoons lemon juice	1	tablespoon wasabi powder
½	cup heavy cream		Salt and white pepper to taste

Combine shallots, wine and lemon juice in sauté pan and bring to a simmer. Reduce until almost dry. Add cream and reduce by half. Turn heat down to low and whisk butter in by small amounts. Ensure butter is emulsified before whisking next amount in. Strain and add wasabi powder. Adjust seasoning.

MAHI MAHI WITH SOURDOUGH CRUST & PAPAYA CHUTNEY

4	7-ounce mahi mahi fillets	1	ounce raisins
1	12-ounce loaf sourdough bread	1	ounce rice wine vinegar
	Salt and pepper to taste	2	ounces salad oil
12	ounces strawberry papaya	½	ounce diced jalapeño
2	ounces diced onion	1	ounce chopped mint
2	ounces diced red bell pepper	8	ounces egg wash
		6	ounces flour

Breading: (the night before) Bake sourdough bread. Cut bread into large pieces and allow to dry overnight. Grind bread into a coarse mixture and set aside.

Papaya Chutney: Peel, seed and dice papaya in large chunks. Heat salad oil in heavy bottomed pot. Add onions and cook until clear. Add bell pepper and jalapeño. Continue to cook for 2 to 3 minutes on medium heat. Add vinegar, papaya and mint and simmer for 4 to 5 minutes, until papaya softens, but does not turn to mush. Adjust seasoning and remove from heat. Add raisins and let cool.

For Fish: Season mahi fillets and dredge in flour. Shake excess flour off and dip in egg wash. Drain excess egg from fillets and coat with bread crumbs. Heat a heavy skillet and coat with oil or clarified butter. Sauté mahi on one side until golden brown. Turn and place in 325 degree oven. Cook for 8 to 10 minutes or until fish reaches desired doneness. If fish is cooked for more than the minimum time, turning fish over to prevent overbrowning may be necessary. Serve with chutney and garnish with mint.

Serves 4.

TENNESSEE BOURBON PECAN & CHOCOLATE PIE

4	each eggs	1	cup semi-sweet chocolate chips
1½	cups brown sugar	2	ounces sweet butter
¾	cup dark corn syrup	2	ounces Tennessee bourbon whiskey
2	teaspoons vanilla extract	2	10-inch pie shells – deep dish (2-inches)
⅓	teaspoon salt		
1½	cups chopped pecans		
1	cup whole pecans		

Mix in a bowl: sugar, eggs, corn syrup, vanilla and salt. Layer chopped pecans and chocolate chips, layer whole pecans on top of chocolate chips. Melt butter, add to batter mix and then add bourbon whiskey. Bake in 350 degree oven uncovered for 15 minutes and then cover with aluminum foil and bake for an additional 40 to 45 minutes or until pie is firm. Remove to cooling rack and let cool for two hours before taking out to serve.

Yield: 2 pies

FAIRBANKS STEAK HOUSE
HOLLYWOOD CASINO & HOTEL

1150 Casino Strip
Tunica, Mississippi 38664

Fairbanks Steakhouse serves choice beef, prime service and an award-winning wine list. Fairbanks was one of two Mississippi winners of the prestigious DiRona Award. Fairbanks is listed in the 1998-1999 guide of the Distinguished Restaurants of North America. The DiRona Award is the only award that results from an independent and anonymous restaurant inspection. The inspection examines the total dining experience from reservation to departure, but emphasizes the quality of food and its presentation.

Marc Silverberg
Food & Beverage Director

Chef Marc is a native of Philadelphia, Pennsylvania. He is a graduate of the Culinary Institute of America in Hyde Park, New York and the Philadelphia Restaurant School in Philadelphia, Pennsylvania. Chef Marc has received the Certified Executive Chef designation from the American Culinary Federation and the Certified Food and Beverage Executive designation from the American Hotel and Motel Association.

DAIQUIRI CHICKEN

2	8-ounce chicken breasts (boneless/skinless)		Seasoned flour (as needed)
		1	ounce clarified butter

Heat butter in hot sauté pan. Dredge chicken breast in flour, shake off excess, and sauté in hot butter until golden brown. Remove from pan and place on a sizzler. Place in the oven.

DAIQUIRI SAUCE

1	ounce shallots, chopped	½	cup strawberries, quartered
3	ounces chicken stock	2	teaspoons mint, chopped
¼	cup currant jelly	3	sprigs fresh mint (for garnish)
½	ounce 151 proof rum		

Drain excess oil from the sauté pan and add shallots. Sauté for 30 seconds and deglaze with chicken stock. Allow to reduce, incorporating the flour and drippings of the chicken. Add currant jelly and stir until incorporated. Add rum and flame. Add strawberries and mint.

Place chicken back in pan with sauce and heat until internal temperature is 165 degrees and sauce is caramelized. At service time, place chicken on the plate, wing side up. Pour sauce and berries over chicken. Finish plate with rice and vegetables. Garnish with fresh mint.

Yield: One portion

LOBSTER SILVERBERG

2	(each) 3-ounce veal medallions	1	ounce seasoned flour
1	(each) 3 to 4-ounce lobster tails	2	ounces clarified butter

Pound veal until very thin. Cut the lobster tail in half and remove the meat. Wrap the veal around the lobster and secure with toothpick. Heat butter in hot saucepan. Dredge veal with lobster in flour, shake off excess and sauté in hot butter until golden brown. Remove from pan and place on an ovenproof dish. Place in oven at 325 degrees and cook till internal temperature is 165 degrees.

Yield: One portion

SUN-DRIED TOMATO SAUCE

2	ounces whole butter	1	tablespoon chopped parsley
1	ounce white wine	1	ounce sun-dried tomatoes
1	ounce lemon juice		

Soak the tomatoes until soft and tender and chop parsley. Mix the rest of the ingredients and bring to a boil and then remove from heat. Add the butter last and let it melt off of the heat.

Yield: One portion

CHARLES JONES

Executive Chef

Chef Charles is a native of Shelby Forest, Tennessee. He graduated from State Tech in Hotel & Restaurant management. Chef Charles attended the Culinary Institute of America in Hyde Park, New York for an advance course in Garde Manger. He was the Chef Garde Manger for six years at the Hyatt Regency Hotels in Ft. Worth, Texas and Memphis, Tennessee. He has 20 years experience in the industry. Until recently, Chef Charles was the executive chef at Harrah's.

CRAB CAKES

(Appetizer)

1	pound lump crab meat	½	tablespoon dry mustard
¾	cup mayonnaise	½	tablespoon Worcestershire sauce
2	small eggs		
⅛	cup green pepper, minced	⅛	cup cilantro, minced
⅛	cup red pepper, minced	¼	cup bread crumbs
¼	cup roasted corn	½	cup seasoned breading
1½	tablespoons Cajun seasoning		

Break up crab meat and remove any shell that may be present. In the same bowl, add all of the listed ingredients (mayonnaise through cilantro) and blend with a cook's spoon till a smooth uniform consistency. Add the bread crumbs and blend till incorporated. Form into 2-ounce patties and dredge in seasoned bread crumbs.

Deep fry cakes at 350 degrees until lightly golden (2 minutes). Remove from fryer basket and place in pie tin. Finish cooking in a 350 degree oven for 3 minutes or until 145 degree internal temperature.

Serve with Creole Remoulade sauce (recipe follows) and Shrimp & Corn Salsa (recipe follows).

Serves 6 (3 crab cakes per serving)

REMOULADE SAUCE

1½	cups mayonnaise	¼	cup ketchup
1¼	cups celery, chopped	1½	tablespoons Worcestershire sauce
1¼	cups green onions, chopped	¼	cup salad mustard
½	cup chopped parsley	¼	cup white vinegar
⅔	cup horseradish, processed	¼	cup fresh garlic
		⅛	cup paprika
1	tablespoon lemon juice	½	tablespoon hot pepper sauce
¼	cup Creole mustard	¾	tablespoon salt

Mix all ingredients in a food processor till smooth. Keep refrigerated (shelf life 3 days).

Yield: 1½ quarts

SHRIMP & CORN SALSA

¾	quart shrimp – cooked baby (250 to 300-count) thawed	3	cloves garlic, fresh minced
3	cups corn kernels, thawed	1½	bunches fresh cilantro, minced
1½	cups red bell peppers, small dice	½	tablespoon cumin, ground
1½	cups green bell peppers, small dice	1½	tablespoons kosher salt
7	Roma tomatoes, small dice	1½	cups olive oil
		½	tablespoon black ground pepper
1½	jalapeño peppers, minced	1	(each) fresh lime juice

Thaw the baby shrimp and drain off the liquid. In a large mixing bowl, combine all remaining ingredients with the thawed and drained shrimp and mix thoroughly. Portion into appropriate containers and cover. Refrigerate (shelf life 3 days).

Yield: 3 quarts

RAYMOND J. DERDERIAN, C.C.C.

Executive Chef

Chef Raymond is a graduate of the New England Culinary Institute. He received his Associates degree in 1993. His degree program included classical cuisine and contemporary American cooking. Chef Ray's signature dish "Cheddar & Broccoli Pork Rolls with Rosemary-Parmesan Sauce" recipe was an award-winning dish (gold medal) in the 1995 Premier Chefs of America contest. He is also an active member of the American Culinary Federation. He is a ACF Certified Chef de Cuisine and has all education points needed for CEC plus 19 experience points. He recently worked for Hollywood Casino in Tunica, MS.

CHEF DERDERIAN'S POTATO NETTED SHRIMP WITH BRANDIED SHRIMP CREAM

Sauce:

2	ounces butter	1	ounce custom gold shrimp base
½	(each) shallot		
2	ounces all-purpose flour	20	ounces hot water
½	ounce brandy	2	ounces heavy cream
	Zest of ¼ lemon	½	ounce brandy

Shrimp:

36	21 to 25-ct. peeled and deveined tail-on tiger shrimp	8	ounces vegetable oil
4½	each (70 count baker's potatoes)	4	lemons (cut into 24 slices)
4	ounces cornstarch	12	purple kale leaves

Step 1: In a 4-quart saucepan, melt butter, add shallots and sweat until clear, deglaze with brandy, add lemon zest and mix in flour to make roux, make stock from water and base, whisk into roux. Bring to a simmer and whisk in heavy cream. Simmer again with brandy, and salt and white pepper to taste.

Step 2: On the crinkle cut part of a mandoline, slice peeled potato lengthwise once then slightly turn potato to produce netting. Repeat procedure until you have 36 netted slices, blanch in hot oil for thirty seconds, drain and cool.

Step 3: Roll shrimp in cornstarch and wrap in potato nets, pan fry in oil until golden brown, place kale leaf in center of plate near upper rim, sauce bottom of plate with 1 ounce of sauce, fan shrimp in sauce and drizzle another ounce of sauce over the shrimp. Finish with lemon twist on either side of plate.

Serves 12 (3 shrimp per serving)

GRILLED PIZZETTA

Ingredients for pizza dough:

4	pounds flour	2	ounces chopped garlic
2½	pints water		
½	ounce sugar	⅛	ounce fresh rosemary
1½	ounces olive oil		
½	ounce salt	1	ounce grated Parmesan cheese
¼	ounce yeast		
¼	ounce dry oregano	¼	ounce dry basil

Mix the sugar, yeast and water. Water should be between 90 and 100 degrees. Cover the mixture with plastic and wait until it foams. This is called proofing the yeast. Then add the herbs, olive oil and cheese. Mix it together with the yeast mixture. Next, add the flour and salt. Add the salt last. Mix the dough together. Chef Ray recommends a dough hook or mix it by hand until the dough is smooth. Let it rise to double the size and cut it into 7-ounce portions. Roll the portions into little balls, cover with plastic wrap and let it rise again. (You can freeze the extra dough, which will be good up to four months.)

Smoked garlic oil to spread on dough: Take eight cloves of garlic and add a tablespoon of olive oil, wrap the cloves in foil and bake in the oven at 350 degrees. Cook until the cloves are golden brown and soft. Then take one cup of olive oil or an olive oil blend and blend it together with the garlic cloves. Add ¼ teaspoon of liquid smoke. This adds a smoky flavor. (Don't add too much.) Next take one 7-ounce pizza dough and roll it into a 10-inch circle. Brush it lightly with the smoked garlic oil. Put the dough on a very hot grill and wait until it starts to rise. Rotate it and wait another 30 seconds. Flip it over and add the toppings.

Toppings: Top it with Roma tomatoes sliced thinly. Then sprinkle with freshly chopped basil and three ounces of shredded Parmesan cheese. If the grill is slow, cover the pizza with a metal bowl to melt the cheese.

Ray Derderian's Cheddar & Broccoli Pork Rolls with Rosemary-Parmesan Sauce

1	teaspoon baking soda	5	teaspoons kosher salt
4	pounds, 8 ounces broccoli florets	5	teaspoons coarse black pepper
20	(6-ounce each) pieces loin of pork, trimmed, sliced, pounded to ⅛-inch thickness		Clarified butter, as needed
		1	tablespoon unsalted butter
1	pound, 4 ounces sharp cheddar cheese, shredded	5	each shallots, coarsely chopped
		½	cup white wine
1	pound pine nuts, coarsely chopped	2	tablespoons fresh rosemary, snipped, divided
20	ounces dry bread crumbs	1	pint heavy cream
6	large eggs	1	cup Parmesan cheese, grated
4	ounces milk		Salt and pepper to taste
1½	tablespoons olive oil		
1	pound, 8 ounces flour	5	pounds hot cooked fettuccine

Dissolve baking soda in 6 quarts boiling water. Blanch broccoli until bright green and still firm. Drain; shock in ice water. Reserve 60 florets for garnish; use remaining for preparation. Alternately layer each pork slice with ½-ounce cheddar, 1 broccoli floret and another ½-ounce of cheddar. Fold ends toward center; roll each pork fillet into snug cylinder. Wrap each tightly in plastic wrap; twist ends. Freeze to set.

Mix nuts with bread crumbs; set aside. Combine eggs, milk and olive oil thoroughly; set aside. Combine flour, salt and pepper. Unwrap pork rolls. Roll in flour until well-coated; dip in egg mix and roll in crumb mixture. Sauté rolls in moderately hot clarified butter until golden, turning as needed. Bake on sheet pan at 350 degrees for 20 to 25 minutes. Hold warm for service.

To prepare sauce, melt butter over low heat; add shallots. Cook until translucent. Add wine and 1 tablespoon rosemary; reduce by half. Add cream; reduce by a third. Strain. Rinse pan; return mixture to heat. Bring to a simmer. Gradually add Parmesan, continuously whisking until smooth. Over low heat, add remaining rosemary, salt and pepper. Hold warm in stainless steel container over hot water bath to prevent curdling. To serve, plate 4 ounces of pasta. Slice pork rolls on the bias into 4 equal sections. Ladle a pool of sauce on pasta; arrange slices on sauce. Drizzle pasta with additional sauce. Garnish with broccoli florets.

Yield: 20 servings, 6-ounces each

Chef Ray's Cajun Corn Bisque with Blackened Chicken

½	pound butter	½	large red bell pepper, small dice
3	ounces celery, diced	¾	pound whole kernel corn, frozen or fresh
6	ounces onions, diced		
2	ounces mushrooms, sliced	4	ounces clarified butter
½	pound whole kernel corn, frozen or fresh	¾	pound boneless, skinless chicken breast
¼	pound all-purpose flour	4	ounces blackening spice
¼	ounce blackening spice	½	teaspoon kosher salt
80	ounces water	1	large red bell pepper (for garnish fine-julienne)
½	large green bell pepper, small dice		

Step 1: Melt butter over medium heat, add celery, onion, mushrooms, ½ pound corn and ¼ ounce of blackening spice, sweat until onions are clear in appearance.

Step 2: Dredge chicken in clarified butter and coat with blackening spice. In a dry hot sauté pan, cook until a dark brown appearance is achieved. Cool and cut into small bite-size pieces and hold.

Step 3: Sprinkle flour over sweating vegetable mix while stirring to make a roux; make stock from water and custom base. While whisking, add half of the chicken stock, now use a blender or immersible blender to purée until smooth. Now whisk in the rest of the chicken stock and bring to a simmer.

Step 4: Add the other ¾ pound corn, small diced red and green peppers and diced chicken. Simmer for 15 minutes to blend flavors. Add salt and simmer five more minutes. Taste and adjust seasoning to taste.

Step 5: Ladle 8 ounces of bisque into bowl and garnish with julienne red peppers.

Yield: 12 8-ounce servings

HORSESHOE CASINO & HOTEL

1021 Casino Center Drive Robinsonville, MS 38664

Joseph Ahearn
Chef de Cuisine

Chef Ahearn was born and raised in Schenectady, New York. He started cooking at an early age, being influenced by his parents and grandmother. He graduated from Schenectady County Community College in 1981. Chef Ahearn graduated from the Culinary Institute of America in 1988. He then accepted a chef's position with the famed Mansion on Turtle Creek in Dallas, Texas. Chef Ahearn has worked with many renowned chefs from Europe and throughout the United States. His present position is Chef de Cuisine at the Horseshoe Casino restaurants in Robinsonville.

PAN-FRIED CORNBREADED QUAIL

4	whole boneless quail, wings removed	½	cup vegetable oil
2	large eggs		Salt to taste
3	cups cornbread crumbs		Ground black pepper to taste

Cut each quail in half, lengthwise, and put in a large bowl. Beat eggs and pour over quail. Toss to coat. Place cornbread crumbs in a medium bowl. Press each egg-coated quail half into cornbread crumbs until fully coated.

Heat oil in a large cast-iron skillet over medium heat. Season quail with salt and pepper and when oil is hot, place quail in skillet. Cook for 4 minutes or until golden brown, then turn and cook for an additional 4 minutes. Don't let quail overcook. Breast should be pink. Remove from skillet and place on towel to drain.

Serves 2.

GREEN BEAN & PEPPER COMPOTE

¼	pound green beans, trimmed	2	ounces country ham, julienne cut
1	tablespoon olive oil		Salt and pepper to taste
½	red bell pepper, seeded, julienne cut		
½	yellow bell pepper, seeded, julienne cut		

Place green beans in boiling salted water for 2 minutes or until cooked with crunch left. Immediately drain into sieve and hold under cold running water. When cool, drain well and pat dry. Heat oil in sauté pan over medium-high heat. When hot, add beans, bell peppers and country ham. Season with salt and pepper.

Serve while hot.

Serves 2 to 4.

SPOON BREAD

3	cups milk	3	eggs, well beaten
2	tablespoons chopped shallots	1	teaspoon salt
1	tablespoon chopped garlic	1¾	teaspoons baking powder
1½	cups cornmeal	1	teaspoon unsalted butter, melted

Preheat oven to 375 degrees. Generously butter a 2-quart casserole and set aside. Combine milk, shallots and garlic in a large saucepan over high heat. Bring to a boil, stirring in cornmeal. Cook for about 5 minutes or until very thick, stirring constantly. Remove from heat and allow to cool. When mixture is cool and very stiff, add eggs, salt, baking powder and melted butter. Using an electric mixer, beat for 10 to 15 minutes. Pour into prepared casserole and bake in preheated oven for 30 minutes or until light brown.

Keep warm for service.

Serves 2 to 4.

PEACH SAUCE

7-8	ripe peaches	1	pint chicken stock
4	shallots, peeled		or broth
	and finely minced	1	tablespoon fresh
1	clove garlic, peeled		chopped cilantro
	and finely minced		or parsley
1	tablespoon finely		Salt to taste
	grated fresh ginger		Fresh lime juice to
			taste

Peel and pit peaches. Cut 2 into ⅓-inch dice and reserve. Place remaining peaches, shallots, garlic and chicken stock in medium saucepan over medium heat. Bring to a boil. Lower heat and simmer for 5 minutes. Remove from heat and pour into a blender. Process until smooth. Strain through a coarse sieve. Add diced peaches, cilantro or parsley. Season with salt and lime juice.

Keep warm until ready for service.

PLUM CRISP

2	pounds fresh Italian prune plums or any plums in season	2	tablespoons brown sugar
¼	cup granulated sugar	2	ounces butter
		¼	cup rolled oats
½	cup plus 2 tablespoons unbleached flour	2	tablespoons sliced almonds
		½	teaspoon almond extract
			Fresh mint sprig for garnish

Preheat oven to 375 degrees. Cut the plums in half and remove the pits. Arrange the plums in a 9 by 9-inch pan with the cut side down. Combine the granulated sugar and 2 tablespoons of flour and pour over the fruit. In a small bowl, combine the remaining flour and the brown sugar. Cut the butter into the flour mixture. Add the oats, almonds, almond extract and combine. Pour this over the plums. Bake for 40 minutes or until the juices bubble and the topping is browned.

Serve warm.

Serves 6 to 8.

GOLD STRIKE CASINO

1010 Casino Center Drive Robinsonville, MS 38664

Gary Riley
Executive Chef

Chef Riley was born in Middletown, Ohio and raised in Carlisle, Ohio. His first culinary experience was in 1977 as a cook and later as a sous chef for the Maxim Hotel in Las Vegas. His apprenticeship was with Chef Guy Kirtley. Chef Riley took Food & Beverage courses at UNLV. In 1988 he joined the Stardust Hotel as assistant sous chef. He became Executive Chef at Sam's Town when it opened in 1994. He joined the Gold Strike Hotel & Casino in 1998 as Executive Chef.

ITALIAN WEDDING SOUP

1	ounce butter	1	teaspoon white pepper
6	ounces diced onion	4	bay leaves
6	ounces diced celery	½	teaspoon thyme leaves
6	ounces diced carrots	1	pound cooked, diced chicken (white and dark meat)
3	8-ounce cans chicken broth		
3	8-ounce cans beef broth		Meatballs (from your favorite recipe or store-bought)
1	pound endive, cleaned and chopped		

Sauté diced vegetables in butter until clear and wilted. Add chicken and beef broth. Add endive. Simmer 10 minutes. Add seasonings and continue to simmer 5 more minutes. Add cooked chicken and meatballs and heat through. Remove bay leaves and serve hot.

Serves 18.

NOTE: Add pasta to soup for an even heartier dish. Makes a meal, served with warm bread and a salad.

CHICKEN DANIELLE

(created by Gary Riley)

Boneless chicken breast (one per person)
Gorgonzola cheese
Avocado
Tomato
Mushrooms (2 to 3 per breast)
White onion
White wine
Heavy cream
Butter
Garlic

Sauté onions and mushrooms in butter on medium high heat for approximately 4 minutes. Remove from skillet and set aside. In same skillet, add enough butter to sauté chicken breasts that have been dusted in flour and lightly seasoned. Brown both sides. Remove chicken.

To prepare cheese sauce:
Use same skillet (on medium-high) add ¼ cup white wine, then ½ teaspoon garlic, ¼ cup gorgonzola (shredded is easiest) and ½ cup heavy cream. Reduce the sauce by a third – then it will be ready.

Place chicken on ovenproof pan, and top with the sautéed onions, mushrooms, sliced tomato, sliced avocado and shredded gorgonzola cheese. Place in a preheated oven on 350 degrees for approximately 4 to 6 minutes or until cheese melts. Put chicken on a plate and drizzle cheese sauce over it.

CHAMOUN REST HAVEN RESTAURANT

U.S. Highway 61 Clarksdale, MS 38614

**Louise Chamoun
Chef Owner**

RICE PILAF WITH NOODLES

(Ruz Bishareyee)

¾	cup vermicelli broken into 1-inch lengths	1¼	cups long grain rice
		3	cups boiling water or chicken broth
3-5	tablespoons butter	1¼	teaspoons salt

Sauté vermicelli in butter until golden brown, stirring constantly. Stir in rice and fry about one minute until glazed. Add water or chicken broth and allow it to boil. Reduce heat, cover and simmer until liquid has been absorbed. Sprinkle with roasted almonds or pine nuts as garnish.

Serves 8.

GREEN BEANS WITH MEAT & TOMATOES

2	pounds stew meat	1	8-ounce can tomato sauce
3-4	cans green beans or fresh green beans	1	large onion, chopped
1	16-ounce can crushed tomatoes	1	teaspoon garlic (freshly crushed or powder)

Brown meat and onions. Add tomatoes, salt, pepper and garlic. Boil until meat is tender. Add beans and cook another 20 minutes. Serve over rice for a main dish.

Serves 6 to 8.

LEBANESE CABBAGE ROLLS

2	medium heads of cabbage	1	16-ounce can tomato sauce
2	pounds ground chuck roast	2	tablespoons salt
2	cups long grain rice	2	tablespoons fresh crushed garlic or garlic powder
1	16-ounce can stewed tomatoes	2	tablespoons black pepper

Heat enough water in a large pot to cover a head of cabbage. Core cabbage heads so leaves can be separated. Drop cabbage into hot water for 5 to 10 minutes. Use a large fork and knife to separate leaves. Place individual leaves aside. Mix all other ingredients except the large can of tomato sauce together. Stuff each individual leaf with mixture and roll lengthwise. Do not overstuff, as rice will expand as it cooks. Layer the rolled cabbage in a pot. Sprinkle a touch of salt on top and pour the can of tomato sauce and 2 cans of water over the cabbage. Cook on high for 10 minutes, then lower heat. Cover and cook for 30 more minutes or until cabbage is tender.

Serves 10.

LEBANESE BREAD SALAD

(Fattoosh)

1	small green pepper diced	2	cloves garlic, crushed
1	cucumber cut into ¼-inch cubes	¼	cup fresh lemon juice
1	cup chopped green onions	⅓	cup olive oil
¾	cup chopped parsley	2-3	medium tomatoes cut into cubes
¼	cup chopped fresh mint	2	large loaves of pita bread toasted and broken into bite-sized pieces

Mix all dry ingredients except bread in a large bowl. Ten minutes before serving, add the toasted bread and toss with lemon juice and olive oil. Add garlic salt and pepper to taste.

Serves 6.

GRILLED EGGPLANT

(Baba Ganoush)

4	medium eggplants grilled	2	teaspoons crushed garlic
2-4	tablespoons of olive oil Juice of 4 to 5 fresh lemons	¼	teaspoon salt Pinch of black pepper

Eggplant can be served whole by putting all ingredients on the eggplant like a baked potato or the eggplant can be peeled and mashed with all ingredients added to it. More oil, lemon or garlic may be added, if desired.

Serves 4.

FRIED KIBBIE

(Lebanese)

2	pounds ground round steak with all fat trimmed (and ground twice)	1½	cups bulgar or cracked wheat Salt & pepper to taste
1	large onion (ground once)		

Cover wheat in water and allow to soak for a few minutes. Drain all water by squeezing with hands. Mix with meat. Add onions and salt and pepper. Mix all ingredients as if kneading dough. Small amounts of cold water may be added until texture is soft and smooth – if onion is ground in blender with 2 cups of cold water, additional water will not be necessary. Form kibbie into patties and deep fry in hot oil until brown, approximately 8 to 10 minutes. Kibbie may also be baked by spreading kibbie in baking dish with a light layer of oil on top. Bake at 350 degrees for approximately 25 to 30 minutes or until golden brown.

Serves 8.

YVONNE ROSSIE ABRAHAM

1209 Miller Drive
Clarksdale, MS 38614

Lebanese-American Chef

LEBANESE SALAD DRESSING

½	cup lemon juice	1	teaspoon salt
½	cup olive oil	1	teaspoon pepper
2	cloves garlic		

Crush garlic to a paste. Add salt and pepper. Mix into oil and lemon juice. Pour over ½ head washed lettuce and cut-up tomato.

Serves 2.

STUFFED GRAPE LEAVES

1	quart grape leaves	½	cup lemon juice
⅔	cup long grain uncooked rice	2	tablespoons cinnamon
1	pound ground lamb or beef		Salt and pepper to taste

Wash leaves to remove brine. Mix other ingredients together. Roll mixture inside leaves in cigar fashion. Place stuffed leaves in pot. Cover with water, lemon juice, salt and pepper. Put two small plates on top of leaves to weight them down and cook 45 minutes on medium heat.

Serves 8.

LENTILS WITH RICE

(Imjadara Roz)

1	cup lentils	1	cup long grain rice
1	quart water	1	large onion
1	teaspoon salt	½	cup oil
½	teaspoon black pepper		

Check lentils for any foreign matter. Wash thoroughly. Put in 2-quart boiler. Bring to boil. Drain and rinse. Return to boiler with 1 quart of water. Bring to boil again. Add salt, pepper and rice. While rice and beans are cooking, brown chopped or thinly sliced onions in oil in skillet. Add oil to rice mixture and use onions to garnish top when served, or stir both onions and oil into rice mixture.

Serves 2.

BAKED SPINACH

2	10-ounce packages frozen chopped spinach	½	cup extra fine bread crumbs
4	tablespoons butter	1	can cream of mushroom soup
½	cup chopped onion	1	8-ounce carton cottage cheese
½	cup chopped celery	⅛	teaspoon oregano
½	pound fresh mushrooms, or 1 4-ounce can sliced	½	teaspoon pepper
5	eggs	¼	cup grated Parmesan cheese

Pour hot water over spinach to thaw; or remove from freezer and put in refrigerator the day before to let it thaw. Strain raw spinach, making sure all water is pressed out. Melt butter. Sauté onion, celery and mushrooms until onion is opaque. Beat eggs. Combine with crumbs, soup, cottage cheese, seasonings and spinach. Mix with onion mixture. Pour into greased 9-inch square pan and sprinkle top with Parmesan cheese. Bake at 325 degrees for 30 minutes. Cool. Cut in 1-inch squares or serve warm in larger squares as a luncheon vegetable.

STUFFED SQUASH
(Koosa Mishee)

8	medium-size squash, room temperature	1	16-ounce can whole tomatoes
1	pound ground beef (or chuck)	1	can water
¾	cup uncooked long grain rice	1	teaspoon salt
½	cup scooped squash	1	teaspoon black pepper
		¾	teaspoon ground cinnamon
		1	tablespoon lemon juice

Wash squash. Cut off enough on rounded end to allow for scooping. Save tip. Scoop out squash, leaving about ¼-inch thickness. (If regular scooper not available, use potato peeler as scooper.) Rinse squash. Combine meat, rice, scooped squash, the whole tomatoes (reserving liquid for later use), salt, pepper and cinnamon. Mix thoroughly, mashing tomatoes well. Stuff squash loosely, about ¾ full. (If packed too tight, squash will burst, as rice must have room to swell.) Place squash in boiler; add cut-off tips and reserved tomato juice, plus 1 can of water. Simmer 30 minutes. Add lemon juice and cook 15 minutes longer.

You may prefer cutting off the neck of the squash and scooping from there. Tiny eggplant, zucchini or bell peppers may be used as squash substitute.

Serves 4.

GARBANZO BEAN DIP

1	can garbanzo beans		Salt to taste
2	cloves garlic	1	tablespoon olive oil (optional)
½	cup lemon juice		
2	tablespoons ground sesame seed paste		

Crush garbanzo beans in blender. Blend all ingredients together and spread olive oil on top. Serve as side dish or dip.

Serves 6.

SADIE ROSSIE'S LEBANESE RICE

½	cup broken thin spaghetti	2	cups chicken broth (may use canned broth)
1	stick butter		
2	cups uncooked long grain rice	2	cups hot water
¼	cup cinnamon (ground)	1	teaspoon salt
		1	teaspoon pepper

Fry spaghetti in butter until brown. Add rice and sauté for two minutes. Add chicken broth, water, cinnamon, salt & pepper. Cook on high for 5 minutes. After it starts to boil, cover and cook on low heat for about 20 minutes. Do not stir. It will cook down.

Serves 10 to 12.

CHICKEN WITH PINE NUTS & RICE

1	whole 3-pound fryer or 8 chicken breasts	2	tablespoons butter (preferably rendered)
	Salt for chicken	2	cups long grain rice
1	pound ground chuck	1	teaspoon black pepper
¼	cup pine nuts	½	teaspoon cinnamon
		2	cups chicken broth

Clean and cut up fryer; season with salt and set aside. Brown meat and drain. Brown pine nuts in butter; add pine nuts, rice and seasonings to meat. Mix thoroughly. Put meat and rice mixture in bottom of 11 x 14-inch pan. Place chicken on top. Pour broth over chicken and rice. Bake at 350 degrees for 45 to 50 minutes until chicken and rice are done.

Serves 8.

*The Chapel at Delta State University
Cleveland, Mississippi*

KC's
Highway 61 at First Street
Cleveland, MS 38732

Wally C. Joe
Executive Chef/Co-owner
Don Joe
Restaurant Manager/Sommelier/Co-owner

Wally and Don were born in Hong Kong and came to this country when they were 4 & 2 years old, respectively. Their father, K. C. Joe opened a small grocery store in Cleveland when the family first came to this country. In 1974, K. C. bought a small restaurant on the property where KC's beautiful new restaurant now stands. His boys grew up in the business, washing dishes, waiting tables and helping their parents cook.

Wally and Don graduated from the University of Mississippi in business and finance. After graduation, both brothers returned to Cleveland to work in their father's restaurant. Wally's interest is primarily in cooking which he describes as "New American." Don had a wine cellar built onto the restaurant to house what has been described as the finest wine collection in the state.

*In 1994, Wally became the first chef in the state of Mississippi to be invited to cook at the James Beard House in New York City, home of the Beard Foundation, where chefs from all of country are invited to showcase their talent. In 1997, Wally appeared on the "Great Chefs of the South" series on The Discovery Channel. In 1998, KC's received a 4-star rating (the top award) from Memphis' **The Commercial Appeal** newspaper for its fine cuisine and extensive wine selection. They also received a 4-star rating from the Jackson, Mississippi **Clarion Ledger's** "Epicurius".*

Two of KC's signature recipes are featured:

1) Roast Rack of Lamb with Sun-dried Tomatoes, Black Olives, Rosemary-Zinfandel Sauce and Goat Cheese Mashed Potatoes

2) Parfait of Jumbo Lump Crab, Avocado, Oven-dried Tomato and Cucumber with Mango Coulis and Basil Oil

ROAST RACK OF LAMB WITH SUNDRIED TOMATOES, BLACK OLIVES, ROSEMARY-ZINFANDEL SAUCE & GOAT CHEESE MASHED POTATOES

Lamb:

1	lamb rack, trimmed of fat and bones frenched	1	teaspoon chopped fresh rosemary
½	tablespoon chopped fresh garlic	1	teaspoon chopped fresh thyme
			Salt and pepper
			Olive oil

Season the lamb rack with herbs and salt and pepper. Brush with olive oil.
Serves 2.

Sauce:

2	cups good quality red zinfandel wine	6	sundried tomatoes
1	shallot, chopped	6	black olives, halved
1	sprig fresh rosemary		Salt and pepper to taste
1	cup veal or lamb stock or beef broth		

Reduce the wine, shallots, and rosemary sprig by ¾. Add the stock and reduce to sauce consistency. Add the tomatoes, olives and season to taste.

GOAT CHEESE MASHED POTATOES

2	medium russet potatoes	2	tablespoons butter
3	ounces fresh goat cheese		Salt and pepper to taste

Boil the potatoes until done. Mash the potatoes, goat cheese and butter with a hand masher. Season to taste.

Assembly: Sear the lamb rack in a sauté pan until browned on both sides. Roast in a preheated 450 degree oven until medium rare for about 10 minutes or until desired temperature. Let the rack rest for about 5 minutes and slice 4 chops per serving. Serve with the mashed potatoes and sauce.

PARFAIT OF JUMBO LUMP CRAB, AVOCADO, OVEN-DRIED TOMATO, & CUCUMBER WITH MANGO COULIS & BASIL OIL

Crab:

12	ounces jumbo lump crab meat, picked clean of debris and shells
10	fresh water chestnuts, peeled and diced

Mix crab meat and chestnuts together.

Vegetables:

2	ripe avocados, diced
8	ripe Roma tomatoes, cored and de-seeded, dried in a 200 degree oven for 6 to 8 hours
1	small cucumber, de-seeded and diced

Keep vegetables separate.

Mango Coulis:

1	ripe mango, pitted
1	lime, juiced

Purée mango with ½ of the lime juice. Pass through a fine mesh strainer. Thin if necessary with a little water. Adjust the sweetness or tartness with honey or remaining lime juice.

Basil Oil:

2	cups fresh basil leaves, tightly packed, blanched and shocked in ice water. This will preserve the bright green color.
2	cups extra virgin olive oil

Purée basil and olive oil together. Pour into a clean jar and infuse overnight. Strain through a cheesecloth into a clean bottle.

Assembly: In an oiled ring mold (or a small empty can such as a tomato paste can), start by layering a small amount of cucumber, 2 tomatoes, crabmeat and finish with the avocado. Be sure to pack tightly or the tower will tumble. Carefully slide the mold off. Drizzle the coulis and oil around the plate in a decorative pattern. Garnish with a sprig of fresh dill and diced red bell pepper if desired. A good quality caviar on top would make it an elegant first course. Serves 4.

INDONESIAN CATFISH SATÉ

16	wooden skewers	¼	teaspoon ground ginger
¼	cup soy sauce		
1	tablespoon vinegar	1	clove garlic, crushed
1	teaspoon packed brown sugar	4	catfish fillets

Soak the wooden skewers in water and refrigerate for 1 hour. This will help to prevent the wood from burning during cooking. Combine the soy sauce, vinegar, sugar, ginger and garlic in a small bowl. Stir well to dissolve the sugar. Set aside.

Cut the catfish fillets, lengthwise into four thin strips. Two of the strips will be longer than the others. Thread 1 catfish strip onto each wooden skewer. Cover the catfish skewers with the marinade and refrigerate for several hours.

When ready to serve, grill the skewers for 3 minutes per side and serve warm on a bed of Cucumber Salad as a first course or from a buffet table with a choice of sauces.

Yield: 16 small skewers

CUCUMBER SALAD

2	cucumbers, thinly sliced	1	teaspoon liquid non-sugar sweetener
1	onion, thinly sliced	1	tablespoon chopped parsley
½	cup vinegar		
¼	cup water		
½	teaspoon salt		

Place the cucumbers and onions in a glass bowl. Add the remaining ingredients and mix thoroughly. Refrigerate for several hours if possible.

This salad will hold refrigerated for several days.

Serves 4 to 6.

SHRIMP-STUFFED CATFISH

1	small onion, minced	⅓	cup flour
3	green onions, minced	2⅔	cups milk
3	tablespoons butter	2	egg yolks
4	ounces fresh mushrooms, sliced	⅓	cup dry white wine
½	cup soft bread crumbs	½	teaspoon dry mustard
3	tablespoons chopped parsley Juice of 1 lemon		Dash of cayenne pepper Salt to taste
		6-8	catfish fillets
⅓	cup butter or margarine	½	pound shrimp, cooked and peeled
		¾	cup grated Swiss cheese

For the stuffing: Sauté the onions and mushrooms in butter until tender. Add bread crumbs, parsley and lemon juice, mixing well. The stuffing will hold at this point, refrigerated, for 24 hours.

Make a rich white sauce by melting the butter in a heavy saucepan over low heat. Add flour and cook for 1 minute, stirring until smooth and bubbling. Slowly add the milk, continuing to stir as the sauce thickens. Beat the eggs with a fork. Stir a little of the hot sauce into the eggs to warm them. Add the egg mixture to the sauce, mixing well. Add the wine and seasonings, stirring until the sauce is smooth. Set aside.

Wash the catfish fillets and pat dry. Spread about 2 tablespoons of the stuffing across the center of each fillet and top with the shrimp. Reserve a shrimp to garnish each serving. Roll the fillets and secure with a wooden pick.

Serves 6 to 8.

GINGER-STEAMED CATFISH WITH SESAME SAUCE

6	catfish fillets		Toasted sesame seeds to garnish
2	teaspoons grated fresh ginger		
2	green onions, finely chopped		

On top of each catfish fillet, put a bit of ginger and green onion, spreading it along the length of the fish. Place catfish fillets on a plate in a steamer with 2 inches of water.

Bring the water to a slow boil and with the pan tightly covered, steam the fillets for about 15 minutes or until they are white and firm to the touch. Serve immediately with the Sesame Sauce and sprinkle with the sesame seeds.

Serves 6.

SESAME SAUCE

¼	cup soy sauce	2	teaspoons rice vinegar
½	teaspoon oriental sesame oil	1	small green onion, finely chopped
½	teaspoon sugar		

Combine all of the ingredients in a small bowl. Stir well to dissolve the sugar. This sauce is rich and should be served in small dipping dishes, or lightly drizzled on top of the steamed fish. Sauce can be made a day ahead.

Yield: ½ cup

The catfish fillets can be served cold as an appetizer. Cut in bite-size pieces, pile onto a serving dish, sprinkle with toasted sesame seeds, and serve with the dipping sauce. It's a good idea to steam a couple of extra fish for an easy lunch the next day to be served with a salad and a bit of the sauce.

CREOLE CATFISH CAKES

1	pound catfish fillets, broiled	1½	cups finely chopped bell pepper
6	tablespoons butter	½	cup finely chopped green onions
¾	cup flour		
2	cups milk		
½	teaspoon salt	½	teaspoon hot pepper sauce
½	teaspoon black pepper	1½	cups fresh bread crumbs
½	teaspoon dry mustard		

Melt the butter in a heavy saucepan. Add the flour. Stir constantly for 2 to 3 minutes, while the roux bubbles. Add the milk slowly, continuing to stir until the cream sauce is thick, 10 to 12 minutes. Add salt, pepper and mustard, mixing well.

Flake the catfish fillets into a bowl. Add the cream sauce and the remaining ingredients, mixing thoroughly. Use the fish mixture immediately or refrigerate for up to 2 days.

Using a large spoon, make cakes with the fish mixture and coat them completely with more fresh bread crumbs. Using a heavy skillet, sauté the patties gently in 1 tablespoon oil and 1 tablespoon butter, until they are browned. Keep warm while you continue cooking the cakes, adding more oil and butter as needed.

Serves 8 or more.

This recipe is perfect for using your imagination! The cakes can be made large enough for a luncheon serving or tiny to serve as pick-up appetizers. They are delicious served with a fruit salsa or use them as a base for poached eggs with a Hollandaise Sauce over the top. Fill mushroom caps with the fish mixture and bake for a great hot appetizer or fill green peppers with the mixture and bake for a wonderful hot main dish.

*Indian Bayou
Indianola, Mississippi*

GREEK CATFISH WITH GARLIC WHITE BEANS

6-8	catfish fillets	1	large clove garlic, crushed
1½	tablespoons ground thyme	2	tablespoons fresh lemon juice
½	teaspoon salt		
½	teaspoon black pepper	½	cup mashed white beans
2	tablespoons olive oil	3	tablespoons minced fresh parsley
5	tablespoons butter		

GARLIC WHITE BEANS

16	ounces dried Great Northern Beans	1	teaspoon garlic powder
2	quarts salted water	½	teaspoon salt
½	cup white vinegar	2	tablespoons minced parsley
½	cup vegetable or olive oil		

In a large heavy saucepan, cook the dried beans in the salted water over medium heat, until almost done – about 1 hour. They should be tender, but not mushy. Drain. In the same saucepan, toss the beans with the oil and vinegar to coat. Add the salt and garlic powder, continuing to toss the beans. Correct the seasonings to your own taste. (We like a lot of both.) Add the parsley and set aside until needed. The beans can be made 2 days ahead and refrigerated. Warm them up to use with this recipe.

Prepare the Garlic White Beans and keep them warm. Wash the catfish fillets and sprinkle them with the thyme, salt and pepper. Refrigerate until ready to cook. When ready to serve, heat the olive oil and 2 tablespoons of the butter in a large heavy skillet. Add the garlic and stir.

Serves 6 to 8.

FLORENTINE CATFISH

6-8	catfish fillets	4	tablespoons flour
3	cups water	2	cups milk
1	lemon, sliced	½	teaspoon dry mustard
1	10-ounce package frozen, chopped spinach	½	teaspoon white pepper
4	tablespoons butter	1	teaspoon salt
1	clove garlic, minced	3	teaspoons lemon juice
3	green onions, finely chopped	1	cup grated Swiss cheese, divided

In a large saucepan, bring the water and lemon slices to a slow simmer. Add the catfish fillets and poach gently for about 8 minutes. Remove fillets and drain well. Thaw and drain the spinach. Place it in a kitchen towel and squeeze the moisture from the spinach. Set aside.

Melt butter in a heavy saucepan. Add green onions and garlic. Cook briefly to soften. Add flour and stir constantly while the roux cooks. Do not brown. Slowly add the milk, continuing to stir until the sauce is smooth and thickened. Add reserved spinach, seasonings, lemon juice and ½ cup of the cheese, mixing well.

The sauce may be prepared ahead to this point and refrigerated until needed, up to 2 days. When you are ready to serve, place the cooked catfish fillets in a lightly buttered 9 x 13-inch baking dish or individual au gratin dishes. Cover with sauce and top with remaining cheese. Bake at 350 degrees for 15 minutes or until bubbly. Finish under the broiler to lightly toast the cheese. Serve immediately.

Serves 6 to 8.

When company's coming, this is a great dish.

SAUTÉED CATFISH FILLETS WITH PECAN-BASIL SAUCE

1	cup fresh basil	2	tablespoons butter, in pieces
1	cup fresh parsley	6	catfish fillets
½	cup olive oil	1½	cups flour
½	cup chopped pecans	1	tablespoon cayenne pepper
2	cloves garlic, minced	2	teaspoons salt
½	cup grated Parmesan cheese	2	tablespoons vegetable oil
½	cup grated Romano cheese	2	tablespoons butter Toasted pecan halves, to garnish

Chop the basil and parsley in a food processor. Add the olive oil, pecans, garlic, cheeses and butter. Process into a paste or thick sauce. Add salt to the sauce as needed and set it aside. The sauce can be refrigerated for several days or frozen until needed.

When ready to serve, put the flour, cayenne pepper and salt in a large bowl and mix well. Wash the catfish fillets, coat with the flour mixture and set them aside while the oil and butter heat in a large skillet. When the butter is foaming, add the fillets and sauté until lightly browned, about 3 to 4 minutes. Turn the fillets over and spread the cooked side with the basil sauce. Continue to cook for another 3 to 4 minutes until the fish is done. Add more butter and oil to the pan when needed for the rest of the fillets. Serve immediately, garnished with toasted pecan halves.

Serves 6.

*Toasted, salted pecans have always been a favorite Southern snack food, traditional parts of holiday nibbling, cocktail buffets and wedding cake plates. Southern cooks have always used almonds on fish and chicken dishes, but only recently begun to use pecans in these same ways! Pecans, wonderful, flavorful, moist and slightly oily, they will substitute for almonds or walnuts in almost any dish! Now if we could just teach the rest of the country how to pronounce – PECAN!

POISSON PROVENCAL

6	catfish fillets	1	cup thinly sliced fresh zucchini
3	cups water	½	teaspoon black pepper
1	lemon, sliced		
2	tablespoons butter or olive oil	¼	teaspoon salt
1	onion, sliced	¼	teaspoon thyme
1	green pepper, thinly sliced	1	tablespoon chopped parsley
2	cloves garlic, minced	½	cup dry red wine
1	16-ounce can sliced tomatoes, with liquid		

In a large saucepan, bring the water and lemon slices to a simmer. Add the catfish fillets and poach gently for about 8 minutes. Remove fillets and drain well.

Discard water. In same pan, melt the butter over medium heat. Add onion, green pepper and garlic. Cook until soft. Add tomatoes, zucchini, pepper, salt, thyme and parsley. Simmer 5 minutes, stirring gently. Add red wine and simmer for another 5 minutes. The sauce can be held, refrigerated, at this point for several hours.

When you are ready to serve, place cooked catfish fillets in a lightly buttered baking dish in one layer, or in individual serving dishes. Cover fillets with the sauce, heaping it on top. Bake at 350 degrees for 15 minutes or until hot and bubbly.

Serves 6.

The Provencal sauce is really versatile. Try simmering fresh peeled shrimp directly in the sauce. Add a bit more red wine if necessary for moisture and the resulting broth is delicious! And this is heart healthy – especially if you use the olive oil. Either way the Catfish or Poisson Provencal is a winner. The Roughtons developed this dish for a dinner meeting of the Mississippi Heart Association.

COLD LEMON SOUFFLÉ WITH RASPBERRY SAUCE

Soufflé:

1	envelope unflavored gelatin	2	teaspoons finely grated lemon zest
¼	cup cold water	1½	cups sugar
5	eggs, separated	1	cup whipping cream
¾	cup fresh lemon juice		

Sauce:

1	can frozen raspberries, in syrup	1	tablespoon water
		2	teaspoons Grand Marnier
1	teaspoon cornstarch		

Sprinkle gelatin over cold water. Mix egg yolks with lemon juice, zest and ¾ cup sugar. Place egg yolk mixture in double boiler over boiling water and cook, stirring constantly, until lemon mixture is slightly thickened (about 8 minutes). Remove from heat and stir in gelatin until dissolved. Chill 40 to 45 minutes or until mixture mounds slightly when dropped from a spoon.

Beat egg whites until they begin to hold shape and then gradually add ¾ cup remaining sugar until all is added and whites are stiff.

Beat whipping cream until stiff, and fold whites and cream into yolk mixture until no white streaks remain. Pour into 2-quart soufflé dish and chill 4 hours or more (may be chilled overnight). Serve with raspberry sauce.

Sauce: Thaw berries and strain through a sieve. Mix cornstarch and water. Add to strained berries and simmer 5 minutes. Add liqueur if desired. Chill. Keeps well in refrigerator. Sauce is also good over sliced peaches or cantaloupe.

Yield: 8 servings

LEMON CAKE

1	package lemon cake mix	¾	cup vegetable oil
1	package lemon gelatin	¾	cup apricot nectar
		4	eggs

Glaze:

2	cups powdered sugar	¼	cup lemon juice

Combine cake mix and gelatin. Add oil and juice and stir until well blended. Add eggs one at a time, mixing well after each addition. Pour into a greased and floured tube pan and bake at 350 degrees for 1 hour.

For glaze, combine ingredients, mixing until smooth. Drizzle over cake.

Yield: 1 cake

Mississippi River Paddlewheeler

JIM'S CAFE
314 Washington Avenue
Greenville, MS 38701

Gus Johnson
Chef Owner

Jim's Café is the oldest restaurant in Washington County. It dates back to the 1920s and was founded by Gus's father. Gus has been the proprietor since he graduated from the University of Mississippi and returned to Greenville to run the family business in 1959.

CAJUN BARBECUE VENISON

Ingredients:

Any cut of venison	Barbecue sauce
Crab boil	Cajun spice

Preparation:
Place roast in pressure cooker with crab boil and ½ pot of water. Cook for ½ hour and place on barbecue rack. Add barbecue sauce and Cajun spice. Brown and serve.

Serves 4 to 6.

TURKEY NOODLE SOUP

1	turkey breast	Salt & pepper to taste
1	stalk of celery	
1	onion	Water to cover turkey breast 1 to 2 inches
	Noodles	

Boil one turkey breast in stockpot with celery and onions until done. Take turkey out of pot and let cool. Strain the juice in a colander and put back in pot. Add noodles and cook until done. Cut turkey from breast and add to soup with noodles. Serve hot.

Serves 8 to 10.

SOUR CREAM DIP

1 cup sour cream
Fresh spring onions
(including green
top)

Salt & pepper to
taste

Combine sour cream, onions, salt and pepper. Place in refrigerator for one hour before serving. Serve with bread sticks or toast. Great on baked potatoes!

OLD GREEK SALAD DRESSING

1 cup yogurt
Seedless chopped
cucumber

Onion
1 clove garlic

Combine and let sit in refrigerator for one hour before it is served on a salad. Often served on gyros sandwiches.

OYSTER LOAF

1 dozen select
oysters (fried)
1 loaf French bread

Relish (recipe
below)
Sauce (recipe
below)

Relish:
Chopped olives
Chopped celery
hearts

Chopped spring
onions

Mix.

Sauce:
Ketchup
Dash of hot pepper
sauce

Fresh lemon juice
(1 lemon)

"Boat" the bread out of the loaf. Remove most of the insides, (save the top). Butter the loaf and sprinkle on garlic salt. Place on broiler and brown. Combine the relish and place in bottom of loaf. Place 1 dozen fried oysters on relish. Place sauce on the oysters and one slice of bread & butter pickles on each oyster. Add leaf lettuce and put top on the loaf. Cut and serve.

Yield: 2 to 3 servings

THE CATFISH INSTITUTE

118 Hayden Street Belzoni, MS 39038

"Catfish: The Cultured Fish"

No longer seafood's poor country cousin, farm-raised catfish has become one of the country's most popular and versatile foods. 140,000 acres of farm-raised catfish ponds have made Mississippi, Louisiana, Alabama and Arkansas the largest catfish-producing states in the U.S.

The Real Beauty Is In The Taste

One of the main differences between farm-raised and wild catfish is their living conditions. Farm-raised catfish are raised in a quality-controlled environment of clay-based ponds filled with pure fresh water pumped from underground wells. Another notable distinction between farm-raised and wild catfish is what – and – how they eat. Farm-raised catfish are fed a "gourmet diet" of puffed, high-protein food pellets (a mixture of soybeans, corn, wheat, vitamins and minerals) that give them a mild, almost sweet taste.

The following recipes are courtesy of The Catfish Institute

Pecan Catfish with Honey Lemon Chili Butter

Oven Catfish w/Sweet Onion Marmalade

Grilled Lemon Grass Catfish

Catfish Brie Soufflé

Cashew Crusted Catfish w/Tomato Basil

Quick Catfish Gumbo

Layered Catfish Dip

Catfish Antipasto Platter

PECAN CATFISH WITH HONEY LEMON CHILI BUTTER

2	U.S. Farm-Raised catfish fillets	1	teaspoon chopped parsley
1	egg beaten with 1 tablespoon milk	1	cup pecans
3	tablespoons oil for frying	1	cup flour
1	tablespoon honey	4	tablespoons chicken stock
¼	teaspoon crushed red chili pepper flakes	1	tablespoon lemon juice
		1	tablespoon melted butter

Trim any loose pieces from the catfish fillets. Chop the pecans very fine. Set up 3 baking dishes or pie pans on a counter and put flour in the first pan, beaten egg in the second and chopped pecans in the third. Bread the fillets by coating lightly in flour, shaking off the excess. Dip them in the egg and finally coat them in the nuts, pressing the pecans into the fillets on both sides. Heat 3 tablespoons of oil in a large pan. Combine the remaining ingredients for the sauce. Pan-fry the catfish over medium-high heat for 3 to 4 minutes per side. If the coating gets too brown too quickly, remove the fillets to a pie pan and finish them in 400 degree oven for 3 to 4 minutes. Place the cooked catfish on dinner plates and pour the sauce over them.

Serves 2.

OVEN-ROASTED CATFISH WITH SWEET ONION MARMALADE

8	U. S. Farm-Raised catfish fillets	½	teaspoon fresh thyme, leaves only (or dried thyme)
2	pounds thinly sliced sweet yellow onions (approximately 8 small onions)	1	quart heavy cream
		2	tablespoons balsamic vinegar
2	cups chicken stock (to taste)		Salt and pepper (to taste)

The Marmalade:
Place the onions in a heavy-bottomed saucepan and add the stock. Cover the pan and cook over moderate heat for 15 minutes. Remove the cover and add the thyme leaves. Continue to cook for about 45 minutes, until the onions start to color and the liquid is almost evaporated. Add cream and continue to cook until the mixture is thick. Add the vinegar and cook for 2 additional minutes.

The Catfish:
Lay the fillets skin side up on a flat surface. Salt and pepper each. Spread 1 tablespoon of sweet onion marmalade on each fillet. Beginning at the small or tail end, wrap the fillet onto itself to produce a tight spiral. Secure with a toothpick.

Place the catfish in a shallow baking dish, keeping them from touching. Top each with 1 tablespoon of sweet onion marmalade.

Bake at 350 degrees for 10 minutes. Remove from oven and let sit for 5 minutes. Place 3 tablespoons of marmalade in each of 4 warm plates and top with the cooked fillet. (Be sure and remove the toothpick.)

Serves 4.

GRILLED LEMON GRASS CATFISH WITH HOISIN-GINGER SAUCE

4   U.S. Farm-Raised catfish fillets

Sauce:
1	tablespoon vegetable oil	1	cup hoisin sauce (available at most supermarkets)
2	tablespoons finely minced yellow onion	½	cup water
1	clove finely minced garlic	⅓	cup rice wine vinegar (or regular white vinegar)
¼	teaspoon ground chili paste (optional)		

Marinade:
1	tablespoon minced fresh lemon grass (or zest of lemon to taste)	1	teaspoon oil

Garnish:
2	green onions, sliced thin diagonally	2	tablespoon chopped roasted peanuts

In a shallow saucepan, heat oil over moderate heat. Add garlic and onions and let sizzle for about 1 minute. (Do not let garlic burn). Add hoisin sauce, water, rice wine vinegar and chili paste. Reduce heat and allow to slowly simmer for about 10 minutes. If it's still too thick, add more water. (Sauce should have a creamy consistency). Set aside. Preheat grill or oven to 400 degrees. Cook the fillets for about 3 minutes on each side. Remove from heat and set aside. On individual plates, place the fillet in the center and carefully spoon the sauce on top. (Don't cover catfish completely). Sprinkle with slivers of green onion and roasted peanuts. Rice and vegetables are a great accompaniment.

Serves 4.

CATFISH BRIE SOUFFLÉ

3	cups water	1	cup freshly grated Parmesan cheese
1	pound U. S. Farm-Raised catfish fillets	¼	cup snipped chives or parsley
6	tablespoons butter or margarine	½	teaspoon finely shredded lemon peel
⅓	cup all-purpose flour	¼	teaspoon salt
1½	cups milk	¼	teaspoon pepper
8	ounces Brie cheese, rind removed and cut into cubes	6	egg whites
		6	egg yolks

In large skillet bring water to a boil. Add catfish. Return to boil; reduce heat. Cover and simmer gently for 5 to 7 minutes or until fish flakes easily. Remove from water. Cool slightly. Finely chop catfish; set aside.

Position a piece of buttered foil around a 1½-quart soufflé dish, letting it extend 2 inches above the top. Fasten the foil with tape.

In a large saucepan melt butter or margarine. Stir in flour. Add milk all at once. Cook and stir until thickened and bubbly. Stir in Brie cheese, a little at time, until cheese melts. Remove from heat; stir in Parmesan cheese, chives or parsley, lemon peel, salt and pepper. Stir in cooked catfish. Beat egg yolks with fork until combined.

Stir into cheese mixture.

In another mixing bowl, beat egg whites until stiff peaks form. Gently fold about 2 cups of the egg whites into the cheese mixture. Gradually pour cheese mixture over remaining beaten egg whites, folding to combine. Pour into prepared soufflé dish. (If desired, chill, uncovered, for up to 2 hours.)

Bake in a 350 degree oven about 55 minutes or until a knife inserted near the center comes out clean. Gently peel off foil; serve immediately.

Serves 4 to 6.

QUICK CATFISH GUMBO

1	cup chopped celery	½	teaspoon dried thyme
1	cup chopped onion		
1	cup chopped green pepper	½	teaspoon ground red pepper
2	cloves garlic, minced	½	teaspoon dried oregano, crushed
3	tablespoons cooking oil	2	pounds Farm-Raised catfish fillets, cut into bite-size pieces
4	cups beef broth		
1	16-ounce can whole tomatoes, cut up	1	10-ounce package frozen, sliced okra
1	bay leaf	4	cups hot cooked rice
1	teaspoon salt		

In a large kettle or Dutch oven cook celery, onion, green pepper and garlic in hot oil until tender.

Stir in beef broth, tomatoes, bay leaf, salt, thyme, red pepper and oregano. Bring to boil: reduce heat. Cover, simmer for 15 minutes.

Add catfish and okra to kettle. Return to boil, cover and simmer for 15 minutes or until fish flakes easily. Remove and discard bay leaf. Serve in bowls over hot cooked rice.

Serves 8.

CASHEW CRUSTED CATFISH WITH TOMATO BASIL CREAM

2   U.S. Farm-Raised catfish fillets (5 to 7 ounces)

Egg Wash:

2	eggs, beaten	½	cup milk

Cashew Mixture:

2	cups crushed cashews	½	teaspoon basil, dried
1	teaspoon cayenne pepper	½	teaspoon black pepper
2	teaspoons garlic powder		

Dip catfish fillets into egg wash, and dredge in cashew mixture. Sauté fillets in oil on medium heat for 5 to 6 minutes on each side or until golden brown. Serve on bed of tomato basil sauce.

Serves 2.

TOMATO BASIL CREAM

3	tablespoons olive oil	½	cup minced onion
2	cups crushed tomatoes	¼	cup minced basil leaves
4	cloves garlic, minced	¼	cup chicken stock
		¼	cup heavy cream

Sauté garlic and onion in olive oil until transparent. Add crushed tomatoes and chicken stock. Simmer for 20 minutes. Add heavy cream, bring to boil, simmer for 5 minutes and add fresh basil.

LAYERED CATFISH DIP

3	cups water	1	tablespoon lemon juice
1	pound U. S. Farm-Raised catfish fillets		Dash garlic salt
12	ounces cream cheese, softened	1	small onion, chopped
2	tablespoons mayonnaise	1	12-ounce bottle chili sauce
2	tablespoons Worcestershire sauce		Parsley (optional)

In a large skillet bring water to a boil. Add catfish. Return to boil; reduce heat. Cover and simmer gently for 5 to 7 minutes until fish flakes easily. Remove from water. Cool slightly. Flake catfish; set aside. In a mixing bowl stir together cream cheese, mayonnaise, Worcestershire sauce, lemon juice and garlic salt. Stir in chopped onion. To assemble, spread cheese mixture over bottom of a 12-inch plate or shallow serving bowl. Spread chili sauce over cheese layer. Top with cooked catfish. Garnish with parsley, if desired. Serve with sturdy crackers.

Serves 12.

CATFISH ANTIPASTO PLATTER

2	cups water	⅔	cup white wine vinegar
8	ounces U.S. Farm-Raised catfish fillets	½	cup olive oil
		3	green onions, finely chopped
4	ounces cheddar or co-jack cheese, cubed	3	cloves garlic, minced
4	ounces Calamata pitted ripe olives, drained	1	teaspoon sugar
		½	teaspoon dried basil, crushed
1	small zucchini, sliced ¼-inch thick	¼	teaspoon pepper
1	9-ounce package frozen artichoke hearts, thawed and halved		

In skillet bring water to boil. Add catfish. Return to boil; reduce heat. Cover and simmer gently for 5 to 7 minutes or until fish flakes easily. Remove from water. Cool slightly. Cut into bite-size pieces. In a large plastic bag combine cheese, olives, zucchini and artichoke hearts. Add catfish. In a small bowl stir together vinegar, oil, onions, garlic, sugar, basil and pepper. Pour over catfish mixture. Seal bag tightly. Cover and chill for 6 hours or overnight, turning bag occasionally. To serve, let marinated catfish mixture stand at room temperature about 15 minutes. Drain mixture and arrange on a lettuce-lined serving platter. Serve with toothpicks.

Serves 4.

CRYSTAL GRILL

423 Carrollton Avenue Greenwood, MS 38930

Mike J. Ballas   John M. Ballas
Deomi L. Ballas

The Crystal Grill has been a dining tradition in the Delta for more than 50 years. This unique restaurant is located in downtown Greenwood in a building which is listed in the Historic Register. The 250-seat Crystal features home-cooked vegetables, homemade desserts, prime steaks and fresh seafood.

CREOLE SAUCE

Prepare in a 3-quart heavy aluminum pot.

Chop:

3	large onions	1	carrot
1	stalk celery	¼	pound margarine or butter
2	bell peppers		
4	garlic cloves		

Add 1 cup of water to the ingredients above and sauté until clear; then add:

1½	ounces chicken base	2	tablespoons Worcestershire sauce
1½	ounces beef base	½	teaspoon mixed pickling spice
½	teaspoon black pepper	¼	cup sugar
¼	teaspoon hot pepper sauce		
2	tablespoons olive oil		

Mix in:

2	cups crushed tomatoes	½	cup ketchup

Simmer for at least one hour, then tighten to consistency desired with cornstarch and water mixture.

YIANNI'S

506 Yalobusha
Greenwood, MS 38930

Yianni & Elaine Isaak
Owners

Yianni's specializes in homemade casseroles, fresh fish, steaks and yeast rolls. The beautiful restaurant has banquet facilities that accommodate 20 to 50 people for business meetings or special occasions.

TIROPITES
(FETA CHEESE TRIANGLES)

1	pound feta cheese	½	teaspoon white pepper
3-4	ounces cream cheese	½	pound filo (phyllo)
8	ounces cottage cheese	2	sticks melted butter
3	eggs, separated (beat whites till stiff)		

Mix all cheeses together. Separate eggs. Beat yolks into cheese. Add stiffly beaten egg whites. Add white pepper. Cut filo into strips 4-inches wide. Brush one strip with melted butter. Place a second strip over the first and brush again. Put 1 teaspoon of filling at one end of strip. Fold both sides over lengthwise sealing the mixture. Fold diagonally until a triangle is formed and continue to fold like a flag.

Brush with melted butter and bake at 350 degrees for 20 minutes. You may freeze before baking and bake frozen.

Yield: 40 to 50

BEEF TIPS WITH ORZO

3	pounds beef sirloin tips	1	teaspoon beef base
1	medium onion Olive oil	1	bay leaf
		½	stick cinnamon Pinch of sugar
1	14-ounce can chopped tomatoes	2	cups orzo (pasta) Salt and pepper to taste
1	small can tomato purée		

Use 3 pounds of beef sirloin tips. Slice one medium onion, mix with beef tips and brown in olive oil. Add enough water to cover meat and bring to a boil. Skim foam from top. Add salt and pepper (to taste), one 14-ounce can of chopped tomatoes, one small can of tomato purée and one teaspoon of beef base. Also add one bay leaf, ½ stick of cinnamon and a pinch of sugar. Cook until almost ready. Add 2 cups of rosemarina or orzo and cook until pasta is ready. You may need additional water.

Serves 8.

(Vegetables may be added to the stew base instead of pasta.)

Typical Cotton Plant

LUSCO'S

722 Carrollton Avenue Greenwood, MS 38930

Andy & Karen Pinkston, Proprietors

The Pinkstons are fourth-generation owners of this nationally known restaurant. It has been at this location since 1933. Lusco's has been featured in **Condé Nast Travelers, Vogue, Southern Living, Gourmet** *and* **G.Q.** *magazines. It has also been featured in* **USA Today**.

Please note: The special Lusco sauces featured in several of the following recipes may be ordered from Lusco's by calling AC 601 453-5365.

OYSTERS BROCHETTE

1	long skewer	13	1½-inch pieces of bacon
12	medium-sized oysters (freshly shucked or from jars of fresh oysters)	½	cup melted margarine Pepper to taste
		¼	teaspoon freshly chopped parsley

Cut bacon in 1½-inch strips. Thread on skewer alternating bacon, oyster, bacon, etc. Cover baking sheet with foil (shiny side down). Lay skewer on piece of foil and spread oysters and bacon out. Pour melted margarine over brochette. Broil slowly until bacon is cooked. Season only with pepper. Remove from skewer and spoon equal amounts of drippings and Lusco's Broiled Shrimp Sauce over the brochette. Sprinkle with parsley and serve with buttered toast points.

Serves 1.

LUSCO'S BROILED SHRIMP WITH CRABMEAT OVER ANGEL HAIR OR RICE (EASY METHOD)

10	peeled, deveined large shrimp	1	stick of margarine Salt and pepper to taste
6	ounces fresh jumbo lump crabmeat		Lusco's Broiled Shrimp Sauce

Melt margarine in large skillet or wok. Place shrimp in melted margarine in skillet and season with salt and pepper. Cook on medium-high, stirring shrimp around until shrimp turn pink. Place jumbo lump crabmeat on top of shrimp and season with salt and pepper. Cover skillet and lower heat to medium-low and allow to cook about 10 more minutes. This will steam the shrimp and warm the crabmeat. Remove skillet from heat and pour in equal amounts (½ cup drippings to ½ cup sauce of Lusco's Broiled Shrimp Sauce and stir. May eat as is with toast points or spoon over rice or angel hair pasta.

Yield: 1 large serving or 2 small servings.

LUSCO'S PASTA SALAD

1	8-ounce package rotini (spiral) pasta	1	small jar stuffed green olives
1	bunch spring onions	1	jar chopped pimiento
1	large bell pepper	1-2	teaspoons dill weed Salt to taste
1	can artichoke hearts		

Cook pasta according to directions. Drain and allow to cool. Chop spring onions (including tops), bell pepper, drained artichoke hearts and drained olives. Drain pimiento. Add chopped ingredients to pasta. Add Lusco's Salad Dressing. Mix well and add salt and dill weed. Taste and add additional dressing and seasoning as needed to suit taste. Keep refrigerated.

Serves 4.

SOME LUSCO FAMILY FAVORITES:

EGGPLANT ROMANO

(so named because Romano or Pecorino cheese is used)

1	large (1 pound) can whole peeled tomatoes	8-10	fresh or frozen basil leaves or 1 to 1½ tsp. dried basil leaves (chopped)
3	medium-sized eggplants		Fresh hot pepper pod (chopped)
1	tablespoon extra virgin olive oil		Salt to taste
1-1½	tablespoons sugar	½	cup freshly grated Romano cheese

Blend can of whole peeled tomatoes in food processor until soupy yet chunky. Place in boiler or large skillet and add oil, sugar, salt and chopped hot pepper. Add torn basil leaves or dried basil. Cook over medium to low heat for 30 minutes or until it thickens. Stir occasionally to keep from sticking.

Peel eggplants and cut lengthwise into ¼-inch thick slices. Sprinkle with salt and soak in cold water for a few minutes. Drain in colander and lay out on paper towels. Pat dry.

In a large skillet, cook eggplant slices in hot oil over medium high heat until golden brown and tender. Drain lightly upon removing from skillet and begin layering in a casserole dish. Spoon tomato sauce over layer of eggplant, and then sprinkle with freshly grated cheese. Continue layering eggplants, topping each layer with tomato sauce and cheese. May serve as is or reheat in oven 350 degrees for 15 to 30 minutes or until heated throughout.

Serves 12.

ITALIAN CHICKEN SOUP

1	whole chicken (cut up) plus additional 2 chicken breasts	1	large stalk celery
1	large (1 pound) can whole peeled tomatoes	1	small (7-ounce) package thin vermicelli
3	pounds onions	1	cup of freshly grated Romano cheese

Chop onions and celery in food processor. Place chicken in 6-quart stockpot with about 4 quarts water. Add chopped onions and celery, and cook over high heat until chicken is cooked. Lower heat and remove chicken from pot and allow to cool. De-bone chicken and tear into bite-size pieces.

Blend can of whole peeled tomatoes in food processor until soupy yet chunky. Add to chicken broth in pot and bring to a boil. Add vermicelli (broken into small pieces) and let cook 10 to 15 more minutes. Add de-boned chicken and let cook a few more minutes. Add 1 cup of freshly grated Romano cheese. Stir well and serve.

Serves 12.

This is called "Italian Penicillin" because it is great when you are suffering from a cold or flu.

ITALIAN BREAD

1	loaf French bread
	Black pepper
	Coarsely grated or sliced fresh Romano cheese
	Extra virgin olive oil
	Italian Herb mixture

Slice loaf of bread in half lengthwise. Brush both sides of inside layer of bread with olive oil. Cover with grated or sliced Romano cheese. Sprinkle with black pepper a small amount of Italian herbs over cheese. Put loaf back together. Wrap in foil and bake in oven at 350 degrees about 20 to 30 minutes or until heated throughout and cheese is melted. Take out of foil, slice and serve.

Great served with the Italian Chicken Soup or Eggplant Romano.

FIORI'S ITALIAN RESTAURANT

Sunset Drive
Grenada, MS 38801

Anthony Glorioso
Chef Owner

SHRIMP & ZUCCHINI

25	medium-sized shrimp (deveined)	1	cup chicken broth
2	whole zucchini, cut in half (seeds removed)		Fresh parsley Salt and pepper to taste
½	cup diced green onions (reserve top of onions)	1	pound of cooked linguini
3	whole cloves of garlic mashed	½	cup of Parmesan cheese

In large saucepan, sauté onions, garlic and zucchini. Add shrimp until it is halfway done. Add chicken broth. Cook until shrimp are tender. Add Parmesan cheese and blend with cooked linguini. Toss till well coated. Serve immediately.

Serves 4.

ITALIAN SALAD

1	head Romaine lettuce	1	medium purple onion
2	tomatoes (pear-shaped)		Black olives Pepperoncini
1	cucumber	4	artichoke hearts cut in half

Clean and cut all the above. Place in bowl and toss with Italian dressing.

Serves 4.

ZABAGLIONE (CUSTARD)

6	egg yolks	4	ounces Marsala wine
1	cup sugar		

In a double boiler, beat egg yolks and sugar until mixture becomes creamy. Add Marsala wine. Stir for 2 minutes. Serve in a champagne glass. Garnish with amaretto cookies.

CEDAR GROVE
MANSION INN & RESTAURANT

2300 Washington Street
Vicksburg, MS 39180
1-800-862-1300

Ted Mackey, Owner
Pam Netterville, Public Relations

Cedar Grove Mansion, featured in numerous publications, consistently voted "Best Antebellum Home" in Vicksburg, "A Top Ten Most Romantic Place", and rated Four-Diamond by AAA, assures guests of the exceptional quality in accommodations and service.

Cedar Grove Mansion (circa 1840) has been featured on TLC's "Great Country Inns". This 50-room mansion has 30 guest rooms and suites all nestled in five acres of gardens. Relax with a Mint Julep or cocktail in the Piano Bar – the perfect prelude to a romantic gourmet candlelight dinner in Andre's at the Cedar Grove' Mansion.

Chef Andre Flowers
Executive Chef

ANDRE'S RASPBERRY FOREST SALMON

4	skinned and boned salmon fillets, 6-ounces each	½	cup butter (1 stick) melted
2	tablespoons minced fresh dill	8	sheets of phyllo dough
1	cup fresh raspberries		Hollandaise sauce (recipe follows)

Rub salmon with fresh dill. Sear salmon on a very hot grill just a few seconds on both sides to give grilled diamond marks. Brush phyllo dough with (1 stick) melted butter on both sides. Place 2 sheets together for each piece of salmon. Place 1 salmon in center of each double sheet of phyllo dough. Top with ¼ cup fresh raspberries and gather up the corners of dough to cover the salmon and raspberries. Twist the pastry gently to seal without splitting dough. Bake at 350 degrees for 30 minutes or until golden brown. Serve over Hollandaise sauce.

Serves 4.

HOLLANDAISE SAUCE

4	large egg yolks	⅛	teaspoon white pepper
1½	ounces warm water	12	ounces butter
1	tablespoon fresh lemon juice	1	tablespoon small imported capers
½	teaspoon salt		

Place the egg yolks, water, lemon juice, salt and white pepper in a blender. Cover and blend on high for about 5 seconds. Heat butter to 175 degrees. This allows the butter to cook the yolks as it is added to them. Turn the blender on and immediately begin to add the butter in a steady stream. Incorporate all of the butter in 20 to 30 seconds. If any lumps are present, strain the sauce through a cheesecloth. Add capers.

ANDRE'S FRENCH ONION SOUP AT THE MANSION

1	cup butter	2½	cups white wine
3	white onions, thinly sliced	1	cup sweet vermouth
3	yellow onions, thinly sliced		Toasted French bread slices, as garnish
3	purple onions, thinly sliced		Mozzarella cheese shredded, as garnish
2	cups chicken stock		Sliced mushrooms as garnish
¾	cup flour		
1	tablespoon white pepper		
½	cup sugar		

Sauté onions in the butter over low heat. Carefully caramelize them thoroughly without burning. Add caramelized onions to chicken stock and simmer 20 minutes. Soup can be thickened by adding flour slowly to soup. Add white pepper, sugar, salt, white wine and sweet vermouth to soup, simmer 5 minutes and serve in warm bowls. Top with toasted French bread and a sliced mushroom. Cover with a thick layer of cheese and place under the broiler or a salamander until the cheese is melted and lightly browned.

Serves 4.

CHEF ANDRE'S BRANDY BREAD PUDDING

2	large loaves French bread (torn into 3-inch pieces) toasted	3	cartons hazelnut creamer
1	whole pound cake (strawberry glazed) torn into pieces	3	tablespoons nutmeg
		2	tablespoons cinnamon
10	whole eggs	1	pound melted butter
2	cans sweetened condensed milk	2	tablespoons almond extract

Toast French bread, add strawberry glazed pound cake. Place in baking pan (17¼ x 11¾ x 2¼-inches). Mix remaining ingredients with a large whisk. Pour over bread and cake. Cover with foil and bake 1 hour at 325 degrees. Uncover and bake 15 minutes at 350 degrees. Scoop out portions and pour hot brandy sauce over pudding. Top with chopped roasted nuts and sprinkle with powdered sugar. Garnish with a strawberry.

CHEF ANDRE'S BRANDY SAUCE

10	egg yolks	2	cups of brandy
2	cartons whipping cream	2	tablespoons almond extract
2	bags of powdered sugar	1	pound of butter (melted)

Mix all ingredients well. Place sauce in a double boiler on medium heat and stir occasionally until it bubbles and serve.

Cedar Grove Mansion
Vicksburg, Mississippi

MONMOUTH PLANTATION

36 Melrose Avenue Natchez, MS 39120

Ron & Lani Riches, Proprietors
Ed Blackburn, Restaurant Manager
Juanita Love-Carter, Chef

*Monmouth Plantation is rated as "One of the Top Ten Romantic Places in the USA" by **Glamour Magazine** and **USA Today**. It has also been named as one the "top 50 U.S. Inns and B & B's" by **Zagat**. It consists of 26 beautifully landscaped acres that include pebble paths bursting with flowers, a white bridge over a small clear pond, Mississippi song birds and moss draped live oak trees. Monmouth has twenty-eight rooms and suites.*

Nights sparkle under candlelight and crystal during five-course dinners that are repeatedly touted as "the best in Natchez". The chef plans the menu daily and often incorporates regional favorites that are prepared in the South's finest culinary tradition. Monmouth is listed on the National Register of Historic Places.

SWEET POTATO CAKES

6	large sweet potatoes	1	teaspoon ground cinnamon
¾	cup sugar	1	teaspoon vanilla extract
¼	cup butter		
¼	cup brown sugar	2	eggs
¼	cup honey	¼	cup flour
		1	cup gingersnaps

Cut potatoes and boil until soft, then drain and let cool. When potatoes are cooled and drained well, add butter to mashed potatoes. Add the other ingredients, making sure that the mixture is thick – then shape to fit muffin tins. (can be made into other shapes) Make sure your pan is greased and put gingersnap crumbs in bottom of muffin pan. Place cake in pan and coat top with gingersnap crumbs. Cook at 350 degrees for 20 to 25 minutes.

Serves 10 to 12.

JUANITA'S FRENCH ZUCCHINI SOUP

A "tad" of chicken base (concentrated chicken stock)	¼ chopped celery
¼ cup water	2 cloves garlic, chopped
8 good-sized zucchini, sliced thin	1 cup heavy cream
	1 cup whole cream
1 cup chopped onions (Vidalia are best)	¼ cup cornstarch
	Curry powder
	White pepper
	Salt

Dissolve the chicken base in the water in a heavy pot. Boil the zucchini, onions, celery and garlic in this liquid until tender and then purée. Return the purée to the pot and add the heavy cream and the whole cream. Stir in the cornstarch to thicken and heat well, but not boiling. Season with curry powder, white pepper and salt. Garnish with a slice of lemon, sprig of fresh dill and an artfully added sprinkle of cayenne pepper.

Serves 2.

JUANITA'S PRALINE SAUCE FOR BRIE

To Toast the Pecans: Dot ½ cup of coarse pecan pieces with half a stick of butter and sprinkle with sugar. Toast in a 300 degree oven for about 30 minutes, until brown but not burned. Set these aside.

The Sauce:

1 stick (8 tablespoons) butter	⅛ teaspoon lemon juice
1 cup brown sugar, packed	¼ cup whole milk or heavy cream
	½ cup pecan pieces

Mix all the ingredients together and bring to a full boil. Boil until it reaches a fixed stage, approximately 3 to 5 minutes, stirring constantly. Please note that it does burn easily. To serve, pour sauce over brie and serve with sliced apples.

CHEF LOVE'S BEEF BRISKET
(with Creole Mayonnaise)

1 6 to 8 pound beef brisket with fat trimmed	2 tablespoons black pepper
	3 medium onions, sliced
3 tablespoons Worcestershire sauce	6 ounces garlic, minced

Wash brisket and pat dry. Rub seasonings into meat, and place onions and garlic around brisket. Place in a greased serving dish large enough to hold the brisket. Cover tightly with foil and bake in a 325 degree oven for 4 hours or until tender. To carve meat, slice across the grain at an angle. Serve with Creole mayonnaise (recipe follows).

CREOLE MAYONNAISE

1 cup mayonnaise	⅓ teaspoon lemon juice
¼ cup Creole mustard or other spice mustard	

Combine all ingredients and serve with brisket.

PHILADELPHIA is home to the Mississippi Band of Choctaw Indians Reservation and Museum. The annual Choctaw Indian Fair has traditional Indian dancing, crafts, weaponry and Indian Princess competitions. It is also known for its annual Neshoba County Fair, affectionately called "Mississippi's Giant Houseparty" with its arts and crafts and entertainment. The fair has often been used to kick off political campaigns of Mississippians from all over the state.

MERIDIAN, a certified retirement city, is well known for its historic homes and buildings, large medical centers and excellent schools. It is home to the Jimmie Rodgers Memorial Festival, an annual country music festival. Stetson hats were first made at nearby Dunn's Falls.

JACKSON, Mississippi's Capitol City, is the hub of state government, a commercial and financial center and a world-renowned medical center. It is also the cultural capitol of Mississippi. The USA International Ballet Competition is held here every four years and special events such as the Splendors of Versailles Exhibition are held on a regular basis. The Mississippi Museum of Art is located here. Jackson is also home to the Mississippi Sports Hall of Fame & Museum as well as the Russell C. Davis Planetarium and Ronald E. McNair Space Theatre. The Jackson Zoological Park is the largest in the state.

HATTIESBURG is the home of the University of Southern Mississippi. Hattiesburg was recently selected by the U.S. Council of Mayors as the "Most Livable Small City in America." It is one of the fastest growing communities in Mississippi. Lush Southern pine forests surround Hattiesburg.

SILVER STAR RESORT & CASINO

P. O. Box 6048
Highway 16 West
Philadelphia, MS 39350

Silver Star currently offers six restaurants including two fine dining outlets, one of which has been recognized as the Premier Fine Dining establishment in Mississippi by The Chaine des Rotsseurs.

Tracy Castleman A.C.F., C.C.A.
Executive Chef

Mr. Castleman has won numerous awards for his creative designs, stylish and beautifully presented foods. He is Chef Grillardin for the Chaine des Rotisseurs and is a member of Euro Toques, the prestigious European Society of Chefs.

Mr. Castleman graduated from the California Culinary School in 1981. He has also worked on the American-Hawaiian Cruise Lines and has held positions at the Newport Beach Four Seasons, Ritz Carlton Laguna Nigiel and the Imperial Palace in Las Vegas.

He was awarded first place in the Mississippi State Dessert Championship in the non-chocolate division in 1996 with a creation named Gateau Riche. He has won numerous statewide awards. He received 4th place in the "Taste of Elegance" Award for the National Pork Producers Association in Washington, D.C. He received 5th place in the salmon competition (1997) in New York City and 4th place in beef competition in the National Chefs Championship in New York City (1998).

ASIAN PORK WRAPS

2	pounds ground pork	2	tablespoons parsley
1½	pounds peeled shrimp (16/20 count)	1	cup green cabbage
		4	each eggs, beaten
½	green bell pepper	2	tablespoons cornstarch
1	carrot	1	tablespoon soy sauce
2	celery		
½	teaspoon fresh ginger	2	tablespoons olive oil
4	green onions	2	teaspoons roasted onion purée/base
4	cloves fresh garlic		
½	fresh jalapeño pepper		

Finely chop all vegetables and set aside. Heat oil and sauté shrimp with garlic and ginger. Cool and finely chop. Sauté pork until done. Add green bell pepper, carrot, celery, green onion, jalapeño and cabbage. Sauté for one minute. Cool mixture. Add shrimp, eggs and cornstarch. Dissolve in soy and roasted onion base. Adjust seasoning. Roll in wrapper. Fry in peanut oil for approximately 3 minutes.

Yield: approximately 40 each

CHICKEN ON A STICK

Marinade 8 ounces of boneless chicken breast for 12 hours in low calorie Kraft Italian dressing.

For batter: (combine and mix)

4	cups all purpose flour	2	teaspoons granulated garlic
1	teaspoon paprika	2	teaspoons season salt
1	tablespoon baking powder	3	cans beer
2	teaspoons black pepper		

Cut chicken breast into strips and put on skewer. Dip into batter and fry at 350 degrees 3 to 4 minutes (5 maximum).

TWIN PEAKS AU PORC SAUCE

8	ounces pork loin	1	each whole egg
5	ounces shredded filo	½	cup flour
1	quart pork stock	7	ounces beer
1	each large red bell pepper		Salt to taste
1	bundle asparagus spears		Pepper to taste
2	bundles large spinach leaves	4	ounces polenta
		1	cup port wine
1	teaspoon sesame seeds	4	ounces heavy cream
1	teaspoon black sesame seeds	1	each garlic clove
		1	tablespoon whole butter
4	ounces Port-Salut cheese	2	tablespoons olive oil
10	each large shallots	2	tablespoons Chablis wine
1	tablespoon Romano cheese	3	sprigs fresh thyme
		1	quart peanut oil

Sauté fresh spinach leaves with chopped garlic and shallots, season to taste and add olive oil and Chablis wine. Set to the side and chill.

Cut the Port-Salut cheese into 6-inch strips ⅛-inch thick. Set to the side.

Prepare a beer batter by incorporating flour, egg and beer. Blend to a smooth consistency. Season to taste then chill.

Prepare a polenta mix with 4 ounces polenta and grated Romano cheese. Season to taste and place into a pyramid mold. Chill.

Reduce port wine & shallots-thyme down to a sec (means dry). Add pork trimmings and stock. Reduce down to a glacé. Strain and add sesame seeds. Keep warm.

Trim pork loin, pound out to ⅛-inch, season. Lay whole spinach leaves to cover the whole loin, add a strip of Port cheese to cover the length of the loin. Roll the loin and tie. Sear the roll to lock in the juices. Untie and roll into the beer batter. Then lightly coat with filo dough (shredded). Place rolled loin into a frying pan with peanut oil and cook until golden brown and place into a 350 degree oven for 8 to 12 minutes.

TAHITIAN VEAL LOIN

1	each veal loin		Flour to coat
	Salt to taste	4	ounces lager beer batter
	White pepper to taste		Peanut oil to fry
6	large leaves spinach	1	ounce jalapeño pepper chili sauce
3	ounces shredded phyllo dough	2	ounces Bel Paese cheese
1	ounce teriyaki sauce (sweet)		

Pound veal loin to ¼-inch flat, season with salt and white pepper. Sauté spinach leaves with garlic oil or peanut oil. Arrange leaves on loin and let cool. Melt down Bel Paese cheese with a little cream till fully free of lumps. Place mixture in a cool area till it is chilled. Roll out cheese into a small rope shape and place this in the center of the loin. Roll the loin up and chill. Now dust the loin with flour and coat into the beer batter and roll it with the phyllo dough. Place into the peanut oil at 350 degrees. When phyllo becomes pork brown you should be ready to serve.

Sauce: Mix together teriyaki sauce with the jalapeño chile sauce and heat.

Yield: 1 portion

SOUFFLÉ DE SAUMON WITH A MUSCADINE SAFFRON SAUCE

1	12-ounce salmon fillet	2	each shiitake mushrooms, medium
3	teaspoons butter	8	ounces vermouth
1	each truffle	8	ounces white wine
		1	tablespoon olive oil

Muscadine Saffron Sauce:

16	ounces white wine	1	sprig fresh thyme
4	ounces muscadine juice	5	each white peppercorns
3	each shallots, medium	1	each bay leaf, small
8	ounces heavy cream	15	threads saffron
6	ounces whole butter, unsalted	½	tablespoon each salt, pepper to taste
1	each plum tomato, brunoise		

Vegetables:

1	each carrot, batonnet	10	each morel mushrooms
1	bundle asparagus tips	3	each basil leaves

Mousse:

4	ounces heavy cream	5	each fresh basil leaves
1	each egg white Salt and pepper to taste		

This recipe will produce two entrees!

Cut the salmon into 6-ounce fillets. Reserve all trim for the mousseline filling. You will need 6 ounces. Chill the fish thoroughly.

Make a mousseline as follows: Purée the salmon in the bowl of a food processor to a smooth paste. Add the egg white, cream, basil and salt and white pepper. Pulse the machine off and on, until the ingredients are all just incorporated. Keep chilled until needed.

You will need a ring mold, 3 inches in diameter. Coat the inside of the ring, liberally with olive oil using the reserved 6-ounce fillet, slice it thin and build into layers, salmon, salt and pepper and the mousseline filling. Repeat the procedure again.

Slice the shiitake mushrooms thin, lightly sauté in clarified butter. Form the slices into a star on the top layer of the mold, slice the truffle and place in the center of the star. Place the finished product into a shallow baking pan and add vermouth and white wine – 8 ounces each. Poach in a 300 degree convection oven for 20 minutes.

To prepare the sauce, combine the wine, muscadine juice, shallots (rough cut), and herbs. Heat and reduce to a sec, (this word means dry). Add heavy cream, reduce to half, add saffron, incorporate the cold butter. Add the brunoise tomato to the sauce, finish sauce with salt and pepper to taste. Set aside and keep warm, do not keep hot or the sauce will break.

Blanch the batonnet of carrots and asparagus tips until tender, shock with ice water immediately and set aside. Slice the morel mushrooms in half and rinse thoroughly, set aside. Take the fresh basil leaves and fry in hot oil until crispy. This will be used as a garnish on the top of the entrée. Sauté the 3 vegetables lightly in butter, season with salt and pepper and set aside (hold hot).

Remove salmon mold out of ring, place on plate. Place the vegetables in a criss-cross pattern. Ladle 1 ounce of the muscadine saffron sauce on base of plate. Garnish with fried basil leaves.

Serves 2.

PHILLIP M
CASUAL FINE DINING

STUFFED PORTOBELLO MUSHROOMS WITH HARVEST RICE STUFFING

8	portobello mushrooms	¼	cup Worcestershire sauce
1	stick butter		Seasoned salt

Wash mushrooms gently and pat dry. Toss with butter and Worcestershire sauce. Sprinkle with seasoned salt. Place in baking dish and bake at 350 degrees for about 8 minutes. Remove from oven and set aside. Stuff with harvest rice stuffing.

1	stick butter	½	cup sliced fresh mushrooms, diced
1	box long grain wild rice	1	can cream of mushroom soup
½	cup chopped onions	2	cups water
½	cup chopped green peppers	4	beef bouillon cubes
½	cup chopped water chestnuts		
¼	cup chopped pecans, toasted		(mix pecans, almonds and walnuts together)
¼	cup chopped almonds, toasted		
¼	cup chopped walnuts, toasted		
	Pimientos and fresh parsley for garnish		

Melt butter. Add onions, mushrooms, water, chestnuts, peppers and sauté 4 minutes. Add half of the toasted nut mixture. Sauté 3 more minutes. Set aside. In a saucepan combine bouillon cubes and water. Bring water to boil to dissolve bouillon cubes. Add cream of mushroom soup and rice and seasoning packet. Stir until mixed. Add the sautéed vegetable mixture. Place in covered casserole and bake at 350 degrees for 20 to 25 minutes until rice is done. Remove from oven and let sit uncovered 10 minutes. Stuff mushrooms with large ice cream scoop. Bake an additional 10 minutes uncovered at 350 degrees. Top with remaining nuts, pimientos and fresh parsley.

Serves 8.

OYSTER ARTICHOKE BISQUE

2	(12-ounce) containers fresh shucked oysters		Dash fresh grated nutmeg
1	cup oyster liquid	⅓	cup all-purpose flour
½	cup butter	1	(14-ounce) can quartered artichoke hearts (not marinated)
2	cups chopped green onions		
4	bay leaves		
⅛	teaspoon dried thyme		Fresh parsley, chopped
⅛	teaspoon crushed red pepper flakes	1½	cups heavy cream
		2	(14-ounce) cans chicken broth

Melt butter. Add green onions, bay leaves, thyme, red pepper flakes and nutmeg. Gently sauté until green onions are slightly tender, but not cooked. Add flour. Stir to blend. Gradually add chicken broth and 1 cup of oyster liquid. Bring to a boil and reduce heat to simmer and continue to simmer uncovered 15 to 20 minutes. Remove bay leaves. Add oysters and artichokes. Simmer 15 minutes. Remove from heat and add heavy cream. Gently simmer until thoroughly heated. Sprinkle with parsley. Serve immediately.

Yields 8 to 9 cups.

SUN-DRIED APRICOT STUFFED PORK LOIN WITH APRICOT BALSAMIC TARRAGON GLAZE

1	large pork loin	¼	teaspoon coarse ground pepper
¼	teaspoon dried tarragon		
½	teaspoon seasoned salt	2	bags dried pitted apricots

Rinse pork loin with cool water. If loin is in two parts, you can separate with a very sharp knife and cut a slit ⅔ to ¾ of the way through the loin being careful not to cut through. Cut this slit in the upper third. Sprinkle tarragon, salt and pepper inside this slit; then stuff with dried apricots. Use cotton twine string to tie the loin in 1-inch intervals. Set aside. Make a reduction glaze. When ready to baste loin with glaze, save ½ of the glaze throughout the cooking process (baste periodically during cooking process) and overglaze when ready to serve.

Bake at 350 degrees for 1 to 1½ hours basting every 15 minutes. Let meat rest 15 minutes after removing from oven before slicing and serving. Use fresh apricots and fresh tarragon for garnish.

APRICOT BALSAMIC TARRAGON GLAZE

1	stick butter	1	cup water
1	(10 to 12-ounce) jar apricot preserves	¼	cup balsamic vinegar
		½	teaspoon tarragon +

Melt butter. Add preserves until melted. Add ½ of the water and tarragon. Gently simmer 8 to 10 minutes, adding small amounts of water if needed. Reduce glaze and add additional tarragon to taste. Glaze loin before baking and during baking. Save ½ cup to use when serving.

CHOCOLATE RASPBERRY TRUFFLE LOAF WITH RASPBERRY SAUCE

2	cups heavy cream	½	cup butter
3	egg yolks	¼	cup confectioner's sugar
16	ounces semi-sweet chocolate		
½	cup light or dark corn syrup	1	teaspoon vanilla

Raspberry sauce:		½	cup light corn syrup
12	ounces fresh or frozen raspberries		
		½	cup sugar

Puree in food processor. Strain. Stir in corn syrup. Put in saucepan and add sugar. Bring to boil. Cool.

Line 9½ x 5½ x 2¾-inch loaf pan with plastic wrap. Mix ½ cup cream with egg yolks in small bowl. Warm chocolate, corn syrup and butter in large saucepan over medium heat until melted. Add egg mixture. Cook 3 to 4 minutes while stirring constantly. Remove from heat and cool to room temperature. Beat remaining cream, sugar and vanilla until soft peaks form. Fold into chocolate until no streaks remain. Pour into pan. Refrigerate overnight.

To serve: Slice and place in pool of raspberry sauce.

WEIDMANN'S RESTAURANT

210 22nd Avenue
Meridian, MS 39301

**Gloria & Poo Chancellor
Owners**

BLACK BOTTOM PIE

Crust:

14	gingersnaps
5	tablespoons melted butter

Crush gingersnaps, roll out fine, add melted butter, pat into 9-inch pie pan. Bake in hot oven 10 minutes and allow to cool.

Custard Filling:

2	cups scalded milk
4	egg yolks, well beaten
½	cup sugar
1½	tablespoons cornstarch
1½	squares bitter chocolate
1	teaspoon vanilla extract

Add eggs slowly to hot milk. Combine sugar and cornstarch and stir into egg yolk mixture. Cook in double boiler for 20 minutes, stirring occasionally, until it coats spoon. Remove from heat. Take out one cup of filling and set the remaining aside. Add 1½ squares bitter chocolate to cup you have taken out and beat well as it cools. Add one teaspoon of vanilla extract, then pour this mixture into pie crust. Chill.

Second Mixture:

1	tablespoon gelatin
2	tablespoons cold water
4	egg whites
½	cup sugar
¼	teaspoon cream of tartar
2	tablespoons whiskey

Dissolve gelatin in cold water, and add remaining custard, and cool. Beat egg whites, sugar and cream of tartar until stiff, add whiskey, then fold into plain custard mixture and spread on top of chocolate mixture. Chill. Cover top of pie with whipped cream with shavings of bitter chocolate.

Serving for 6 to 8.

THE GOVERNOR'S MANSION

300 East Capitol
Jackson, MS 39201

**Luis Bruno
Chef de Maison**

Chef Luis Bruno is the Executive Chef at the Mississippi Governor's Mansion. Chef Bruno's employers, of course, are Governor and Mrs. Fordice. He describes his employers as "the best that he has ever had". Bruno is a native New Yorker and has worked in Florida and New York before moving to Jackson, his wife's hometown. Kathleen Bruno is the culinary chef instructor at the Jackson campus of Hinds Community College. Chef Bruno received a diploma in Culinary Arts from Pinellas Technical Education Center in Clearwater, Florida, and completed a 30-hour course at the Culinary Institute of America at Hyde Park, New York.

CRAB & AVOCADO EMPANADAS WITH PAPAYA MOJO

For the filling:

8	ounces jumbo lump crabmeat
2	tablespoons lemon juice, freshly squeezed
1	ripe, firm avocado, diced small
8	green onions, tops only, chopped
3	plum tomatoes, seeds remove, diced small
4	tablespoons fresh parsley, chopped Salt and pepper to taste

Pick through crab for any shells. Carefully rinse under cold water. Squeeze lemon juice over diced avocado to prevent discoloration. Toss all filling ingredients together.

(see next page)

For the dough:

2	cups all-purpose flour	½	teaspoon salt
½	cup shortening	½	cup iced water
2½	tablespoons unsalted butter, cold	1	large egg, beaten, for egg wash

In a large bowl, combine the flour with the shortening, butter and salt. Mix lightly with your fingertips until the dough forms pea-sized pieces. Stir in the iced water. Lightly knead, handling dough as little as possible, until the dough forms a ball. Add a little more iced water if necessary. Cover with plastic wrap and allow to rest for about one hour in refrigerator.

To assemble the empanadas:

Remove dough from refrigerator and roll out to a thickness of about ⅛-inch. Use a 6-inch round cutter to cut out about 10 circles. Place 1 to 1½ ounces of filling into the center of each dough round. Brush edges of circle with egg wash. Fold over to form a half-moon and seal edges with fork. In a large, heavy pan, fry empanadas in 325 degree oil until golden brown, about 3 to 4 minutes. Serve with papaya mojo.

Yield: 10 empanadas

Papaya Mojo:

2	cloves garlic, minced	⅛	cup fresh cilantro, chopped
2	tablespoons olive oil	2	teaspoons granulated sugar
½	cup lime juice	1-2	teaspoons crushed red pepper flakes
1	firm, but ripe, papaya, peeled, seeded and diced		Salt and pepper to taste

Cook garlic in olive oil over medium-low heat for one to two minutes. Add the lime juice and cook one more minute. Add the papaya, cilantro, sugar, crushed red pepper flakes, salt and pepper, and cook another 30 seconds. Remove from heat. Transfer to cool, clean container. Chill before serving.

GONDULES WITH CHORIZO & COLLARDS

½	pound gondules* (may substitute dried black-eyed peas)	1	ham hock, scored
		2-3	bay leaves
		¾	cup sofrito**
1½	quarts chicken broth	1	teaspoon salt
		1	teaspoon pepper

Pick through gondules for any debris, then soak overnight. Drain and rinse gondules, then add broth, ham hock, bay leaves, sofrito, salt and pepper. Bring to a boil, then lower heat to medium-low and let simmer for about one hour or until beans are very tender but not mushy.

Gondules, or Spanish pigeon peas are available in the ethnic food section of many grocery stores.

**Sofrito is a mixture of chopped vegetables such as onions, garlic, tomatoes and herbs cooked together in olive oil.*

COLLARDS WITH CHORIZO

1	cup chorizo (Spanish sausage; may substitute regular sausage)	3	bunches collard greens, ribs and stems removed, cut into 1-inch strips
1	tablespoon vegetable oil	1	cup chicken broth
2	small onions	1	tablespoon sugar, more if desired
2	garlic cloves		Salt and pepper to taste
1½	teaspoons crushed red pepper		

Cook chorizo in vegetable oil over medium heat. Add onions, garlic and crushed red pepper. Cook until onions are soft and translucent. Add greens in batches, stirring each batch to wilt before adding more. Add chicken broth. Cover and cook, stirring often until wilted, about 15 minutes longer. Add the sugar, salt and pepper to taste. Lower heat to medium-low, cover and cook until greens are completely tender and sugar is fully dissolved.

PECAN CRUSTED VEAL CHOP WITH BARBECUE DEMI-GLACE

Barbecue Sauce:

1	cup ketchup	1	tablespoon Dijon mustard
½	cup vinegar	3	teaspoons Tabasco
¼	cup Worcestershire Sauce	½	cup brown sugar
		2	cups veal stock

In a food processor, place the first 6 ingredients. Puree, set aside. Reduce veal stock to about ⅓. Add 3 tablespoons barbecue sauce to stock reduction, simmer for about 2 to 3 minutes and set aside.

Veal Chops:

4	(6-ounce) veal chops	Salt and pepper to taste	
1	cup crushed pecans		

Preheat oven to 400 degrees. Season the veal chops with salt and pepper. Grill veal chops, slightly char on each side for 2 minutes. Remove veal, brush each side with barbecue demi-glace. Sprinkle crushed pecans on the veal. Place veal in a roasting pan and finish baking for about 6 to 8 minutes or until desired temperature.

Serves 4.

FLAN

1	can sweetened condensed milk	1	tablespoon vanilla extract
1	can evaporated milk		Caramel Sauce (recipe below)
2	eggs, whole		
6	eggs, yolks only		

For the Caramel Sauce:
1 cup granulated sugar

Preheat oven to 375 degrees. Combine all ingredients (other than caramel sauce) and mix in blender until smooth.

In small pan, stir sugar over medium high heat constantly with wooden spoon until lumps are gone and light amber color is achieved. Should take about 15 minutes.

When sauce is ready, immediately pour into ramekins or pan and coat interior. Sauce will harden immediately. Pour custard mixture into coated ramekins or pan and cook in water bath at 375 degrees for 15 minutes. Then lower heat to 325 degrees for an additional 25 minutes. If custard is browning, cover with aluminum foil. Cook flan until a knife inserted into the center comes out clean. Allow to cool for several hours or overnight, then run a small knife around the rim to release the edges. Unmold onto serving plate. Enjoy.

Yield: 1 large flan or 6 individual portions

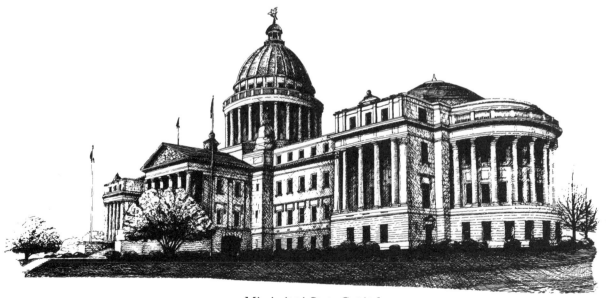

Mississippi State Capitol
Jackson, Mississippi

BRUCE CAIN
Former Executive Chef
For Huntington's Grille, Jackson, MS & Baton Rouge Country Club

MARINARA SHRIMP & CORN SOUP

4	dozen 50-ct. shrimp, peeled and deveined	2½	cups marinara sauce
3	cups whole kernel corn	2	whole bay leaves
1	cup oil	1	teaspoon thyme
1	cup flour	1	teaspoon basil
2	cups chopped onions	3	quarts shellfish stock
2	cups chopped celery	1	cup sliced green onions
1	cup chopped bell pepper	1	cup parsley
¼	cup diced garlic		Salt and cracked black pepper to taste

In a two gallon stock pot, heat oil over medium-high heat. Add flour and using a wire whisk, stir constantly until roux is golden brown. Add corn, onions, celery, bell pepper and garlic. Sauté 5 to 10 minutes or until vegetables are wilted. Add marinara sauce, bay leaves, thyme and basil. Add shellfish stock, one ladle at a time, stirring constantly until all is incorporated. Bring to a low boil, reduce to simmer and cook for thirty minutes. Add shrimp, green onions and parsley and continue to cook for 10 additional minutes. Season to taste using salt and cracked black pepper.

Serves 12.

SALMON PASTA

3	tablespoons unsalted butter		Juice of ⅓ large lemon
1	tablespoon finely chopped shallots	2	ounces Scotch whisky (optional)
1	cup heavy cream Salt to taste		White pepper, a goodly amount
12	ounces bow tie pasta (butterfly pasta, cooked al dente)		Fresh ground black pepper Diced pimientos and chopped parsley for garnish
3	ounces finely diced smoked salmon		

Place butter in a large frying pan over low heat. When melted, add salmon and shallots and cook for about 2 minutes. Add lemon juice and mix well. Stir in cream and whisky. Raise heat just long enough to let alcohol evaporate. Add salt and pepper and stir. Combine butterfly pasta with the salmon sauce until pasta is well coated. The sauce should be smooth and creamy and should cling to pasta but pasta should not "swim in it." If sauce is too dry, add a little cream. Top with fresh ground pepper, diced pimientos and chopped parsley.

Serves 6.

SHRIMP SCAMPI FIRENZI

12	10 to 15-ct. cleaned shrimp	½	cup seafood stock
2	tablespoons paprika	½	cup medium strength demi-glace
½	tablespoon cayenne pepper	½	cup heavy cream
¼	pound butter	¼	cup fresh lemon juice
½	tablespoon finely minced garlic		Cracked black pepper to taste
½	cup brandy		Garnish with fresh parsley and tri-color confetti
½	cup anisette		

Season shrimp with paprika and cayenne pepper. Pan sauté shrimp on medium-high heat until just pink, flambé with brandy then anisette. Add seafood stock, demi-glace and cream. Bring to rapid boil, remove shrimp and reduce mixture until thick and creamy. Replace shrimp, add lemon juice and cracked pepper. Serve with plenty of sauce.

Serves 4.

DIJON PORKLOIN ORLEANS

2	7-pound porkloins, trimmed	½	cup finely diced green onions
2	cups died andouille sausage	3	tablespoons diced garlic
2	cups crawfish tails	1	cup bread crumbs
½	cup finely diced onions	1	cup Dijon mustard
			Salt and pepper to taste

Combine all ingredients except porkloin. Season to taste. Using a sharp knife, cut a pocket through the center of the porkloin, stuff tightly with stuffing.

To cook:

2	stuffed porkloins	1½	cups white wine
½	cup melted butter	2	cups demi-glace
½	cup Dijon mustard	1	cup Dijon mustard
⅓	cup cracked black pepper		Salt and pepper to taste
2	tablespoons diced garlic		

Season the stuffed porkloins with butter, mustard, pepper and garlic rubbing well into the meat. Place in a preheated 450 degree oven and bake thirty minutes or until 155 degree internal temperature.

Deglaze pan with white wine. Add demi-glace and Dijon mustard; then pour into a saucepan. Reduce over medium heat until well thickened. Season to taste. Slice stuffed porkloin into 2 ounce slices; 3 per person. Serve with 2 to 3 ounces of the white wine demi-glace Dijon sauce.

Serves 12.

PORK, VEGETABLE & CHEESE STRUDEL

4	ounces carrots, diced	4	ounces yellow squash
4	ounces mushrooms	4	ounces zucchini
		4	ounces broccoli

Blanch and drain.

1	pound diced pork tenderloin	2	tablespoons butter
4	ounces red bell peppers, diced	2	tablespoons shallots, diced
		1	tablespoon garlic

With butter, brown pork. Add vegetables; sauté two minutes and reserve.

12	ounces phyllo	1½	cups Swiss cheese, grated
5	ounces butter, melted		Salt and pepper to taste
10	ounces Mornay sauce, tight		

Stack phyllo sheets 5 layers thick, buttering each layer; spread thin layer vegetables and lace with Mornay sauce and sprinkle with Swiss cheese. Roll and bake at 400 degrees until golden brown. Slice and serve.

Serves 12.

Merrillls' Store – 1834
Carrollton, Mississippi

CRAWFISH & BLEU CHEESE MOUSSE WITH CAJUN BEURRE BLANC

½	pound cream cheese	½	cup parsley, finely chopped
¾	pound bleu cheese	½	cup shallots
6	eggs	1	tablespoon garlic
4	ounces heavy cream		White pepper to taste
1	pound crawfish tail meat, chopped		Red pepper to taste
1	cup pimientos, chopped		Salt to taste

Combine cream cheese and bleu cheese in food processor until smooth. Add eggs and heavy cream and mix well. Add all of the other ingredients and mix well.

Fill timbales or molds. Poach in bain-marie until 170 degrees or line timbales with poached julienne vegetables if desired.

CAJUN BEURRE BLANC SAUCE

2	ounces butter soft (clarified)	2	ounces heavy cream
1	tablespoon chopped garlic	¾	pound solid butter
4	inch slices of andouille sausage		Salt to taste
½	pound crawfish tails		White pepper to taste
1	cup green onions		Cayenne pepper to taste
1	ounce white wine		Lemon juice to taste
½	ounce hot pepper sauce		

Sauté butter, garlic and andouille sausage on medium heat. Add crawfish tail meat and green onions and sauté. Add white wine and hot pepper sauce and reduce by half. Add heavy cream and reduce by ¼. Mount butter into reduction on low heat, strain through fine chinois (conical-shaped sieve). Season to taste with salt, white pepper, cayenne pepper and lemon juice.

Serves 10.

PLANTATION PORK & SQUASH PUDDING

3	cups finely chopped squash	¼	cup minced garlic
3	cups finely chopped green zucchini	2½	cups chicken stock
		½	cup pimientos
3	pounds diced pork tenderloin	½	cup parsley
		½	cup green onions
½	cup finely chopped onion	3	tablespoons hot pepper sauce
½	cup finely chopped bell pepper	4	cups bread crumbs to tighten

Poach yellow and green squash until tender, reserve. In a one gallon stock pot on medium heat, brown pork. Add onion, celery, bell pepper and garlic and cook until wilted. Add chicken stock, reserved squash and cook on medium heat ten minutes. Add pimientos, parsley, green onions and pepper sauce. Tighten with bread crumbs. Fill 12 2-inch ramekins and bake 5 to 8 minutes in 450 degree oven. Turn out and serve at once. For garnish, ramekins may be inlaid with different colors of vegetables, etc.

Serves 12.

PORK MEDALLIONS WITH STRAWBERRIES

12	6-ounce pork tenderloin medallions	1	cup dry white wine
		2	cups sliced strawberries
¾	cup melted butter	4	cups demi-glace
2	cups flour	1	cup heavy whipping cream
1	cup green onions		
2	tablespoons diced garlic		Salt and cayenne pepper to taste
1	cup sliced mushrooms		

Dust medallions with flour. Sauté with butter over medium heat 5 to 6 minutes on each side. Remove medallions from pan. Reserve. Add onions, garlic and mushrooms and sauté until vegetables are wilted. Deglaze, add strawberries and demi-glace. Bring to boil and reduce to slightly thicken. Add cream and reduce 5 minutes on medium heat. Season to taste.

Serves 6.

PORKLOIN STUFFED MIRLITON "CHIOTE SQUASH"

12	mirlitons	1½	cups rich chicken
2	cups porkloin		stock
	diced ½-inch cubes		Mirliton meat
½	pound butter		from 6
1	cup chopped	1½	cups seasoned
	onions		bread crumbs
1	cup chopped celery	½	cup chopped
½	cup chopped bell		parsley
	pepper		Salt, cayenne or
1	cup sliced green		black pepper to
	onions		taste
½	cup diced garlic		

Boil in lightly salted water till meat is tender enough to scoop from shells. Remove seeds from center of mirlitons and gently scoop all meat out of shells. Reserve meat and save shells for stuffing later. Brown pork cubes in butter. Add onions, celery, bell peppers, green onions and garlic. Cook until vegetables are wilted. Add stock, mirliton meat and cook on medium heat until all vegetables and pork are well blended. Remove from heat. Add bread crumbs, parsley and season to taste. Stuff reserved mirliton shells and top with 1 teaspoon melted butter and bread crumbs. On baking pan, bake until golden brown.

Serves 12.

PORK TENDERLOIN WITH MISSISSIPPI FIGS

¼	cup vegetable oil	1	cup mushrooms
1	cup flour	2	tablespoons garlic
	Salt and cayenne	2	ounces port wine
	pepper to taste	1	cup fig preserves
12	3-ounce pork	2	cups demi-glace
	tenderloin		Salt, white pepper
	medallions		and cayenne
1	cup green onions		pepper to taste

Heat oil in large skillet. Season pork, toss with flour and sauté until golden brown. Add to skillet and pork, green onions, mushrooms and garlic. Sauté two minutes. Deglaze with port wine and add fig preserves and demi-glace. Reduce until slightly thickened (about 5 minutes). Season to taste.

Serves 12.

PORK TENDERLOIN MARDI GRAS

24	2-ounce pork	½	cup each of
	tenderloin		crawfish tail meat
	medallions		and crab meat
½	pound butter	¼	cup diced
½	cup sliced		pimientos
	mushrooms	1	cup white wine
2	tablespoons	½	cup cream
	minced garlic		Salt and pepper to
½	cup green onions,		taste
	chopped	4	cups cooked
½	cup tomatoes,		rainbow rotini
	diced		pasta
½	cup raw 90/110-ct.		
	shrimp		

Sauté on medium heat pork medallions in butter until golden brown on both sides. Take out and reserve. Add in same skillet, medium heat, mushrooms, garlic, onions, tomatoes. Add shrimp and sauté for 10 minutes. Add pimientos, parsley, crawfish, crab meat and white wine. Reduce by ¼, then add cream and cook until creamy (3 minutes). Season to taste. Add pasta to sauce and pork medallions. Serve at once.

Serves 12.

FIG GLAZED LOIN OF VEAL

1	5 to 6 pound	1	cup mushrooms,
	center cut veal loin,		minced
	trimmed	2	tablespoons garlic,
	Salt and pepper to		minced
	taste	2	ounces port wine
	Flour to dust veal	½	cup fig preserves
	loin lightly	1	cup fresh figs,
¼	cup vegetable oil		minced
1	cup green onions,	2	cups demi-glace
	minced		

Season veal loin with salt and pepper to taste, dust with flour and pan sauté over medium heat until medium rare and brown on both sides. Add onions, mushrooms, garlic; sauté for 2 minutes. Deglaze with port wine, add fig preserves, fresh figs and demi-glace. Continue cooking until sauce is slightly thickened. Slice into 10 portions. Serve underlayed with fig glaze.

Serves 10.

LEMON & LIME BARBECUED BREAST OF CHICKEN WITH A SHALLOT, CRAB & HORSERADISH SAUCE

5   whole boneless chicken breasts, skinned, trimmed and halved

Marinade:

½	cup white wine	Salt and pepper to taste
¼	cup lemon juice	
¼	cup lime juice	
½	teaspoon finely minced garlic	

Sauce:

2	tablespoons diced shallots	2	cups demi-glace	
½	tablespoon minced garlic	2	tablespoons lemon juice	
4	cups thin sliced oyster mushrooms	1	tablespoon lime juice	
½	cup white wine		Salt and pepper to taste	
¼	cup Worcestershire sauce	1	pound jumbo lump crab meat	
2	tablespoons tomato paste	1	cup fresh shredded horseradish	

Prepare chicken breast: Combine marinade mixture and marinade chicken for 2 hours.

Heat a large cast iron skillet until very hot. Quickly add chicken, browning on both sides. Add shallots, garlic, mushrooms, tossing and turning the chicken rapidly. Deglaze with the white wine and Worcestershire sauce. Add tomato paste and demi-glace, lemon and lime juice and crab meat. Reduce heat to lowest setting. Finish with a flick of fresh horseradish and serve at once.

Serves 10.

BREAD PUDDING

32	slices toasted bread; light brown on each side; diced	4	tablespoons ground cinnamon	
8	cups homogenized milk	30	ounces (1 pound, 14-ounces) fruit cocktail	
8	eggs, slightly beaten	6	tablespoons 60/40 butter, melted	
6	cups granulated sugar	1	recipe brandy sauce (recipe follows)	
1	cup raisins			
¼	cup vanilla extract			

Preheat convection oven to 270 degrees. Put 3 table-spoons of melted butter in full size stainless steel steam table pan. Beat milk and eggs until foamy. In a separate bowl, mix sugar and cinnamon. Add to milk mixture and beat until foamy again. Add vanilla extract. Mix toasted bread well to soak. Pour into pan and add fruit cocktail and raisins. Bake in 270 degree oven for one hour. Brush with three tablespoons melted butter and put into oven another 15 minutes or until brown.

BRANDY SAUCE

1	cup white granulated sugar	3	cups whole white milk	
4	tablespoons cornstarch	1	teaspoon vanilla extract	
1	dozen egg yolks	½	cup brandy	
½	pound melted 60/40 butter			

In a double boiler with about a quart of water in the bottom of the double boiler, not on stove, mix cornstarch and sugar. Add egg yolks, melted butter, milk and vanilla extract. Beat until eggs foam on top. Put double boiler on medium heat. Stir constantly until thick. When thick, stir in ½ cup brandy. Cook and stir 2 minutes longer. Remove sauce from heat. Pour into storage containers, let cool and put in refrigerator until ready to serve.

SWEET POTATO NUTTY BUDDY

Almond Cones:

⅓ cup butter	⅓ cup light brown sugar, packed
3 tablespoons light cornstarch	

Heat above ingredients in skillet. Heat until well blended. Remove from heat.

1½ cup all-purpose flour, sifted	1 cup toasted almonds, crushed

Add flour and almonds and mix until smooth. On a well heated and greased cookie sheet, place 1 tablespoon of mixture for each cone. Spread each one 3 inches apart, not exceeding 6 per pan. Cook in 350 degree oven until golden brown. Allow cones to cool for 2 to 3 minutes. Remove one cookie at a time and form cone. Repeat until all of mixture has been used. If cookies harden, place back in oven until soft. Can be made 48 hours in advance and kept in airtight container.

Sweet Potato Filling:

2 cups canned sweet potatoes	½ teaspoon salt
½ cup light brown sugar, packed	½ teaspoon cinnamon
2 tablespoons vanilla extract	¼ teaspoon nutmeg
	¼ teaspoon allspice

Place above sweet potato filling ingredients in a sauté pan and cook until dry. Remove from heat and cool completely.

12 ounces cream cheese	1 cup whipping cream

In a mixing bowl, blend ¾ cream cheese and whipping cream together until smooth. Add cooled sweet potato mixture to cream cheese mixture and blend until smooth.

Topping:

Chocolate syrup	Walnuts or pecans chopped

Fill each cone with sweet potato mixture, top with chocolate syrup and chopped nuts. Serve.

ORANGE SOUP WITH STRAWBERRY ICE CREAM

1½ cups thawed frozen concentrate orange juice	1 tablespoon cornstarch
2 cups water	8 ounces fresh, cleaned and quartered strawberries
⅓ cup sugar	Strawberry ice cream
1 orange, peeled and thinly pared	

Place orange juice concentrate, water and sugar in a medium saucepan. Bring to a boil, blend cornstarch and a little cold water. Stir into soup. Return to a boil. Simmer over medium heat for 1 minute. Add strawberries. Remove from heat, add orange and refrigerate until very cold.

To serve: Place a spoonful of strawberry ice cream in the center of each bowl of fruit soup.

Serves 4.

PRIMOS RESTAURANTS

4330 North State Street
Northgate
Jackson, MS 39206

Don Primos
Owner/Operator

Primos Restaurants were started in September of 1929, as Primos Bakery at 236 East Capitol Street by Angelo "Pop" Primos and Mildred Primos. Primos changed to a full service restaurant about 1935. Again, as times changed, Primos changed and expanded in 1948, a second and third location were opened at 1916 North State Street and at 415 North State Street. In 1964, Northgate was opened as the South's latest concept of fine dining with restaurants and private dining rooms in one complex. Northgate also has a deli specializing in bakery items.

PORTOBELLA MUSHROOM WRAP

Portobella mushrooms	Mayonnaise
Cooking oil	Herbs
Balsamic vinegar	2 garlic cloves
Salt and pepper to taste	12-inch tortilla
Onions	Shredded lettuce
Canned Roasted Red Peppers	Diced cooked bacon

Briefly marinate portobella mushrooms in oil, balsamic vinegar and salt and pepper. Grill mushrooms for 3 minutes on each side, or until soft. Slice mushrooms into strips. Slowly sauté ½ rounds of onions in oil, salt, pepper and sugar for 20 minutes. Season prepared mayonnaise with fresh herbs and a couple of garlic cloves. Heat mushrooms, onions, peppers and tortilla. Spread tortilla with herbed mayonnaise, line with shredded lettuce, bacon, mushrooms, onions and peppers. Roll up. Slice in half. Serve with cut fresh fruit.

Serves 1.

CRAWFISH STUFFED CHICKEN

1	ounce olive oil	2	ounces good quality demi-glace (infused with basil)
1	teaspoon chopped fresh basil		Flour
2	ounces Primos crab stuffing		Salt and pepper
1	5-ounce skinless chicken breast		

Cut pocket in chicken breast at fat end. Combine crab stuffing, crawfish, basil, place into chicken pocket. Preheat sauté pan. Add olive oil. Flour and season chicken. Sear both sides golden brown. Finish in 400 degree oven for 10 minutes. Top with basil demi-glace (chicken can be sliced).

Serves 1.

SEAFOOD BURRITO

1	8-inch flour tortilla	2	ounces grated cheddar cheese
½	teaspoon chopped garlic	4	26/30 count shrimp
½	chopped green onion	4	40/60 count scallops
1	tablespoon olive oil	1	ounce lump crab meat
2	ounces white wine	2	medium mushrooms, sliced
4	ounces good quality marinara sauce		

Sauté shrimp, scallops, lump crab, garlic, mushrooms and green onions in olive oil until shrimp and scallops are translucent. Deglaze with white wine. Add 2 ounces marinara sauce. Sauté 15 seconds more. Add salt and pepper. Wrap seafood and vegetables in flour tortilla. Top with remaining 2 ounces marinara sauce and cheese. Bake in 400 to 450 degree oven for approximately 5 minutes. Top with a sauté of julienne vegetables.

Serves 1.

CARROTS WITH HORSERADISH

8	large carrots, cut into julienne strips	1	teaspoon lemon juice
½	cup mayonnaise or salad dressing	¼	teaspoon salt
2	tablespoons grated onions	¼	teaspoon cracked black pepper
2	tablespoons prepared horseradish	½	cup fine dry bread crumbs
		1	tablespoon butter or margarine, melted

Preheat the oven to 350 degrees. In a 3-quart sauce-pan, cook carrots in ½ cup boiling salted water, covered, for 5 to 7 minutes or until crisp-tender. Drain, reserving ¼ cup of the cooking liquid. Arrange carrots in 12 x 7½ x 2-inch baking dish. In a small bowl, combine mayonnaise, onion, horse-radish, lemon juice, salt, pepper and reserved cooking liquid. Pour mayonnaise mixture over carrots. Sprinkle with bread crumbs. Drizzle with melted butter. Bake for 15 to 20 minutes or until heated through.

Serves 6.

PENNE PASTA WITH SMOKED CHICKEN, ALMOND & GRAPES IN CREAMY RASPBERRY VINAIGRETTE

2	pounds penne pasta cooked firm in chicken stock (use stock for other pasta)	1	cup almonds (sliced) toasted in oven
1½	pounds smoked chicken cut in 2-inch long French fry thick	2	cups seedless green grapes soaked 4 hours in brandy
		⅛	cup raspberry vinegar
		⅜	cup olive oil
		1½	cups mayonnaise

Mix the raspberry vinegar and olive oil well. Use ½ of the raspberry and oil mix with 1½ cups of mayonnaise and mix together well. Use 1 cup in the pasta and above mix with all ingredients. Serve cold.

Serves 5 to 6.

AMERIGO'S

6592 Old Canton Road Jackson, MS 39211

Al Roberts & Bill Latham Proprietors

The original – opened in Jackson in 1987. The traditional and distinctively Italian menu features veal, chicken and pasta dishes along with a heavy emphasis on fresh fish and seafood. Amerigo's has sister restaurants in Nashville, Memphis and Atlanta.

BOWTIE PASTA CAESAR SALAD

1	pound chopped romaine lettuce, rinsed and drained	1	pound cooked bowtie pasta
8	ounces Caesar salad dressing	4	ounces walnut pesto (recipe follows)
3	5-ounce chicken breasts, seasoned and oven roasted, then cooled and sliced thinly	4	ounces balsamic vinaigrette
		2	ounces diced sundried tomatoes

Toss salad and Caesar dressing. Separate onto 4 plates.

Toss remaining ingredients and place equal portions over Caesar salad.

Top with croutons and Parmesan cheese if desired.

BASIL & WALNUT PESTO

3	ounces fresh, whole basil leaves	2	tablespoons chopped fresh garlic
1	cup extra-virgin olive oil	1	teaspoon salt
⅓	cup chopped walnuts	½	cup finely grated Parmesan cheese

Place all ingredients into food processor, and purée until smooth. Store in airtight container in refrigerator.

GRILLED PORTOBELLA MUSHROOM SALAD

8	ounces fresh baby greens	4	large portobella mushrooms, stems removed
4	ounces roasted walnuts		Olive oil
4	ounces goat cheese		Salt and pepper
8	ounces balsamic vinaigrette		

Rub mushrooms with olive oil, and season with salt and pepper.

Grill until desired doneness.

While mushrooms are cooking, arrange mixed greens on 4 plates.

Remove mushrooms from grill, and slice each one into 6 to 8 slices. Place slices on side of lettuce mix.

Top with balsamic vinaigrette, goat cheese and roasted walnuts. Salad can be served with cheese toast or garlic crostinis.

For vinaigrette: Utilizing any good quality dried Italian dressing mix, substitute balsamic vinegar for red wine vinegar. Hold in refrigerator until ready to use.

SPICED CRAWFISH PASTA

1	16-ounce package fresh angel hair pasta cooked according to instructions	1	pound crawfish tail meat with fat
1	quart heavy cream	2	teaspoons spiced seasoning mix (recipe follows)
2	cups finely grated Parmesan cheese	1	cup diced scallions
			Salt to taste

Place all ingredients except pasta in saucepot, and bring to slow boil. After pasta has been cooked, drain well, add to sauce and cook to desired consistency. Place in 4 bowls, and top with grated Parmesan cheese. Serve with green salad and French bread.

Serves 4.

SPICED SEASONING MIX

3	tablespoons barbecue spice	10	bay leaves
3	tablespoons paprika	½	tablespoon garlic powder
1	tablespoon black pepper	½	tablespoon thyme
1	tablespoon white pepper	½	tablespoon rosemary
1	tablespoon red pepper	½	tablespoon basil
½	tablespoon onion powder	½	tablespoon oregano
		½	tablespoon cilantro

ROASTED GARLIC & SUN-DRIED TOMATO MEATLOAF

5	pounds ground chuck	6	cups bread crumbs
1½	ribs celery, diced	3	cups ketchup, divided
2	medium onions, diced	3	whole eggs
2	tablespoons olive oil	1	cup milk
1	large or 2 small green bell peppers, diced	1	tablespoon tarragon, dried
1	cup whole garlic cloves, chopped	4	teaspoons oregano
1	cup sun-dried tomatoes, diced	1	teaspoon fresh sage, chopped
		4	teaspoons salt
		3	teaspoons pepper

Place garlic, celery, onions and pepper with olive oil in 400 degree oven and roast for 15 to 20 minutes. Remove from heat, cool and drain. Blend all ingredients except 1 cup ketchup well. Divide mixture equally into two loaf pans, making sure meat is packed tightly. Cook at 350 degrees for 1 hour or until internal temperature reaches 150 degrees. Remove from oven and top with remaining ketchup. Allow to rest at room temperature for 15 minutes. Remove from loaf pan and slice as needed. Best served with mashed potatoes and fresh vegetables.

Serves 10.

RISOTTO WITH VEGETABLES AND SMOKED OR GRILLED CHICKEN

2	cups risotto (cooked according to directions with chicken stock)	4	5-ounce boneless chicken breasts, smoked or grilled, sliced thinly
½	cup green bell pepper, diced	2	tablespoons chopped fresh basil
½	cup red bell pepper, diced	3	tablespoons chopped scallions
½	cup each zucchini and yellow squash, diced	1	teaspoon chopped fresh sage
½	cup tomatoes, diced	3	tablespoons butter, divided
	Salt and pepper to taste	1	cup grated Parmesan cheese

As risotto finishes cooking, place peppers, squash and tomatoes in a sauté skillet with one tablespoon of the butter. Lightly sauté vegetables. Blend vegetables into risotto, and continue to finish cooking. At end of cooking process, stir in last seven ingredients, including remaining butter, and remove from heat. Season to taste. If risotto is too sticky, add a touch of chicken stock. Allow risotto to sit for about 10 minutes to incorporate all flavors. Serve in bowl and top with grated Parmesan cheese and cracked black pepper.

Serves 4.

SHAPLEY'S RESTAURANT

863 Centre Street
Ridgeland, MS 39157

Scott Koestler
Chef/Owner

When Jacksonians think of steak, most think of Shapley's. Opened by Mark and Mary Shapley in 1985 in Centre Park, this restaurant has since moved twice to its present beautiful new location at 863 Centre Street. It was purchased by Scott Koestler in 1998. Scott is a graduate of the University of Mississippi. Scott received most of his culinary experience as a chef/manager at Shapley's. In addition to steaks, Shapley's menu offers rack of lamb, veal, chicken and a variety of seafood.

TUNA & CRABMEAT SALAD

	Enough lettuce (any variety) for three salads	⅔	pound jumbo lump crabmeat
1	10-ounce tuna steak at least 1-inch thick		

HONEY-MUSTARD BALSAMIC VINAIGRETTE

1	cup extra virgin olive oil	2	tablespoons light brown sugar
⅔	cup balsamic vinegar	1	teaspoon basil
½	teaspoon garlic		Salt and pepper to taste
¼	cup honey		
2	teaspoons Dijon mustard		

Blend all ingredients well. Marinate the tuna in a small amount of the salad dressing for 1 hour. Over a very hot fire or in a skillet, leaving the tuna rare to medium-rare, sear the tuna. After searing the tuna let it cool and slice as desired. Remove cartilage or shells from crabmeat. Add tuna, crabmeat and vinaigrette to lettuce. Toss and serve.

Serves 3.

FRIED SOFT-SHELL CRAB IN A CREOLE MUSTARD CREAM SAUCE

(Appetizer)

Creole Mustard Cream Sauce:

¼	cup chopped onions	3-4	teaspoons horseradish
¼	cup red or yellow bell pepper	½	teaspoon red pepper flakes
1	clove garlic		Salt and white
1	cup heavy cream		pepper to taste
1	cup chicken or fish stock	2	tablespoons butter
¼	cup Creole mustard		

Sauté in 1 tablespoon of butter the onion, garlic and red or yellow bell pepper. Add the chicken stock, heavy cream, Creole mustard, horseradish and red pepper flakes then reduce by ½. Once reduced, whisk in the remaining butter and season with salt and white pepper.

Fried Soft-Shell Crab:

2	soft-shell crabs (the larger the better) halved or quartered if large enough	1	egg
		1½	cups milk
			PEANUT OIL for frying
1	cup flour seasoned with salt and pepper or Shapley's seasoning		

Mix egg and milk. Carefully dust the crab in the seasoned flour. Dip in the egg wash. Re-batter the crab in the flour and gently shake off any excess flour. Fry in peanut oil until golden brown. Remove and place on paper towels to drain and cool slightly. After the crab has cooled, place on a plate and generously spoon the sauce over the crab.

Serves 2.

BEEF TENDERLOIN WITH BLUE CHEESE BÉARNAISE & BACON & CRAB MASHED POTATOES

1   8 to 10-ounce center cut filet seasoned and grilled as desired

Form a bed of mashed potatoes to place the grilled filet. Top with Béarnaise sauce and serve.

BLUE CHEESE BÉARNAISE SAUCE

Combine:

2	tablespoons shallots	2	tablespoons water
½	teaspoon black pepper	4	egg yolks
		1⅔	cups melted unsalted butter
1½	tablespoons tarragon	1-2	tablespoons chervil
⅓	cup tarragon vinegar		Salt, pepper & blue cheese to taste

In a double boiler or a small mixing bowl over lightly simmering water, reduce vinegar, shallots, pepper and tarragon until almost dry. Remove from heat. Refresh reduction with the water. Add egg yolks and cook, whisking constantly over **lightly** simmering water until egg yolks begin to thicken and lose frothiness (be careful not to scramble yolks). In a thin stream whisk in melted butter until thickened and very warm. Add tarragon, chervil and blue cheese. Reserve in a water bath or double boiler in **warm** water until needed.

BACON & CRAB MASHED POTATOES

4	potatoes, skinned	½	teaspoon black pepper
¼	cup chopped bacon		
		4	tablespoons butter
½	cup sour cream	¾	pound jumbo lump crab meat
1	teaspoon salt		

Boil potatoes until tender. Mash cooked potatoes and add 3 tablespoons butter, sour cream, salt, pepper and bacon. Mix well. Sauté crab meat in remaining tablespoon of butter and lightly salt. Gently fold in crab meat, being careful not to break up the lumps.

Serves 4.

THE PARKER HOUSE RESTAURANT

1060 East County Line Road Ridgeland, MS 39157

Please note: In the fall of 1999, the Parker House will be moving to a new location, "Olde Towne" in Ridgeland, Mississippi. The new location will be on Jackson Street, between Highway 51 and the railroad. It is only 5 minutes from their present location.

Steve and Barbara Parker, both native Mississippians, opened their first restaurant "The Parker House Restaurant" on April 14, 1994. Steve's love of good food and cooking gave them the idea for their new business venture together. Having no formal training or restaurant experience did not deter the couple from bringing The Parker House into the forefront of fine dining in the Jackson Metropolitan area.

As co-owner/executive chef, Steve leads the kitchen in the preparation of traditional "continental/American" cuisine with a Southern flair. Barbara's attention to detail has helped to create an elegant atmosphere of home some have described "as romantic a setting to be found" in the Jackson area. Barbara has worked to create a service staff that assures the guest a wonderful dining experience.

OYSTERS MESCALERO

1	dozen fresh shucked oysters	1	each red, yellow, green bell pepper
4	cups Hollandaise sauce	2	each green onions
6	10-inch flour tortillas	3	tablespoons minced garlic
2	cups fresh whole kernel corn	1	medium red onion
			Salt to taste
			White pepper

Tortillas: Julienne the flour tortillas into long strips. Deep fry the tortilla strips at 350 degrees for about one minute. Set aside.

Relish: Finely dice equal amounts of peppers, onion, green onion and combine. Add minced garlic and fresh corn. Season to taste. Your favorite Southwestern seasonings should be added to taste at this time. Refrigerate and allow flavors to marry for one hour.

Sauce: A traditional Sauce Hollandaise (Dutch sauce) should be prepared. In a large stainless steel bowl, over a bain marie, beat 5 egg yolks, 2 tablespoons water, salt and pepper until thick. Slowly add small amounts of softened unsalted butter (1 pound). Whip the butter into the egg mixture, adjusting the temperature by moving the bowl off and on the heat until the butter is incorporated. Be sure not to allow the sauce to get too hot. To this mixture add your favorite Southwestern seasonings to taste.

Oysters: Salt and pepper oysters, dip in fresh milk or cream and dredge in corn flour. Deep fry at 350 degrees until done. Drain.

Presentation: On large serving plate, ladle approximately 4 ounces of the Southwestern Hollandaise on the bottom of the plate. In the middle of the plate, place a generous amount of the fried tortillas topped with the corn relish. Place the fried oysters around the relish. Garnish and serve.

Serves 6.

HERB & PARMESAN CRUSTED BLACKFISH WITH LEMON BEURRE BLANC

2	fresh fish fillets	2	teaspoons minced garlic
1	cup fresh bread crumbs	1	lemon
4	tablespoons Parmesan cheese	3	minced shallots
2	tablespoons minced fresh basil	⅓	pound unsalted butter
1	tablespoon minced fresh oregano	¼	cup white wine
			Salt to taste
			White pepper to taste

Presentation: Place fish fillets on serving plate. Sauce can be presented covering the fish or by surrounding the fish. Must be served immediately. Make sure the plate is not too hot so as not to "break" the sauce.

Crusting: Combine bread crumbs, basil, oregano, garlic, Parmesan and juice from lemon and lemon zest. Set aside.

Beurre Blanc: Simmer the shallots and white wine, until reduced by three-fourths. Add the butter, and incorporate into the reduction by stirring continuously, until fully emulsified. Season to taste with salt and pepper and fresh lemon juice.

Crusting and preparing the fish: Dredge the fish fillets in flour, then in milk, cover them completely. Then cover the fillets with the bread crumb mixture.

In a hot sauté pan with a small amount of oil, lightly brown the fillets on top of the stove. Once the fillets are lightly browned, place on oven dish, uncovered into a 450 degree oven.

Cook until a finger lightly pressed into the fish will break through.

Serves 2.

BRICK OVEN CAFÉ
862 Avery Boulevard Ridgeland, MS 39157

Grant Nooe
Chef/Owner

Music was Grant's first love. Initially, his work in a variety of restaurants, from classic French to Southern café-style supported his musical training and study. But, it wasn't long before Grant discovered that preparing and serving fine food and later the challenge of restaurant ownership was an art in and unto itself. A growing desire to further please this new audience led him to the Culinary and Hospitality Institute of Chicago. While in Chicago, Chef Nooe was privileged to work on the restaurant teams of nationally acclaimed chefs, including Michael Foley of Printers Row and Monique Hooker of Monique's Café. Chef Nooe's recipes have been featured in **Food Art Magazine, Nations Restaurant News, Alliant Food & Service Ideas** *and the* **Chicago Tribune**. *Nooe's most recent venture is the Brick Oven Café. The new American restaurant's menu includes wood-fired pizzas, fresh pasta, rotisserie meats and unique desserts.*

BUTTERNUT SQUASH BISQUE

2	butternut squash (approximately 3 pounds)	1	pinch of nutmeg (approximately ⅛ teaspoon)
4	ounces butter		Salt and white
½	cup chopped onion		pepper to taste
4	ounces flour	4	ounces sliced
2	tablespoons minced garlic		almonds (toasted)
2½	quarts chicken stock	1	bunch chives (sliced into small pieces)

Cut squash in half, remove seeds and place on a sheet pan flesh side down. Pour enough water in pan to fill ¼-inch. Roast in a 400 degree preheated oven until the squash can be pierced easily with a fork (approximately 20 minutes). Remove and place in the refrigerator until cool. Meanwhile sweat onions in butter until translucent. Add flour and make a light roux. Add garlic then pour in hot stock, bring to a simmer, then add flesh of roasted butternut squash. Purée squash and stock then continue simmering for approximately five minutes. Pass purée through a strainer and set aside until ready to serve. Ladle 8 ounces into a bowl and garnish with toasted nuts and fresh-cut chives.

Serves 8.

CUMIN SEARED TUNA WITH MANGO, PAPAYA, ARUGULA, ASIAN VINAIGRETTE & CARAMELIZED RED ONION

2½	pounds fresh sushi grade tuna loin		and cut into 1 to 2-inch medallions)
½	cup cumin powder Salt and pepper	2	cups Asian vinaigrette (see recipe)
1	ounce light sesame oil	2	cups caramelized red onion (see recipe)
6	bunches fresh arugula (approximately 1 quart)	1	cup wasabi (mixed so that it will spread through a squeeze bottle)
2	small ripe mangoes (seeded, peeled and cut into 1 to 2-inch medallions)	3	tablespoons black sesame seeds (slightly toasted)
2	small ripe papayas (seeded, peeled		

Trim tuna loin until all dark blood line is removed. Cut so that there are long loins approximately 2 inches in diameter. Cover thoroughly with cumin and season with salt and pepper. Heat a skillet with oil until almost smoking. Add seasoned tuna loin and sear until golden brown on all sides. Place in refrigerator and let cool until ready to serve. Meanwhile place arugula in center of plate. Slice chilled seared tuna into medallions (about the size of a silver dollar). Place around arugula with alternate layers of mango and papaya until fanned neatly. Drizzle 1 teaspoon of vinaigrette on arugula and 2 ounces on plate surrounding tuna. Place three dollops of caramelized red onion on vinaigrette and garnish with wasabi and toasted sesame seeds.

Asian Vinaigrette: In a food processor combine 2 cups light sesame oil with ¾ cup rice vinegar. Blend while adding 1 tablespoon fresh chopped ginger and 1 tablespoon mustard. Continue blending until emulsified.

Caramelized Red Onion: Thinly slice 5 large red onions, and place in a saucepot with 1 cup Mirin and ½ cup red wine. (Mirin is a sweet rice wine seasoning found in Asian groceries.) Simmer covered for about 10 minutes then remove lid and continue simmering until liquid is evaporated and onions are completely done. Stir often so that it does not stick and burn. Put in a refrigerator and let cool until later use.

Serves 8.

ROASTED LAMB LOIN WITH POLENTA, WILD MUSHROOMS & SPINACH, ROSEMARY DEMI-GLAZE

8	trimmed lamb loins (6 to 8-ounce loin after silver skin is removed)	2	quarts (approximately 3 pounds) thin sliced mushrooms such as portobellas, shiitakes, etc.
5	ounces olive oil		
4	bunches rosemary (approximately 5 ounces, chopped)		
		4	ounces port wine
8	slices polenta (cut with round cookie cutter) (see recipe)	3½	cups demi-glaze (see recipe)
			Salt and pepper to taste
1½	gallons washed fresh spinach, stems removed		

Rub lamb loins with 2 ounces olive oil and 3 ounces chopped rosemary. Place in refrigerator for at least 12 hours. In a large sauterne, heat 2 ounces of oil to the point of almost smoking. Season lamb loins with salt and pepper then sear until golden brown. Place seared loins and polenta slices on sheet pans then roast in a preheated 400 degree oven for about 5 to 10 minutes. Meanwhile, place mushrooms in a large saucepan and add port wine. Cover and simmer for about 3 minutes, remove lid, continue simmering until mushrooms are done and liquid has evaporated then season with salt and pepper. Place spinach in a large pot with 3 ounces olive oil, stir well, cover then slowly simmer until spinach is wilted. Remove roasted lamb loins from oven and let them rest for 3 to 5 minutes. On a large plate, place hot polenta in the center, top neatly with spinach, then mushrooms. Slice lamb loin into medallions then fan medallions atop mushrooms. Ladle 3 ounces of rosemary demi glaze around tower of lamb. Garnish with roasted pearl onions and baby carrots.

Rosemary Demi-Glaze: Fresh stocks are great to have on hand. You may want to double the stock recipe and freeze in ice trays for later use. The grocery meat market will often have veal bones. Roast 4 pounds veal bones in a 400 degree oven until they are golden brown. Add 3 cups each: chopped celery, chopped carrots and onions. continue roasting for about 5 more minutes. Place bones and vegetables in a stock pot and cover with 4 quarts cold water. Bring to a boil, immediately reduce heat, then skim surface with a ladle to remove any fat. Add two fresh chopped tomatoes, one bunch fresh parsley, fresh thyme and oregano, 1 teaspoon black peppercorns and 4 bay leaves. continue simmering until reduced by half. Add 2 ounces chopped rosemary and reduce again by half. Strain through a strainer and set aside for later use.

Polenta: Polenta is good to have around. It can be kept in the refrigerator and later grilled or baked. Double recipe and eat some later. In a saucepot bring 2½ quarts of chicken stock to a boil. Add 2½ cups cornmeal, stir for 5 minutes then add ½ cup grated Parmesan, season with salt and pepper. Pour mixture in a 9 x 12-inch greased baking pan. Bake for 10 minutes in a preheated 350 degree oven. Remove and place in a refrigerator until cool and firm. When ready for service, cut with a 4-inch cookie cutter.

Serves 8.

RASPBERRY CRÈME BRÛLÉE

1	quart heavy cream	⅛	teaspoon almond extract
9	egg yolks		
1½	cups sugar	1	pint raspberries
1½	ounces raspberry liqueur		

Slowly heat cream until it scalds. Combine sugar, egg yolks, raspberry liqueur and almond extract, then mix thoroughly. Slowly pour cream into the egg mixture and continue mixing. Fill an 8-ounce soup cup with custard then place 6 to 8 raspberries in each cup. Place cups of custard in a baking pan and put enough hot water in the pan to partially submerge cups ¼ of the way up sides. Bake in a preheated 350 degree oven for about 45 minutes or until the custard is cooked enough so that you can place a knife in and remove without mixture sticking to blade. Once the custard is done place in the refrigerator and let them cool completely. For service sprinkle sugar on the top of custard and place under broiler until sugar is caramelized.

Serves 8.

MONTE'S SEAFOOD & PASTA

896 Avery Boulevard
Ridgeland, MS 39157

Monte Agho
Chef/Owner

Chef Agho grew up in Bennin City, Nigeria. He arrived in Jackson as a student when he was 22 and enrolled in Jackson State University. He studied finance and general business, and eventually earned a master's degree in business in 1982. To make extra money while in school, he worked in restaurants.

TROPICAL SEAFOOD STEW

2	fresh whole tomatoes	2	8-ounce cans tomato sauce
1	green bell pepper	1	teaspoon cayenne pepper
1	each yellow and red bell pepper (optional)	2	tablespoons fish base
1	yellow onion	1	gallon water
1	12-ounce can tomato paste	1½	pounds fish chunks, shrimp (whatever seafood you prefer)
½	cup vegetable oil		

In a blender or food processor, purée onions, bell pepper and tomatoes. Combine mixture and water in a saucepan with tomato paste and tomato sauce. Cook for about 45 minutes to 1 hour. Halfway through cooking time, add seafood, fish base and cayenne pepper to taste. Toward end of cooking time (about 10 minutes), add vegetable oil and let simmer for rest of cooking time.

Can be served over pasta but is best over rice.

Serves 6.

BLACK-EYED PEA MOUSSE

2	cups black-eyed peas	1	teaspoon chicken base
½	cup yellow or white onion, chopped		Pinch of salt and crushed red pepper
3	bay leaves		

Soak peas overnight in water. Drain and remove black-eyed pea shells. In blender or food processor, purée peas, onions and bay leaves. Add salt, pepper and chicken base to mixture. Pour mixture into molds. Place in baking pan containing approximately ¼-inch water. Bake at 375 degrees for 1 hour.

SALMON ELLENA
WITH LEMON BUTTER SAUCE

(Appetizer)

2	pounds fresh salmon fillets	5	leaves fresh basil
¼	pound fresh cheese preferably mozzarella, sliced	½	cup lemon juice
		½	pound fresh unsalted butter, cubed
½	pound fresh lump crab meat	¼	cup white wine

Pound the fillet of salmon between film wrap until paper thin. Arrange the sliced fresh cheese across one end of the pounded salmon. Place the basil and crab meat on top of the cheese. With the help of the film wrap, roll the pounded salmon; then poach in hot boiling water for about 10 minutes. Take out of water and cool in refrigerator until needed.

Sauce: Pour the lemon juice and white wine into saucepan. Reduce on medium heat to half the size, whip in fresh butter until it resembles a cream sauce. It can be served hot or cool, but is better served hot. Cut the salmon about ½-inch thick, two to a plate. Warm up in microwave for about 20 seconds. Serve with lemon wine butter sauce. Garnish with lemon wedges and fresh parsley sprigs.

Serves 6 to 8.

SHRIMP & PASTA DÉ MONTE'S

6	large shrimp (21 to 25-ct.)	2	sun-dried tomatoes (cut in strips)
	A handful of mixed vegetables (zucchini, mushrooms, carrots, peppers and broccoli)	1	teaspoon Parmesan cheese
		½	teaspoon chopped garlic
¼	cup olive oil	1	teaspoon green peas
8	ounces cooked fettuccini		Salt and pepper to taste

In a 10-inch skillet, sauté the mixed vegetables, garlic and shrimp until tender. Toss in fettuccini, salt and pepper to taste. Garnish with sun-dried tomato, green peas and Parmesan cheese.

Serves 1.

RICE PILAF

3	cups rice, cooked	1	medium green bell pepper
1	teaspoon chicken base	1	medium red bell pepper
1	medium yellow onion, chopped	2	tablespoons fresh parsley, chopped

Sauté onion, bell peppers and chicken base. In separate bowl, mix rice, vegetables and parsley.

Yield: 10 servings

STRAWBERRY CREPE WITH BRANDY BUTTER SAUCE

1	pound fresh strawberries, sliced	¼	pound cream cheese
3	teaspoons sugar	¾	cup powdered sugar

In a bowl mix the strawberries and sugar and set aside. Take the cream cheese at room temperature and whip until softened. Add powdered sugar and whip until blended; then add the berries and mix. Take a thin crepe, roll the filling in it and set aside.

Sauce:

½	pound fresh butter, unsalted	1	ounce brandy
½	pound powdered sugar		

In saucepan, combine butter and sugar over medium heat. Cook until thickened. Add brandy while stirring the mixture. Stir for a couple of minutes and set aside. Warm the berry crepe in microwave for about 20 seconds. Pour the brandy butter sauce over the crepe. Serve two crepes per plate. Garnish with fresh berry slice and sprinkle with powdered sugar.

Observatory – Millsaps College
Jackson, Mississippi

NICK'S

1501 Lakeland Drive
Jackson, MS 39216

Nick Apostle
Chef/Owner

Nick Apostle graduated with a degree in business from the University of Mississippi. He then attended the Culinary Institute in Hyde Park, New York for a six week Continuing Education Program, offered by the CIA. He started working in his father's restaurant while in high school and college. After graduation he went to work full-time. He worked for Paul's Restaurant from 1974 until he became owner of Nick's in Jackson in 1983. In 1986, Nick helped establish, and now is part-owner of the Crescent City Seafood Grill, Mahogany Bar and the Purple Parrot Café in Hattiesburg, Mississippi. Mr. Apostle has served as President and now is Chairman of the Board of the Mississippi Restaurant Association. Nick's has been featured on the Discovery Channel's "Great Chefs" series (The Great Chefs of the South).

NICK'S PAN-FRIED SOFT-SHELL CRAWFISH WITH FRESH CHIVE & TARRAGON BUTTER SAUCE

CHIVE AND TARRAGON BUTTER SAUCE

2	shallots, finely minced	3	tablespoons tarragon, rough chopped
¼	teaspoon garlic, finely minced	¾	pound butter, cut into pieces and room temperature
½	cup white wine, dry	¼	cup heavy cream
1½	cup fish stock, shrimp stock or bottled clam broth	1	tablespoon (rounded) fresh chives, finely sliced
2	teaspoons balsamic vinegar	1	tablespoon fresh tarragon, finely chopped
3	tablespoons chives, rough chopped		

Wilt shallots and garlic in a saucepan. Add white wine, stock, vinegar, rough-chopped tarragon and chives; reduce to a glaze in pan; then reduce heat to very low. Add heavy cream and work butter in, in small increments, whisking until fully incorporated. Strain through a bouillon strainer. Adjust seasoning with fresh tarragon and chives. Salt to taste, if needed.

SEASONING MIX

2	tablespoons salt	1	teaspoon garlic powder
2	teaspoons onion powder	1	teaspoon black pepper
2	teaspoons sweet paprika	½	teaspoon dried oregano leaves
1	teaspoon cayenne pepper	½	teaspoon dried thyme leaves
1	teaspoon white pepper		

PAN-FRIED SOFT-SHELL CRAWFISH

18	extra large soft-shell crawfish, cleaned of stones	2	cups milk
3	cups flour		Seasoning mix
4	eggs		Vegetable oil for frying

Make chive and tarragon butter sauce and set aside either in a thermos or controlled temperature bain-marie arrangement. Combine the milk and egg until well blended. In a small bowl, thoroughly combine the seasonings. In a separate pan add 3 tablespoons of the seasoning mix to the flour and mix well. Sprinkle some of the remaining seasoning mix on the crawfish. Heat about 1 inch of the oil in a very large skillet to about 350 degrees. Dredge each crawfish in seasoned flour, shaking off the excess, and drop in the egg/milk wash. Drain off the egg/milk wash and dredge once more in the flour, shaking off the excess. Fry the crawfish about 2 minutes, drain on paper towels. While still draining, and very hot, spread a little sauce on warm plates and place three crawfish on each. Serve immediately.

Serves 6.

NICK'S PANÉED MISSISSIPPI CATFISH FILLETS WITH CRAWFISH STUFFING IN AN HERBED BUTTER SAUCE

12 2 to 4-ounce catfish fillets or tilapia, rainbow trout, salmon trout or any other small freshwater fish fillets

SEASONING MIX

1	teaspoon salt	½	teaspoon onion powder
½	teaspoon white pepper	¼	teaspoon dried thyme leaves
¼	teaspoon cayenne pepper	⅛	teaspoon dried oregano leaves
¼	teaspoon black pepper		

CRAWFISH STUFFING

4	ounces margarine	1	pound crawfish tails with fat, coarsely chopped
1	cup finely chopped onions		
½	cup finely chopped celery	1	cup very fine bread crumbs, in all
½	cup finely chopped green bell peppers	4	tablespoons unsalted butter
½	cup finely chopped green onions	2	eggs, in all
1½	teaspoons minced garlic	3	tablespoons finely grated Parmesan cheese

MILK WASH FOR FILLETS

½	teaspoon salt	1½	cups milk
½	teaspoon white pepper		

SEASONED FLOUR

3	cups all-purpose flour	1½	teaspoons garlic powder
1	teaspoon white pepper	1½	teaspoons dried thyme leaves
3	teaspoons onion powder	⅜	teaspoon dried oregano leaves
1	teaspoon cayenne pepper		Clarified butter for pan frying

HERB BUTTER SAUCE

1	tablespoon clarified butter	2	bay leaves
2	shallots, finely minced	1¼	cups fish stock or clam broth
		¾	cup white wine
2	cloves garlic, finely minced	½	tablespoon fresh lemon juice
2	tablespoons fresh thyme	1	pound butter, cut into pieces
1	tablespoon fresh oregano	¼	cup heavy cream

Stuffing: Thoroughly combine the seasoning mix ingredients in a small bowl; set aside. Place margarine in a large skillet over high heat. When half melted, add the onions, celery and bell peppers. Sauté about 4 minutes, stirring occasionally. Add the seasoning mix, green onions and garlic. Cook about 3 minutes, stirring occasionally. Add the crawfish and continue cooking for 5 to 7 minutes, stirring infrequently. Let mixture caramelize without scorching or burning. Add ½ cup of bread crumbs. Stir well and then let cook without stirring until mixture sticks, about 1 minute. Stir and scrape pan bottom well. Then add butter and continue cooking until butter melts, stirring and scraping pan bottom continuously. Stir in the remaining ½ cup bread crumbs and remove from heat. Cool slightly. Combine 1 beaten egg with the Parmesan. Add to mixture in skillet, mixing well. Transfer to a shallow pan and refrigerate until chilled.

Herb Butter Sauce: Wilt shallots, garlic, thyme, oregano and bay leaf with a touch of clarified butter. Add white wine and stock. Reduce to a glaze. Reduce heat to lowest setting and add heavy cream. Then work in the butter piece by piece. Strain and hold sauce in warmed thermos or controlled temperature bain-marie arrangement. While the reduction for butter sauce is on the fire, combine the milk and the remaining egg in a pan. In another pan, combine the seasoned flour ingredients, mixing well. The butter sauce reduction should be ready to be finished and put away for service. Sprinkle the fillets of fish with the salt and pepper. In a large skillet heat enough clarified butter to sauté the catfish fillets. Soak the seasoned fillets in the egg/milk wash, then dredge into the seasoned flour. Pan sauté the fillets until lightly golden. Stuff the fillets by placing 1 fillet on baking sheet, putting 3 ounces of stuffing, then lay another fillet over the stuffing, leaving the stuffing exposed. Bake in the oven at 400 degrees for 5 minutes or until stuffing is heated through. Using a spatula, pick up the stuffed catfish, then ladle the butter sauce over it. Serve with chunky garlic and fresh parsley boiled potatoes and fresh asparagus or broccoli.

Serves 6.

NICK'S NEW ENGLAND CLAM CHOWDER

1	quart warm water plus 3 quarts clam juice	4	pounds diced potato ⅜-inch square
2	#5 cans chopped clams	1	pound salt pork, ground
½	teaspoon white pepper	2¼	pounds onions, diced
2	tablespoons Worcestershire sauce		

Bring water/clam juice to boil and season. Remove enough of the above stock to cover potatoes, cook potatoes. Place salt pork in soup pot, cook until partially rendered. Add onions, sauté until transparent. Add flour and roux and cook 5 to 6 minutes. Add clam stock to roux and stir until smooth. Add potatoes, clams, milk and cream. Adjust seasoning and add melted butter.

Yield: 4 quarts

WHITE CHOCOLATE MOUSSE

1½	cups sugar	4	ounces Grand Marnier
½	cup water		
¼	teaspoon cream of tartar	18	ounces white chocolate, finely chopped
¾	cup egg whites		
1	quart whipped cream		

Combine sugar, water, cream of tartar and bring to a rapid boil for 2 to 3 minutes (235-240 degrees or soft ball stage). Beat egg whites to soft peaks, then slowly drizzle sugar/water mixture into them. Add white chocolate, folding gently and freeze for 10 minutes. Whip cream and add Grand Marnier and fold into egg whites and white chocolate mixture. Freeze.

RASPBERRY SAUCE

1	package frozen raspberries in heavy syrup (about 10 ounces)	1	tablespoon powdered sugar

Place raspberries in blender and blend well. Put this mixture through a fine strainer and mix well with a tablespoon of powdered sugar. Serve with your mousse.

TIMES CHANGE

4800 I-55 North Jackson, MS 39211

Thomas J. Lambing, Jr.
Chef/Owner

Times Change was given a "4-Star" rating by the Clarion Ledger's "Epicurius". This rating is reserved for the best restaurants in the state. Tom and his wife Kimberly opened this popular upscale Jackson restaurant in 1990. In addition to steaks, *Times Change* offers boar, elk, caribou, musk ox, pheasant, rack of lamb, salmon, and the fresh catch of the day – all grilled over mesquite.

THAI TARTARE

GINGER SLAW

(Recipe for ginger slaw can be found with "Scarlet Shrimp" recipe on next page.)

THAI SAUCE

1	cup molasses	1	tablespoon minced fresh ginger
¼	cup vinegar		
¼	cup lemon juice	1	teaspoon Oriental chile paste
½	cup Dijon mustard		
⅓	cup ketchup	1	tablespoon fresh thyme
1	tablespoon minced garlic		

Combine all ingredients and let sit for 1 hour. Refrigerate.

MEAT

1	8-ounce beef tenderloin, room temperature

Slice beef across grain into ¼-inch medallions. Pound out until paper thin. Cut into ¼-inch strips.

To serve: Place sauce in small bowl in the center of a plate. Arrange beef around sauce, put ginger slaw on the side. Garnish with croutons and stir-fried snow peas.

Serves 4.

SCARLET SHRIMP, GINGER SLAW

Shrimp Sauce:

1	pound shrimp, peeled and deveined	¼	cup chicken stock, chilled
¼	cup minced onion	1	tablespoon sugar
3	green onions, minced including stalks	1½	tablespoons dry sherry
1½	tablespoons minced ginger	½-1	tablespoons chile paste
¼	cup ketchup	3	tablespoons peanut oil

Combine all ingredients except shrimp and peanut oil; set aside. Heat peanut oil in a 10-inch skillet over high heat. Add shrimp and stir until pink. Add sauce and cook until shrimp are opaque. Remove shrimp from sauce. Cook sauce over high heat until sauce thickens (approximately 1 to 2 minutes). Pour sauce over shrimp and serve.

GINGER SLAW

1	small head napa, chopped	1	tablespoon minced fresh ginger
1	small head radicchio, cored and chopped	1	teaspoon powdered ginger
½	cup mayonnaise	1½	teaspoons dry mustard
½	cup sour cream		

Combine napa and radicchio, set aside. Combine remaining ingredients and refrigerate for 15 minutes. Add dressing to napa a little at a time until a creamy consistency is obtained. Serve immediately. Serves 4 to 6.

YUKON GOLD POTATO STUFFED WITH LOBSTER TOPPED WITH CRÈME FRAÎCHE

4-8	2-inch potatoes	¼	pound softened butter
1-1¼	pound live lobster		Salt and pepper

Place lobster in cold water over high heat until water begins to simmer. Remove and place in ice bath to stop cooking, clean and set aside. Bake potatoes until soft to the touch (about 35 minutes). Remove from oven and prick top to release steam, cool. Using melon baller hollow out potatoes, careful not to break the skins, set aside. Chop lobster into very small dices and place in mixing bowl with potato flesh and butter. Using your hands, work together lobster and potato mixture until you can form a meatball-like consistency. Carefully refill potato skins allowing a small amount to mound out the top. Place on a cookie sheet and refrigerate for at least 2 hours to solidify. Preheat oven to 425 degrees, bake, using center rack, for 12 to 15 minutes. Top with a dollop of crème fraîche and garnish with chives or caviar.

CRÈME FRAÎCHE

1	pint heavy whipping cream	¼	cup buttermilk

Mix together in a plastic or glass bowl. Cover with plastic and poke 2 or 3 holes with a small knife. Leave sitting out at room temperature for 24 to 48 hours. Uncover, whip quickly with a wire whip and refrigerate.

Will keep for 1 week refrigerated and tightly covered.

Old State Capitol Museum
Jackson, Mississippi

ROASTED RACK OF LAMB

2	racks of lamb (room temperature) approximately 1½ pounds each, trimmed and frenched	Salt and pepper

Preheat oven to 450 degrees (350 degrees if using convection oven).

Place racks on flat roasting pan bone side down and salt and pepper. Bake in preheated oven for 10 minutes using the center rack. After 10 minutes turn racks over and bake for 5 additional minutes. Remove from oven and preheat broiler. Place racks under broiler, still using center rack, bone side down for an additional 2 minutes. Foil may be wrapped around bones to protect from burning. Let lamb rest for 5 minutes before slicing and serving.

Serves 4.

DIJON MUSTARD SAUCE

2	tablespoons minced yellow onion	½	cup demi-glace
½	cup dry white wine	2-3	tablespoons Dijon mustard

Sauté onions in dry skillet for 1 minute. Add white wine; bring to a boil and boil for 3 minutes. Add demi-glace and boil for 3 minutes. Remove from heat and stir in Dijon (will thicken up standing). Serve immediately.

ROSTI POTATOES

8	par-boiled chilled new potatoes	2	tablespoons butter
1½	cups grated Emmenthaler cheese	½	teaspoon house seasoning to taste
		½	cup medium diced onion

Preheat 8-inch non-stick skillet over medium-high heat. Cut potatoes into quarters and then slice thinly. Melt butter in hot skillet. Add potatoes and toss to coat with butter, spread evenly over bottom of skillet. Let potatoes brown for approximately 5 minutes (swirl skillet . . . crisp potatoes create a scratching sound). Toss potatoes, then add onions. Continue cooking for 5 minutes until onions are tender. Add seasoning and toss – then add ½ of the cheese and toss through. Cover top of potatoes with remaining cheese and cover pan. Cook over medium heat until cheese melts. Once cheese has melted, remove lid and turn up heat until potatoes move freely in skillet in one piece, invert then serve.

Serves 4.

PRALINE KEY LIME PIE

1	8-inch graham cracker pie crust	¼	cup unsalted butter
½	cup pecan pieces	6	egg yolks
½	cup light brown sugar	1½	cans sweetened condensed milk
		⅓	cup key lime juice

Melt butter in saucepan over medium heat. Stir in pecans and cook for 2 minutes. Stir in sugar and melt until smooth. As soon as it comes to a boil, remove from heat, spread evenly over bottom of pie shell. In a mixing bowl, combine yolks, sweetened condensed milk and juice; then whip together until you get a custard consistency. Pour over praline layer and lightly tap on counter to remove air bubbles. Bake on cookie sheet in a preheated 350 degree oven for 12 minutes. Remove and cool before refrigerating.

Serves 8 to 10.

OPTIONAL TOPPINGS

Meringue: Top pie with beaten egg whites and bake at 400 degrees until lightly browned, use top rack of oven.

Whipped Cream: May be piped or dolloped before serving.

STEAM ROOM GRILLE

5402 I-55 North
Jackson, MS 39211

Steam Room Grille has something for everyone. Steam Room Grille offers only the finest aged hand-cut, prime beef, prepared blackened or grilled and served on sizzling platters. For those desiring lighter fare, Steam Room Grille had a wide array of salads and appetizers and a large selection of fresh grilled fish. As the name implies, the steamed seafood available includes live Maine lobster, Alaskan king crab, Dungeness crab or jumbo Gulf shrimp. Stone crabs, snow crabs, oysters, clams and mussels round out the steamed offerings.

SHRIMP MAGGIE

3½	pounds butter	3¾	tablespoons cayenne pepper
11¼	cups diced onions		
7	pounds peeled shrimp (51/60-ct.)	1	tablespoon minced garlic
5⅔	pounds mushrooms, sliced and drained	2½	tablespoons sweet basil leaves
1½	cups all-purpose flour	15	cups sour cream (1 gallon + 1 cup =15)
5	tablespoons salt	⅔	cup Italian parsley, minced

Melt butter, add the onion and shrimp. Sauté until the shrimp turn pink. Add the mushrooms, stir and cook for 5 minutes. Sprinkle the flour over the cooking product. sprinkle in all spices and stir well. Add the sour cream and stir until the sour cream is completely smooth and emulsified. **Cook for 10 minutes. Do not boil.** Add parsley and stir. Place in ice bath immediately.

Yield: 2 gallons

CRAWFISH & CORN BISQUE

4	cups flour	1	cup egg paste
2	cups oil	1	tablespoon cayenne pepper
6	pounds crawfish tails, thawed and drained	1	teaspoon black pepper
6	cups diced onions	1	tablespoon salt
4	cups diced bell pepper	3	tablespoons seafood seasoning
2	cups diced celery	1	tablespoon hot sauce
2	tablespoons minced garlic	4	cups cream corn
3	gallons chicken stock	1	cup parsley, minced
8	cups cut corn		
2	tablespoons Worcestershire sauce		

Put the oil and flour into a braiser pot and cook the roux until it reaches a tan color. Add the onions, bell pepper, celery and minced garlic and cook over high heat for 10 to 15 minutes or until veggies become tender. Add the chicken stock to the vegetable/roux mixture one gallon at a time and then bring the soup to a slow boil. Add the frozen and cream corn and cook uncovered over low heat for 30 minutes allowing it to reduce and thicken. Add the seasonings and egg paste and cook for 10 minutes. Add the crawfish and parsley and cook for 10 minutes. Remove and cool in an ice bath immediately.

Yield: 2 gallons

NEW ORLEANS CAFÉ
1536 East County Line Road
Ridgeland, MS 39157

NEW ORLEANS CAFÉ
SEAFOOD GUMBO

3	pounds shrimp and/or crab meat	2	teaspoons minced garlic
1	package frozen okra	1½	yellow onions, minced
1	16-ounce can chopped tomatoes	½	cup Worcestershire sauce
1	small bunch celery, minced	½	cup browning additive
2	green bell peppers, minced	½	cup parsley
1	red bell pepper, minced		

Roux:

3	cups peanut oil	3	cups flour

Roux Prep: Mix peanut oil and flour and stir over low heat slowly until mixture turns to a medium tan color. Don't overcook.

Preparation: Heat 1 gallon of water with all veggies, crab and seasoning added until cooked. Add shrimp, roux and tomatoes. Add more water if needed. Heat until shrimp is cooked. Be careful not to overcook shrimp.

Serves 8.

BRAVO!
ITALIAN RESTAURANT & BAR
244 Highland Village
Jackson, MS 39211

Chef Dan Blumenthal
David Blumenthal   Jeff Good
Proprietors

Bravo! is a two-time recipient of the **Wine Spectator** *"Award of Excellence" and one of only three recipients in the state!* **Bravo!** *was also named "1997 & 1998 Restaurant of the Year" by the Jackson Convention & Visitors' Bureau. This nouveau Italian restaurant features a wood oven for its pizzas, pasta, seafood, steaks, etc.*

ROMAN STYLE SHRIMP
WITH MINT & BASIL

1	pound shrimp, 16 to 20 ct.	1	tablespoon mint leaves, chopped
1	tablespoon garlic, minced	1	tablespoon basil leaves, chopped
2	teaspoons shallots, minced	1	tablespoon butter
¼	cup dry white wine	2	tablespoons extra virgin olive oil
1	tablespoon lemon juice		Salt to taste
			Red chili flakes

Peel shells off shrimp, leaving the tail on. Butterfly and devein shrimp. Preheat sauté pan on the stove over high heat. Add oil and butter. Fold in the garlic and shallots, then immediately add the shrimp. Sauté the shrimp for several minutes, moving them around the pan so they cook evenly. Deglaze with the white wine and lemon juice. Add the mint, basil, salt and chili flakes. The shrimp are done when they turn from gray to pinkish-white. This dish can be served warm or at room temperature as an appetizer, or increase the portion size by 50% to serve as an entrée.

Serves 4.

CITRUS VINAIGRETTE

6	ounces freshly squeezed orange juice	2	ounces red wine vinegar
1	tablespoon freshly squeezed lemon juice	1	tablespoon Dijon mustard
			Salt and pepper to taste
		1	cup olive oil

Mix well.

SWEET & SOUR CHICKEN

8	each boneless, skinless chicken breasts	½	cup honey
¾	cup flour	⅓	cup chicken broth (not bouillon cubes)
⅓	cup olive oil	½	cup golden raisins
1	tablespoon garlic, minced	2	teaspoons chopped fresh rosemary (1 teaspoon dried)
1	small red onion, chopped finely		
⅓	cup white wine	2	tablespoons cold butter
½	cup balsamic vinegar		Salt and red chili flakes to taste

Prepare the chicken for cooking by dusting lightly with flour, shaking off any excess. Heat olive oil in a skillet. Add the chicken and brown over medium-high heat on both sides. Add the onions then garlic to the skillet, taking care not to burn the garlic, as this will give the sauce an acrid flavor. Add the white wine, balsamic vinegar and chicken broth. Turn the heat up to high and reduce these liquids. After a minute or so, add the honey, salt, chili flakes, rosemary and raisins. Reduce the sauce until it thickens. When the sauce is thickened, finish by adding the cold butter and swirling the skillet over medium heat until it is incorporated into the sauce.

Serves 4.

CHOCOLATE MASCARPONE PUDDING

4	egg yolks	½	pound mascarpone cheese
½	cup sugar		
1	teaspoon vanilla extract	¼	cup Marsala wine
¼	cup unsweetened cocoa		

In a large metal bowl, beat the yolks and sugar with a whip until they are light and fluffy. Place the bowl over a saucepan half-filled with simmering water and whisk until "ribbons" form. Continue whisking while adding the vanilla, cocoa and mascarpone. Whisk until smooth. Add the Marsala, whisking constantly until the custard thickens. Remove from the heat and spoon into serving bowls. Chill until set. Garnish with whipped cream and some toasted, chopped walnuts.

Serves approximately 5.

IRON HORSE GRILL
320 West Pearl Street Jackson, MS 39203

Kenneth B. Crotwell
Chef/Owner

Chef Crotwell is a Louisiana native born in New Orleans, reared in Denham Springs, with ties to Mississippi. Ken is quick to tell you that he learned the art and appreciation of gracious dining from his Mississippi-born mother. Ken graduated from Mississippi College with a degree in business in 1986. It was during that time as a student, he subsidized his income by becoming Food and Beverage Director of the Jack Nicklaus-designed Annandale Golf Club of Mississippi, one of the top 100 golf clubs in America. After college, Ken returned to Louisiana and began a catering business from his home. Later, he worked his way up through a well-established Louisiana-based seafood restaurant chain. He returned to Mississippi and became general manager of the Iron Horse Grill. In July of 1995, Ken and his wife Kay purchased the Iron Horse Grill.

CHOCOLATE BREAD PUDDING

4	ounces chocolate chips	3	each whole eggs
10	ounces cream	1	teaspoon vanilla
2	tablespoons granulated sugar	2	ounces raspberry liqueur
4	each day old croissants		

Bring ¼ cup of the cream to a simmer and remove from the heat. Pour over the chocolate chips and allow to set for thirty seconds until the chocolate is melted. Whisk until smooth. Whisk in the vanilla and liqueur. Whisk the eggs, cream and sugar and then the chocolate mixture. Cut the day old croissants into ¼-inch slices and place on a sheet pan. Toast in a 325 degree oven for ten minutes until crispy. Allow the croissants to cool. Spray a 1 quart heart-shaped pan with all vegetable pan spray. Dipping the croissant slices into the batter, line the entire pan with all of the croissants. Place the pan in a 4-inch hotel pan with enough boiling water to come halfway up the side of the heart pan. Bake in a preheated 325 degree oven for 20 to 25 minutes or until set. Remove from the oven and from the water bath to a baker's rack to cool.

GLAZE

4	ounces chocolate	½	teaspoon vanilla extract
4	ounces cream		
1	tablespoon light corn syrup		

Bring the milk and syrup to a simmer, remove from the heat and pour over the chips. Allow the chips to melt and then whisk in the vanilla until smooth.

Assembly: Invert the pan onto a baker's rack and allow the pudding to cool to room temperature. Pour the pudding, insuring total enrobing. Allow the glaze to set almost until firm. Garnish with a band of red raspberries around the outer edge of the heart, a red ribbon around the side edge of the heart, and a whimsical drizzle of white chocolate inside the rim of raspberries.

WAY TOO HEALTHY BANANA NUT BREAD

2	cups all-purpose flour	30	packs artificial sweetener (a brand that can be cooked)
2	cups whole wheat flour		
1	teaspoon baking soda	1	cup egg substitute
1	tablespoon and 1 teaspoon baking powder	2	cups banana purée
		¾	cup hot water
1	cup applesauce	1½	cups walnut pieces (optional)

Sift the all-purpose flour and re-measure. Mix the two flours and the baking powder and soda. In a mixer blend the applesauce, egg substitute, sweetener and banana purée until smooth. Add the flour, mix alternately with the hot water until totally incorporated and smooth. Add the nuts and mix briefly. Pour into two 9-inch loaf pans sprayed with vegetable pan spray. Bake in a 325 degree oven for one hour or until a toothpick inserted in the center comes out clean. Do not overbake, as this bread will dry easily.

SOUTHWESTERN CEVICHE

1	pound medium shrimp, deveined and shelled	½	cup ¼-inch diced green bell pepper
1	pound jumbo lump crab meat	½	cup ¼-inch diced red bell pepper
1	pound salmon fillet, cut in ½ diced cubes	1	cup ½-inch diced mango
4	cups fresh lime juice (must be fresh not bottled)	½	cup ½-inch diced red onion
4	limes, peeled and segmented	2	tablespoons minced jalapeños
1	cup ½-inch diced tomatoes	1	cup chopped cilantro
		2	tablespoons sugar Fresh ground pepper and salt to taste

Parboil shrimp in water to cover for 3 minutes, drain and lightly dice.

In a large, non-reactive bowl, combine the shrimp, salmon, tomatoes, red and green bell peppers, onions, mango, jalapeño and lime juice. Marinate for 4 hours in refrigerator.

Just before serving, drain off juice and add remaining ingredients to mixture – making sure to gently fold in crabmeat, orange and lime sections so as to not break them up.

Serves 6 to 8.

CHESTERFIELD'S

U.S. Highway 49
Hattiesburg, MS 39401

519 Azalea Street
Meridian, MS 39301

(Mississippi Locations)

Len Moore
Director of Operations

BAKED BEANS

½	cup bacon bits (precooked/diced)	1	cup ketchup
1½	cups vegetable mix (chopped green peppers, chopped yellow onions, cut into ½-inch chunks)	1	cup barbecue sauce
		½	box light brown sugar
		3	16-ounce cans baked beans

Mix all ingredients in pan until well-dissolved. Bake at 300 degrees for 30 minutes.

Yield: 20 to 25 servings

BAKED STUFFED AMBERJACK

6	amberjack fillets	Salt as needed
1	pound Maryland crab meat	Lemon pepper seasoning as needed
1	cup dry bread crumbs (Italian-style)	Paprika as needed
2	cans cream of mushroom soup	Liquid margarine (melted) as needed

Wash and dry fillets. Cut fillets in half (lengthwise). Place one half on each side of casserole dish.

Mix crab, bread crumbs and soup (for stuffing).

Place 1 cup of stuffing in the center of each casserole dish. Brush fish and stuffing with melted margarine. Salt and season (lemon pepper seasoning) to taste. Sprinkle with paprika. Bake in oven at 350 degrees for 20 to 25 minutes until golden brown.

Serves 6.

PURPLE PARROT CAFÉ, CRESCENT CITY GRILL & MAHOGANY BAR

3810 Hardy Street
Hattiesburg, MS

Robert St. John
Chef/Owner

PASTA JAMBALAYA

1	pound andouille sausage (½-inch dice)
2	duck breasts (skinless, boneless and pounded to ½-inch thick)
2	4-ounce boneless, skinless chicken breasts (pounded to ½-inch thick)
1	pound cooked crawfish tails
2	yellow onions, chopped fine
2	green bell peppers, chopped fine
2	red bell peppers, chopped fine
2	garlic cloves, minced
1½	pounds 31 to 35-ct. shrimp, shells reserved
1¼	quarts duck stock
4	tomatoes, seeded and chopped
2	tablespoons Creole seasoning

Cook andouille in medium-high skillet 5 minutes, drain and transfer to stainless steel bowl. Lightly flour and sauté duck and chicken in 1 tablespoon butter using the andouille skillet. Cook until firm and brown, slice against the grain to ½ pieces and transfer to bowl with sausage. Add crawfish to meats. Sauté onions, peppers and garlic in 2 ounces butter until onions are clear and translucent. Add shrimp to vegetables and cook until they become opaque, transfer all to bowl with meats and mix thoroughly. In a 3 quart saucepan bring duck stock and reserved shrimp shells to a rolling boil reducing by half. Strain shells from stock and add tomatoes and Creole seasoning cooking another 5 to 10 minutes. At this point you should have one bowl with meats and vegetables and one bowl of duck/shrimp stock. This can be made ahead of time and will refrigerate for up to two days.

Serves 18 to 20.

To serve, heat equal parts of the jambalaya meat mixture and the stock and serve over fettuccini with crusty French bread.

DUCK STOCK

2½	pounds duck bones	2	stalks celery
2½	quarts water	1	bay leaf
½	large onion	1	teaspoon thyme
1	medium carrot	2	sprigs parsley

Bring duck and water to a boil and lowering heat and skimming foam, add remaining ingredients and simmer 2 to 3 hours. Strain and cool quickly. Keep refrigerated below 40 degrees Fahrenheit.

University of Southern Mississippi
Administration Building
Hattiesburg, Mississippi

FATHERREE'S

1311 Hardy Street
Hattiesburg, MS 39401

Nathan L. Clark, III
Owner/Executive Chef

Chef Clark is a Hattiesburg, Mississippi native. He has been a chef at several local restaurants as well as in Colorado prior to opening his upscale Fatherree's restaurant in Hattiesburg, Mississippi.

PANÉED POMPANO
WITH LEMON SAUCE

(This recipe works well with rainbow trout, orange roughy or any other firm flat fish)

1	teaspoon kosher salt	1	teaspoon white pepper
	White flour	1	ounce clarified butter
1	lemon, juiced		
1	ounce white sauce*	3	tablespoons white wine
5	7-ounce fresh skinned and boned pompano fillets		

Sprinkle fish with kosher salt and white pepper. Lightly dredge the fish in white flour. Add clarified butter to a medium-hot skillet (it is important not to get the skillet so hot that you burn your butter). Shake excess flour off of the fish before placing it into the skillet. Cook each side for approximately 2 minutes. Before removing fish, squeeze ½ of the lemon's juice over fish. Take skillet off of the heat and place the fish onto a warm service plate. Return the skillet to medium heat and deglaze it with the white wine. Next add the white sauce* and the other half of the lemon's juice plus a pinch more kosher salt and white pepper. Reduce the sauce by a ⅓ and pour over fish. Garnish with fresh chopped parsley, paprika and lemon wheels.

*Our white sauce is made from a Béchamel Sauce but can be substituted with heavy whipping cream. Serving for 5.

CREAMY HORSERADISH SHRIMP

½	ounce clarified butter		butterflied, deveined
1	tablespoon Italian bread crumbs	2	tablespoons horseradish
1	teaspoon kosher salt	1	ounce white sauce*
6	shrimp (medium-large) peeled,	1	teaspoon white pepper

In a hot sauté skillet add butter and horseradish then shrimp, sauté the shrimp until done (approximately 1-1½ minutes). Add kosher salt and white pepper then white sauce. When the sauce begins to bubble finish with bread crumbs to thicken. Garnish with fresh chopped parsley, paprika and lemon wheels.

Serves 1 or 2.

SEAFOOD PASTA

1	ounce clarified butter	6	shrimp (medium-large) peeled, butterflied, deveined
¼	cup diced tomato		
2	tablespoons chopped green onion	1	ounce lump crab meat, picked
3	tablespoons white wine	¼	cup julienne onion
2	teaspoons Cajun seasoning	2	ounces white sauce*
1	teaspoon white pepper	1	teaspoon kosher salt
6	crawfish tails, cooked and peeled	4	ounces pre-cooked linguini pasta

Add butter to a hot skillet. To the butter add onions and tomato, sauté these together. Then add shrimp, crawfish, Cajun seasoning, kosher salt and white pepper, sauté these together until shrimp are done approximately 1-1½ minutes). Next add green onions and crab meat, sauté these together then deglaze with white wine and add white sauce. Now add your pasta and sauté it into the other ingredients, reduce heat and continue cooking until pasta is warmed through (approximately 2 minutes). Finish by adding Parmesan cheese to thicken the sauce. Serve this up in a large pasta bowl or serving plate. Garnish with fresh chopped parsley, paprika and lemon wheels.

Serves 1.

BAY ST. LOUIS is home to the NASA John C. Stennis Space Center. The Saturn booster rocket, a vital part of the nation's moon project, was tested here. "Old Town" Bay St. Louis is known as an art colony. It attracts artists and artisans from all over the area. A casino gaming and golf resort is located near Bay St. Louis.

GULFPORT – The CEC/Seabee Memorial Museum is located at the Naval Construction Battalion Center. At the Gulfport Oceanarium, dolphins are trained and sent to other marine aquariums all over the country. The annual Mississippi Deep Sea Fishing Rodeo is held in Gulfport. It is the oldest and largest fishing rodeo in the country. The Mississippi State Port is located in Gulfport. The Port of Gulfport is the largest tropical fruit port in the Gulf of Mexico. It handles more than 500,000 tons of fruit annually. Regularly scheduled excursion boats are available to Ship Island from Gulfport. Ship Island, one of the barrier islands (Gulf Islands National Seashore) has been recognized by USA Weekend as one of the top 10 beaches in the country.

BILOXI observes its Tricentennial anniversary in 1999. Pierre Le Moyne Sieur d'Iberville led the expedition team that dropped anchor on Ship Island on February 12, 1699. A landing was made on the shore of present-day Biloxi. Iberville's landing marked the beginning of a series of activities that led to the exploration and strategic occupation of the lower Mississippi Valley by the French. The Biloxi Tricentennial will be a year-long celebration to pay tribute to Iberville's landing. It will be a non-stop jubilee commemorating 300 years of this historic and diverse city. Biloxi is home to Keesler Air Force Base, the largest electronics training center in the world. Biloxi is also a major gaming destination on the coast.

OCEAN SPRINGS is known for its moss-draped live oaks on scenic shoreline drive and its beautiful homes. It has been recognized for its art colony, quaint shops and internationally-known Shearwater pottery. The Gulf Islands National Seashore facility is located at Davis Bayou. Ocean Springs is celebrating the area's Tricentennial in 1999.

PASCAGOULA is home to the coast's ship building and oil refining industry. It is a Navy Home Port and some of the Navy's finest ships are built here. Pascagoula's Old Spanish Fort and Museum is the oldest existing structure in the Mississippi Valley (1718).

TRAPANI'S EATERY

116 North Beach Boulevard
Bay St. Louis, MS 39520

Anthony Trapani, III & Steven D. Pucheu
Chef/Owners

Established in 1994. Awards: First Place in the Annual Red Beans & Rice Cook-off sponsored by the American Cancer Society 4 years in a row. Top Bean Award – Judges Choice Award for the best restaurant in Bay St. Louis. 1999 Celtic Festival Culinary Competition – First place Peoples Choice Award and 2nd Place Judges Choice Award. Mentioned in the "Best of the Coast" article in **Southern Living** *as having the best Po-Boys on the coast.*

FRIED SPECKLED TROUT WITH CRAWFISH ÉTOUFÉE

Étoufée:

1	pound butter and 2 cups flour to make roux (light brown)	2	cups chopped yellow onions
2	cups chopped celery	1½	cups chopped bell peppers
		3	cloves garlic, chopped
		8	bay leaves

Add the above ingredients to roux until tender (about 20 minutes). Stir often.

4	cups chicken stock		Salt and pepper to taste
1	small can spicy tomatoes (diced)		Creole seasoning to taste
2	pounds cooked crawfish tails		

Add to étoufée mixture the chicken stock and spicy tomatoes. Simmer for 15 minutes (should be thick). Add cooked crawfish tails, salt, pepper and Creole seasoning to taste.

1	egg		Seasoned corn flour
1	cup milk		
8	8-ounce trout fillets		

Mix egg and milk and put over trout fillets. Dip fish in seasoned corn flour and deep fry at 350 degrees until golden brown. Place on platter and top with crawfish étoufée.

Serves 8.

GRILLED SNAPPER PASTA

Marinade:

⅓	cup soy sauce	2	teaspoons chopped garlic
	Juice from 3 lemons	⅔	cup water
10	dashes hot pepper sauce		

Fillet of red snapper	Parmesan cheese
Angel hair pasta	Bell pepper
Onions	Mushrooms
Butter	Crawfish tails
Garlic	Cajun seasoning

Step #1: Marinade fillet for 10 seconds. Grill snapper and baste with marinade (one time when flipped).

Step #2: Pasta Bed (Angel Hair) – Mix pasta with butter, garlic, Parmesan cheese. Place on plate when ready to serve.

Step #3: Sauté onions, bell pepper, mushrooms, crawfish tails with Cajun seasoning (to taste), ½-ounce of marinade added with butter and garlic to sauté these ingredients.

Step #4: Place grilled fish on pasta bed and scoop sautéed mixture on top of fish.

Step #5: Lightly cover fish with Hollandaise sauce and serve.

HOLLANDAISE SAUCE

6	eggs	Juice of 3 lemons
1	pound butter	(remove seeds)
1	pinch cayenne pepper	

Place all ingredients in double boiler except butter. Whisk eggs and pepper in boiler until thick, then continue to whisk until all butter has been melted in egg mixture.

Serves 1.

CASINO MAGIC

711 Casino Magic Drive
Bay St. Louis, MS 39520

Glenn Adams
Director of Food & Beverage

Chef Adams joined Casino Magic in 1994 as director of food and beverage. Prior to joining the company, he served as vice president of food and beverage at Grand Casino Gulfport and general manager of K-Paul's Kitchen, owned by the famous chef, Paul Prudhomme. He received his B.S.B.A. degree in accounting and finance from the University of Florida, graduating in the top 10 percent. His background in food and beverage includes ownership of Creative Culinary Concepts, a food service consulting firm.

ROASTED TOMATO & GARLIC SOUP

4	medium Creole tomatoes	1	tablespoon roasted garlic
1	teaspoon olive oil	½	cup milk
1½	teaspoons all-purpose flour	¼	teaspoon dried basil
½	large onion, chopped	¼	teaspoon sugar
1	quart vegetable broth	¼	teaspoon salt
		1	dash white pepper

1. Heat broiler. Slice tomatoes in half and squeeze out juice and seeds: place skin side up in a jelly roll pan. Broil 10 minutes, or until skins blister and blacken. Remove from oven and allow to cool slightly. Slip off skins and discard. Purée in blender or food processor.

2. In stock pot, heat oil over medium heat; sauté onions until tender, then sprinkle evenly with flour. Stir with a wire whisk and cook 1 minute longer. Stir in tomato purée and broth; cook, stirring frequently, until mixture comes to a boil. Add roasted garlic, basil, white pepper and salt and sugar; simmer 10 to 20 minutes. Turn off heat and stir in reserved milk.

Serves 4.

BASIL-SESAME DRESSING

3	garlic cloves, minced	¼	cup chopped fresh basil
3	tablespoons balsamic vinegar	2	tablespoons chopped Italian parsley
1	tablespoon lemon juice	½	cup olive oil
2	tablespoons grated Parmesan or Romano cheese	½	teaspoon sesame oil
			Fresh ground black pepper to taste

Whisk together all ingredients. Add pepper.
Yield: ¾ cup or 1 serving

SWEET PICKLED SHRIMP

3	pounds fresh shrimp	2	bags shrimp/crab seasoning
6	quarts water	2	tablespoons black pepper
¼	cup salt	1	large lemon, halved

Marinade:

1½	cups olive oil	1	pound Vidalia onions, sliced thin
¾	cup balsamic vinegar	2	cloves garlic, minced
2	teaspoons salt	2	tablespoons capers
2	tablespoons Worcestershire sauce	2	teaspoons celery seed
½	teaspoon jalapeño sauce	3	jalapeño peppers, minced

In a large pot, bring the water, salt, crab boil and pepper to a boil. Squeeze in the lemon juice and add the rinds. Pour in the shrimp, all at once. Bring back to boil, over HIGH heat. Boil 3 minutes – NO MORE. Remove from heat. Add 3 to 4 cups ice cubes to pot to stop cooking. Let stand 5 to 10 minutes. Remove shrimp. When cool enough to handle, peel, leaving last tail segment attached. Set aside.

In a large bowl, stir together the remaining ingredients. Add shrimp to marinade. Toss to coat well. Cover tightly. Refrigerate overnight or up to two days, tossing occasionally in marinade. Drain. Serve on a large platter or decorative bowl lined with lettuce leaves.

Serves 6.

CRAB CAKES

Great with Creole Mustard Sauce or Chorron Sauce

1	cup mayonnaise	¼	teaspoon Cajun seasoning
2	each eggs, beaten	¼	teaspoon baking powder
1	tablespoon Worcestershire sauce	1	teaspoon dry mustard
2	tablespoons white wine	1	quart Japanese bread crumbs
1	tablespoon lemon juice	1	pound jumbo lump crab meat (well picked)
¼	cup fresh parsley, minced		

1. Mix the first five (5) ingredients together and whip until smooth and creamy.

2. Add the next four (4) ingredients to the creamy mixture and whip until smooth.

3. Fold the bread crumbs and crab meat into the wet mixture. Do not overwork. Form into individual patties and pan fry until golden brown.

Serves 6.

STRAWBERRIES WITH PASTA & CREAM

1	cup strawberries, thinly sliced	4	ounces angel hair pasta, cooked
⅓	cup dark brown sugar, divided	4	tablespoons roasted pecans, chopped
¾	cup whipping cream		

1. In a small bowl, gently toss the sliced berries and 1 tablespoon of the sugar. Cover and set aside.

2. In a medium saucepan, mix the cream and the rest of the sugar. Bring to a boil, stirring constantly. Lower the heat and simmer until the sugar has dissolved, cream has turned light brown and mixture is smooth. Remove from the heat.

3. Cook the pasta per package instructions, omitting the salt. Be sure to drain the pasta completely.

4. Over medium heat, add the pasta to the sauce mixture and toss until coated. Before serving, spoon the berries with their juice over the pasta and sprinkle with the chopped nuts. Serve immediately.

Serves 4.

CRABMEAT SAUCE VERT

(Appetizers)

1½   pounds jumbo lump crab meat

Sauce:

4	ounces spinach	½	capful balsamic vinegar
10	leaves fresh basil		Juice of ½ lemon
3	teaspoons tarragon	2	eggs
1	teaspoon thyme leaves	2	cups olive oil
4	anchovies	½	cup vegetable oil
3	garlic cloves	6	dashes Worcestershire sauce
4	teaspoons capers		
1½	cups parsley	1	teaspoon sugar
½	bunch green onions (green part only)	1	teaspoon cayenne pepper, or to taste

In a food processor, combine first nine sauce ingredients. Run on pulse. Add eggs. With machine on, slowly pour in oils. When thick, add lemon juice, vinegar, sugar, Worcestershire, cayenne and salt to taste.

Arrange picked-through crab meat on top of finely shredded lettuce. Cover with sauce. Garnish with lemon if desired.

Serves 8.

BRIE, OYSTER & CHAMPAGNE SOUP

8	cups chicken stock	4	cups white roux
½	bottle champagne	4	pints whipping
½	gallon oysters		cream
2	onions, finely diced	½	wheel ripe brie cheese, room temperature
6	celery stalks, finely diced		Salt, white pepper
8	garlic cloves, finely diced		and cayenne pepper to taste
2	tablespoons dried thyme		

In a pot, combine chicken stock, ¼ bottle champagne, oyster liquid, diced vegetables and thyme. Bring to a boil until reduced by ¼. Slowly add roux until thickened (almost the consistency of whipped cream). Cook for 15 to 20 minutes. Add whipping cream and brie. Reduce heat. Once brie is melted, add remaining champagne. In a colander, strain warm oysters gently until open. Add to soup, and serve.

Serves at least 8.

ROAST TENDERLOIN

Whole beef tenderloin	12	shallots, diced
Salt	¼	cup olive oil
Pepper	1	bottle good red wine
Granulated garlic		
Dried thyme	8	cups strong beef stock
Flour		

Trim fat from and tie one whole beef tenderloin. Season with salt, pepper, garlic and thyme. Lightly flour. Sear in roasting pan on all sides. When brown, put in 500 degree preheated oven for 15 to 20 minutes. Remove, and add shallots to pan. On stovetop, being careful not to burn, stir juices and add wine and beef stock. Reduce to a syrupy consistency (coats the back of a spoon). Strain to remove shallots. Keep warm and serve.

Serves 8.

SIDE DISHES

ARTICHOKES

Cook artichokes (one per person) in salted water until done, or about 25 minutes. Clean and reserve bottoms and hearts, removing the "choke". Toss lightly in butter and lemon juice, using about one stick of butter and the juice of one lemon. Reserve.

ROASTED NEW POTATOES

Cook 3 pounds of potatoes (leaving skin on) in salted water. When done, drain and place in roasting pan with olive oil and 2 medium sliced onions. Roast at 425 degrees until onions are cooked and potato skins are crispy. Reserve.

GREEN BEANS ALMANDINE

Cook green beans in salted water until done. Refresh in ice water and drain. Toss with butter, lemon juice, Worcestershire and sliced almonds. Reserve.

To assemble: Slice beef tenderloin and place on platter. Surround by artichokes, alternating with roasted new potatoes. Top with sauce, reserving some for individual servings. Serve green beans in a separate casserole dish.

EGGPLANT ELOISE

This is another dish that looks like Mardi Gras on a plate: fried eggplant stuffed with shrimp-crab meat filling, topped with a rosy Choron sauce and garnished with bright green snow peas, carrot and shreds of red cabbage. This dish could also serve as the main course at lunch or brunch.

BEER BATTER

2	eggs		Pinch of baking
1½	cup (12 ounces) beer		powder
1	cup all-purpose flour	1	tablespoon seafood seasoning

SEAFOOD FILLING

3	stalks celery	6	ounces fresh cooked crab meat
1	small onion		
1	small peeled carrot	2	green onions
1	small green bell pepper, seeded and deribbed	4	dashes Worcestershire sauce
2	cloves garlic	1	tablespoon seafood seasoning
4	tablespoons butter		
1	cup medium shrimp (30 count), shelled and deveined	1	eggplant Seafood seasoning to taste Flour for coating
3	tablespoons dry white wine		Beer batter
		2	quarts vegetable oil

CHORON SAUCE

6	egg yolks	Salt to taste
	White wine	Cayenne pepper to taste
2	pounds butter, clarified	Juice of ½ lemon
	Dash Worcestershire sauce	

TARRAGON REDUCTION

4	tablespoons minced fresh tarragon leaves	2	tablespoons minced shallots
2	tablespoons minced fresh chervil	4	teaspoons dry white wine
		1	teaspoon cracked pepper

In a small sauté pan, combine all ingredients and reduce 3 to 4 minutes or until the wine evaporates.

TOMATO REDUCTION

2	medium tomatoes peeled, seeded and diced	1	tablespoon dry white wine

Cook tomatoes in wine in a medium skillet for 5 minutes or until softened and most of the liquid is evaporated. Purée the tomatoes and pass through a fine sieve.

To make the beer batter: In a medium bowl, whisk together all of the ingredients until mixture is smooth.

To make the filling: Finely dice the celery, onion, carrot, bell pepper and garlic. Melt 2 tablespoons of the butter in a medium sauté pan or skillet and sauté until tender, about 5 minutes. Add the shrimp and cook until pink, then add the wine. Add the crab meat, then the remaining butter and green onions. Season with Worcestershire sauce and seafood seasoning.

To make sauce: In a medium saucepan whisk egg yolks over medium heat until thickened, about 3 to 4 minutes. Gradually whisk the warm clarified butter into the egg yolks. Season with Worcestershire, salt, cayenne and lemon juice. Add tarragon reduction and tomato reduction.

Peel the eggplant and cut into 1¼-inch thick crosswise slices. Using a spoon or melon baller, hollow out the center of each eggplant slice. Sprinkle with seafood seasoning and dip in flour, then beer batter. In a large, heavy pot or deep fryer, heat the oil to 375 degrees and deep fry the eggplant for 3 to 4 minutes, or until golden brown.

To serve: Fill the fried eggplant slices with the seafood mixture and top with Choron sauce. Garnish with snow peas, shredded red cabbage and carrot.

Serves 8 (about 8 eggplant slices)

BAKED MERINGUE

3   egg whites
    Salt
    Cream of tartar
    Confectioners'
    sugar
2   cups crème
    anglaise

Raspberries or
strawberries to
garnish
Favorite
homemade ice
cream

On a cookie sheet, place one sheet of wax paper. Place 3 egg whites at 65 to 70 degrees or room temperature, in mixing bowl. Add pinch of salt and a knife tip of cream of tartar. Beat until thick. Add ⅓ to ½ cup confectioners' sugar and continue to beat until stiff, not dry. Using a pastry bag, pipe out 6 circles onto paper and pan, about 3 to 4 inches round. Cook in a 200 degree oven for one hour. Turn off oven and let sit overnight. Remove from pan and place in plastic airtight bags. To serve, place custard sauce on base of plate, adding meringue in middle. Scoop ice cream on top of meringue and garnish with fruit.

VRAZEL'S OYSTER DRESSING

2   pints stewing
     oysters with broth
16   ounces butter
1   cup finely sliced
     green onions

2½   pints fresh coarse
     French bread
     crumbs
     Salt and pepper to
     taste

Place butter in saucepan and melt over medium-high heat. Add oysters and cook until the edges start to curl or about half cooked. Remove from heat and add green onions and one pint of the bread crumbs. Dressing should be soggy but no liquid showing. You may need more or less bread crumbs depending on the amount of liquid that needs to be absorbed. Place soggy dressing into baking pan and bake in 350 degree oven till browned. At this point the dressing should have a moist and wet consistency.

SPINACH TOUFFLÉ

6	ounces cream cheese	2	cups bread crumbs
4	ounces butter		Salt and pepper
10	ounces frozen chopped spinach		Parmesan cheese

Melt butter and cream cheese. Add chopped spinach (uncooked) and season with salt and pepper. Add bread crumbs until soggy and place in casserole dish. Top with Parmesan cheese. Bake at 350 degrees for 15 minutes.

Serves 4.

SEAFOOD A LA VRAZEL

12	ounces butter		Salt and pepper to taste
1	teaspoon minced garlic	4	ounces white wine
1	teaspoon parsley	8	ounces thin spaghetti, cooked
16	shrimp		Endive and lemon wedge
16	scallops		
16	ounces crab meat		

Place butter, garlic and parsley in sauté pan, add shrimp and scallops and cook till done. Add crab meat, salt and pepper and white wine. Bring to a boil and serve on spaghetti. May garnish with endive and lemon wedge.

SNAPPER PONTCHARTRAIN

4	extra large soft shell crabs	1	pint seasoned flour (salt and pepper)
4	4-ounce fresh snapper fillets or other fresh Gulf fish		Egg wash (3 eggs and 1 pint of milk, beaten together)
		1	pint frying oil (canola or olive oil)

Clean soft shell crabs and dip in ice water and place in flour. Then dip the crab in the egg wash and back into the flour. Place in sauté pan with oil on medium-high heat. Then take fresh snapper and place in egg wash and then into seasoned flour and sauté in pan with crab. When nicely browned and crispy, top with lemon butter.

Serves 4.

CRAWFISH ÉTOUFÉE

8	ounces butter	1	teaspoon hot pepper sauce
1¼	cup yellow onions (medium diced)	2	tablespoons Worcestershire sauce
½	cup bell pepper (medium diced)	1	pound fresh crawfish tail meat with fat
3	tablespoons chopped garlic	½	cup water
3	medium bay leaves	½	bunch sliced green onions
1	tablespoon whole leaf thyme		
	Salt and pepper to taste		

Place butter in a saucepan and melt on medium heat. Turn heat to medium-high and add onions, bell pepper, celery, garlic, bay leaves, thyme, pepper sauce and Worcestershire sauce. Cook until vegetables are tender. Add crawfish, salt and pepper to taste. Pour ½ cup water into the container crawfish came in and add to mixture. This is to assure that all flavorings from the crawfish are in your recipe. Bring back to a simmer, turn your fire off and add green onions. Serve over rice pilaf (see following recipe).

RICE PILAF

4	ounces butter	1	cup long grain rice
1	cup yellow onions (medium diced)	2	cups water
¼	cup bell pepper (medium diced)	6	cubes beef bouillon

Place butter in saucepan and add onions and bell pepper. Sauté until onion turns clear. Add rice and cook for 3 to 5 minutes until rice is good and hot. Add 3 cups water and bouillon cubes. Simmer over medium heat until all liquid is absorbed by rice (about 5 to 8 minutes). Stir occasionally.

Serves 4.

MISSISSIPPI MUD CAKE

2	sticks margarine	1	pinch salt
½	cup cocoa	1	teaspoon vanilla
4	eggs	¾	cup chopped
½	cup plain flour		pecans
2	cups sugar		

Melt butter and cocoa in skillet until blended slightly. Beat eggs in bowl, add sugar, then cocoa and butter, flour and nut pieces. Add vanilla. Bake in greased and floured 10 x 15 x 2-inch pan for 30 minutes at 350 degrees. While hot, cover with marshmallows, then icing mix.

ICING

1	package powdered	⅓	cup cocoa
	sugar	½	stick margarine
½	cup milk		

Melt butter and blend with other ingredients. Spread over cake.

Yield: 1 cake

STRAWBERRIES LA CRÈME

15	ounces frozen strawberries thawed with juice	3	ounces powdered sugar (measure after sifting)
15	ounces sour cream	½	ounce grenadine syrup
1	ounce vanilla extract	2	ounces half-and-half cream

Mix strawberries and sour cream. Beat slowly until well mixed. Add grenadine, vanilla and sugar while mixing until smooth consistency. Add half-and-half last mixing only until well blended. Chill and serve, mix well before serving.

L. B.'S STEAKHOUSE GRAND CASINO

West Beach Boulevard Gulfport, MS 39501

**Robert "Robbie" Bellew, Jr.
Executive Chef**

Chef Bellew graduated from Long Beach (MS) High School in 1987. He graduated from the Mississippi Gulf Coast Community College (1987-1990) in Hotel & Restaurant Management. He is a 1994 graduate of the Disney Culinary Apprenticeship program in Orlando, Florida. He is an active member of the American Culinary Federation.

ROASTED GARLIC & POTATO SOUP

2	pounds potatoes, peeled and diced	½	pound onions, diced
8	cloves garlic, peeled	¼	pound flour
		¼	pound butter
2	quarts heavy cream	1	teaspoon salt
		1	teaspoon pepper

Roast the garlic in an oven until it turns light brown. In a soup pot, melt the butter and sauté the onions and the potatoes. Add the roasted garlic and flour. Stir the mixture well and add the cream. Simmer the mixture and season with salt and pepper. Serve.

Serves 6.

BRAISED RABBIT WITH FIGS & APRICOTS

1	each rabbit tenderloin (fresh or frozen)	2	ounces onions, diced
1	each rabbit hind quarter (fresh or frozen)	1	ounce rosemary (fresh) chopped fine
4	ounces fresh figs, quartered	1	ounce thyme (fresh) chopped fine
3	ounces rabbit stock (veal stock can be used as a substitute)	½	ounce sugar
		½	ounce salt
		½	ounce black pepper (fresh cracked)
2	ounces bourbon (any brand will do)	1	ounce oil (of your choice)
2	ounces carrots, diced		

Heat oven to 325 degrees. Heat a heavy ovenproof straight-sided pan with a lid. Mix all dry seasonings and rub into the cleaned rabbit. Add the oil to the pan and let it heat to the point where it almost smokes. Sear the rabbit in the oil. Brown on all sides. Remove the rabbit from the pan. Add the carrot and onion and sauté. Deglaze the pan with bourbon (note: this will flame). Add the stock, figs and apricots. Add just the leg quarter (the tenderloin will go in later). Make sure the meat is covered with liquid. Cover the pan and place in the oven for 1 hour. After an hour of cooking, add the tenderloin and cook for 20 more minutes in the oven. Remove from the oven and serve.

Yield: 1 portion

Note: This can be served with rice, potatoes or grains.

RABBIT STOCK

1	ounce cooking oil	½	pound celery, diced
2	pounds rabbit bones (cut up into 2-inch pieces)	½	pound leeks, diced
		½	pound carrots, diced
½	pound onions, diced	2½	gallons water

Seasonings*:

2	each bay leaves	½	ounce rosemary (fresh or dry)
½	ounce whole peppercorns	½	ounce thyme (fresh or dry)
½	ounce salt		

Heat stock pot and add oil. Sauté the bones till golden brown. Add all vegetables and sauté. Add seasonings and cover with water. Simmer the stock for at least 6 hours. After simmering remove and strain (cheesecloth). Chill down to 40 degrees.

*This mix can either be put in a cheesecloth bundle or right in the stock pot.

FRESH WILD GREENS IN HERB TUILE SHELL WITH GOAT CHEESE

8	ounces fresh wild greens	2	ounces lemon/honey vinaigrette (recipe follows)
1	each tuile shell (recipe follows)	2	ounces goat cheese

Toss greens with vinaigrette. Place the shell on the plate and put the greens into the shell. Sprinkle the goat cheese on top of the greens.

Serves 1.

HERB TUILE SHELL

⅛	cup milk	¼	cup sugar
16	each egg whites	1	tablespoon melted
½	cup flour		butter

¼	teaspoon fresh basil, chopped fine	¼	teaspoon fresh thyme, chopped fine
¼	teaspoon fresh rosemary, chopped fine	⅛	teaspoon salt
		⅛	teaspoon fresh cracked pepper

Mix all except the seasonings. Strain the mixture through a fine sieve and then add the seasonings. Heat oven to 325 degrees. On a teflon-coated sheet pan, place about 2 ounces of the batter on it and bake in the oven for about 5 minutes. The shell should be done when it is light brown. Pull the shell off of the pan with tongs (it will be very hot). Then form it over an inverted glass or bowl. Let it cool. The shell will be very fragile. Serve.

Serves 4 to 5.

LEMON HONEY VINAIGRETTE

1	cup fresh lemon juice	3	cups canola oil
½	cup fresh honey	1	teaspoon salt
¼	cup white vinegar	1	teaspoon fresh cracked pepper
1	teaspoon dry mustard		

In a food processor place the dry mustard and lemon juice. Start mixing. Alternate the honey, vinegar and oil. Once all of those are mixed, add the salt and pepper. Chill and serve.

Serves 4 to 5.

ROBBIE'S APPLE COBBLER

Filling:

1	cup apples	½	cup dark rum
¼	cup sugar	1	ounce butter
1	teaspoon cinnamon		

Dough:

2	cups flour	1	teaspoon baking soda
1	cup sugar		
¼	pound butter		Ice water as needed
1	teaspoon salt		
1	teaspoon baking powder		

Heat a sauté pan and sauté the apples in the butter till they become soft. Add the sugar and cinnamon and sauté till a syrup forms. Add the rum and reduce till the syrup is thick. Cool mixture down and reserve.

For the dough: Place all ingredients in a food processor except the ice water. Mix well in the processor. Once all of the ingredients are thoroughly mixed, start adding the ice water very slowly till the mixture forms a ball in the mixing bowl. The dough is now finished. Pull the dough out and pat it smooth form ½-inch thick. Cut the dough to the size of container that you are going to use. Fill the container with the chilled topping and top with the dough. Bake the cobbler in an oven heated to 350 degrees. It should take about 20 minutes. Serve with fresh vanilla ice cream.

Serves 4.

THE FATHER RYAN HOUSE
BUILT CA. 1841

1196 Beach Boulevard
Biloxi, MS 39530

**Anita Velardi Huey
Resident Chef**

Chef Huey is a 1983 graduate of the California Culinary Academy, San Francisco, California. She has also worked as Head Chef for Ocean View Enterprises, Inc., Berkeley, California DBA Bette's Catering: Café Manix. Chef Huey has also been a winery and food consultant in Sonoma, California.

TROPICAL FRUIT CUSTARD

5	eggs	1	cup heavy cream
3	egg yolks	¼	cup shredded
¾	cup granulated		coconut
	sugar	1	teaspoon banana
1⅓	cup papaya-		extract
	pineapple nectar		

Whisk eggs, yolks and sugar in large mixing bowl until light yellow. Add papaya-pineapple nectar and cream. Whisk until incorporated. Add coconut and extract. Mix thoroughly. Pour custard into 8 4-ounce ovenproof ramekins. Place ramekins in rectangular cake pan and fill bottom of pan with 1-inch water. Bake at 325 degrees for 40 to 50 minutes or until knife inserted into center of custard comes clean.

To serve: Place warm or cool ramekins on dessert plates and garnish plate with sliced kiwi and mandarin oranges. Dust top of custard with powdered sugar just prior to serving.

Serves 8.

SOUTHERN BLACK-EYED PEA-TOMATO SALSA
(Breakfast Accompaniment)

2	tablespoons vegetable oil	2	teaspoons lime juice
1	medium onion, diced	1½	teaspoons paprika
1	medium green pepper, diced	1	teaspoon oregano flakes (or equivalent fresh)
1	7-ounce jar red pimiento	2	teaspoons fresh parsley, chopped
1	4-ounce can green chilies	3	"shakes" hot sauce
1	28-ounce can diced tomatoes, drained		Salt and pepper to taste
2	15-ounce cans black-eyed peas, drained		

Using heavy bottom sauté or fry pan, sauté onion and green pepper in vegetable oil on medium heat. Cook for approximately 2 minutes or until slightly translucent. Add spices, salt and pepper. Stir and taste. Add chilies, pimiento, tomatoes, black-eyed peas, lime juice and hot sauce. Cook on medium heat for approximately 5 minutes. Reduce heat to low and cook additionally for 15 minutes, allowing liquids to reduce. Stir occasionally during time period. Check for seasoning and adjust according to taste.

To serve: Using slotted spoon, place salsa on plate and serve with fried or scrambled eggs, country ham and corn or flour tortillas.

Serves 4 to 6.

*Father Ryan House
Biloxi, Mississippi*

CAPTAIN'S QUARTERS RESTAURANT
TREASURE BAY CASINO RESORT

1980 Beach Boulevard
Biloxi, MS 39531

Matt Meadows
Executive Chef

Treasure Bay Casino Resort has moved its fine dining restaurant from its hotel to an upscale location inside its medieval fort. Within the castle walls and iron grating entrance on the third floor, the design and décor provide a luxurious, old-world ambiance where guests can enjoy an elegant dinner amid the Captain's mixture of treasures.

GRILLED DUCK SALAD

2	ounces duck meat without skin	1	each brie
2	ounces salad mix with spring mix	1	each croutons
½	each Belgian endive	2	ounces raspberry vinaigrette
3	each cucumber	4	each red onions
3	each Roma tomatoes	1	tablespoon pecan halves

Marinate duck breast overnight in vinaigrette with rosemary and minced garlic. Grill to medium and cool. Core out cucumber slices and Roma tomato slices. Grill endive by basting with olive oil and sprinkling with salt and pepper. Prepare crouton by cutting spitwick into ¼-inch slice longways and toast. Sprinkle finished product with pecans. Cut brie into a 1½ wedge and stand up on the plate.

Serves 1.

ROASTED TRIPLE CHOP

2	each pork loins	1	cup mashed potatoes
1	cup jerk seasoning		
2	cups demi-glace	2	cups spinach leaves
⅓	cup honey	1	tablespoon garlic
2	teaspoons rosemary	¼	cup black beans, cooked
3	tablespoons green peppercorns	¼	cup red onions

French the pork loin so that the bones are clean and one inch is exposed. Rub the loin with the jerk seasoning and roast on a bed of sliced onions for 2 hours on 250 degrees until internal temperature reaches 145 degrees. Make the mashed potatoes and mix dried chives into the mix and put into a pastry bag. When pork is done keep in a 160 degree oven until ready to serve. Sauté red onions, garlic, beans and spinach quickly until warm. combine demi, honey, rosemary and warm, strain out rosemary and add the peppercorns. For serving, cut three chops off of the loin and stand up on the plate. Put potatoes next to the pork, pour sauce over the pork and potatoes and put spinach on the plate.

Serves 6.

RASPBERRY VINAIGRETTE

2	cups raspberry jam	½	teaspoon garlic powder
2	cups raspberry vinegar	¼	teaspoon onion powder
¾	cup raspberry liqueur	1	teaspoon thyme
½	cup brown sugar	1	teaspoon salt
2	tablespoons shallots	6	cups salad oil

Combine all ingredients until well emulsified. Mince shallots and add. Stir thoroughly before serving.

Serves 30.

PIRATE'S PASTA

12	ounces scallops, medium sized 21 to 25-count	½	cup cilantro, chopped
12	ounces raw lobster meat, preferably tail meat	½	tablespoon red chili paste or Hunan sauce
12	ounces shrimp 12 to 20-count, peeled and deveined	½	cup Bermuda onions (red), julienne strips
12	ounces smoked chicken, fillet julienne strips ⅛-inch	½	cup red bell pepper, julienne strips
⅛	cup olive oil	½	cup yellow bell pepper, julienne strips
⅛	cup clarified butter	2	cups heavy cream
2	cups Creole tomatoes, finely diced		Salt and pepper to taste
1	tablespoon shallots, minced	4	cups red pepper penne pasta, cooked al dente
1	cup lime juice, freshly squeezed	1	cup freshly grated Parmesan cheese
		1	tablespoon garlic, minced

In a large sauté pan, heat the olive oil to almost smoking. Sear the lobster, scallops and shrimp for 2 minutes, shaking the pan vigorously. Remove seafood and set aside. Add butter, diced tomatoes, shallots, garlic, Bermuda onions and both peppers and sauté for 2 minutes, then add lime juice and cilantro. Add smoked chicken and Hunan sauce and toss. Add seafood, heavy cream and reduce for 3 minutes, add paste and salt and pepper, taste, adjust. Serve and top with freshly grated Parmesan cheese.

Serves 4.

FARRADDAY'S RESTAURANT
ISLE OF CAPRI CASINO CROWN PLAZA RESORT

151 Beach Boulevard Biloxi, MS 39530

Mitch Schenkel
Sous Chef

Chef Schenkel is a native of Niagara Falls, Canada. He became interested in cooking while working at his family's Cavalier Hotel at the age of 13. Mr. Schenkel has worked in food service for the Sheraton Corporation and graduated from the Air Force Culinary School in 1985.

CHOP CHOP SALAD

4	ounces chop chop lettuce mix	1	tablespoon red onion, chopped
1	tablespoon chopped tomatoes	2	leaves Belgian endive
1	tablespoon European cucumber, seeded, peeled and chopped	2	ounces poppy seed burgundy dressing
		2	each grilled garlic croutons Radish shaved, for garnish

Mix the lettuce, tomatoes, cucumbers and red onion together in a bowl and toss with the poppy seed dressing. Place this mixture in a large bowl. Line the bowl with Belgian endive and top the salad with the shaved radish. Add the garlic croutons for a crispy added texture.

Serves 1.

CHICKEN SATAY & DIPPING SAUCES

(Appetizers)

Note: Pre-soak bamboo skewers in water for a minimum of 10 minutes before preparation.

3	pounds chicken breasts, skinless boneless	½	bunch shaved scallions, for garnish
1	pound linguine, raw	2½	ounces sesame seeds, toasted for garnish

MARINADE
(For One Gallon)

1   gallon – combine equal parts of peanut sauce and oriental hot sauce (soy base) (2 quarts of peanut sauce to 2 quarts of Oriental hot sauce)

CUCUMBER DIPPING SAUCE
(For One Gallon)

20	ounces cucumber, skin removed, seeded and diced	1¼	pints orange juice
2½	quarts Oriental hot sauce	6	ounces scallion, chopped

Combine all the cucumber dipping sauce ingredients together.

Peanut Sauce: Serve as is needed.

For the Chicken:

1. Trim the fat and remove the center cartilage from the chicken breast. Lightly pound out the chicken breast with a mallet.

2. Cut the chicken breast into strips 3 to 4 inches long (1.5 ounces each for a total of 30 pieces).

3. Place the chicken in a bowl and coat it with the marinade. Do not submerge, just coat.

4. Remove the skewers from the water and weave the chicken onto the skewers, place them into a hotel pan. Cover with clear wrap and reserve for service.

For the Noodles:

1. Place 2 quarts of water in a saucepan and bring to a boil. Drop the pasta in the boiling water and cook until al dente. Strain through a colander and run cold water over the pasta to cool it down.

2. Place the pasta in a container to hold for service. Lightly coat the pasta with oil so it doesn't stick.

Reserve for service. Pre-portion the pasta in bags at 3 ounces per.

Pre-Preparation: Place the dipping sauces in the ramekins prior to service. Place 2 cups of peanut sauce in a squeeze bottle for service.

Yield: 10 servings

PORTOBELLO MUSHROOM ON FIELD GREENS

20	ounces portobello mushrooms, stem removed, membrane removed, cleaned	1	each red pepper, seeded and cut in julienne strips
5	fluid ounces olive oil, placed in a squeeze bottle	1	pint poppy seed burgundy dressing (place in a squeeze bottle)
½	cup salt and pepper, for seasoning	1	ounce garlic, chopped Cracked black pepper for garnish

For the Mushroom:

Remove the stems from the mushroom. Take a serving spoon and scrape the inside of the mushroom cap to remove the black membrane. Rinse under cold water to clean.

Coat with the olive oil lightly, season with salt and pepper and rub with just a small amount of minced garlic.

Place the mushrooms on the char-broiler to cook. Broil on both sides for approximately 4 to 5 minutes on each side. Remove and cool them down in the cooler.

Pre-slice the mushrooms very thin before service and hold. Cover with clear wrap.

Yield: 10

CAJUN SPICED FETTUCCINI

14	ounces fettuccini, cooked al dente Hot water as needed, to heat the pasta	1	ounce olive oil
2	ounces portobello mushrooms, sliced	2	ounces Alfredo sauce
¼	each green peppers, seeded, chopped	1	ounce whole butter
		2½	tablespoons Cajun spice, to taste, seafood
¼	each red peppers, seeded, chopped	1	teaspoon Parmesan cheese Salt and pepper to taste Chopped parsley, for garnish
1	tablespoon diced tomato		
1	teaspoon garlic, minced	2	each grilled garlic croutons

Dip the pasta into the hot water to heat up. Place a sauté pan on the burner and begin to heat the olive oil to a smoke point. Add the mushrooms, peppers, tomato, garlic and sauté until translucent. Drain the pasta very well and add to the hot vegetables maintaining the heat. Add the Alfredo sauce and heat well. Mount with thebutter, season with the Cajun spice, salt and pepper. Add the Parmesan cheese. Garnish with crouton, cheese and chopped parsley.

Present in large bowl.

Serves 1.

STIR FRIED VEGETABLES WITH NOODLES

12	ounces linguine, cooked al dente Hot water as needed, to heat the pasta	1	ounce peanut oil
		3	ounces noodle sauce blend
5	ounces vegetable blend oil for stir fry	3	ounces vegetable broth, mirepoix base
3	each shiitake mushrooms, stem removed, quartered	3	ounces whole chicken breast, sliced, precooked Scallion, for garnish, shaved fine
1	teaspoon garlic, minced		Toasted sesame seeds, for garnish
½	teaspoon ginger, minced		

Present in large bowl.

Heat the linguine in the hot water. In a sauté pan, heat the peanut oil to the smoke point and sauté the garlic and ginger. Add the stir fry vegetable blend, shiitake mushrooms and the vegetable stock to heat the vegetables. Drain the pasta well from the water and combine with the vegetable mixture. Stir well to incorporate the ingredients, add the cooked chicken and the noodle sauce blend. Heat this and mix it all well. Garnish with scallion and toasted sesame seeds.

Serves 1.

Beauvoir – Jefferson Davis Home
Biloxi, Mississippi

IMPERIAL PALACE HOTEL & CASINO

870 Bayview
Biloxi, MS 39530

David Crabtree
Executive Chef

David Crabtree, CWC, is the Executive Chef for the 7 full service restaurants in the Imperial Palace. Chef Crabtree is an active member of the Gulf Coast chapter of the American Culinary Federation. He has an Associate degree in Applied Science/Culinary Arts from Delgado C.C. in New Orleans, Louisiana.

THE SEAHOUSE

The Seahouse is one of five restaurants that make up the dining plaza at the Imperial Palace. It features the best seafood from the Gulf of Mexico and sister water outlets.

PECAN CRUSTED GULF TROUT WITH CRABMEAT

10	each 5-ounce Gulf trout fillets	2	each limes
1	tablespoon Creole seasonings	⅛	cup minced red and yellow peppers
½	cup honey	¼	cup soft unsalted butter
⅛	cup lime juice		
½	cup all-purpose flour	¼	cup roasted pecans
		½	cup lump crab meat
¼	cup blue corn flour	1	tablespoon minced tarragon
1	cup pecan meal		
½	cup clarified butter		

Season trout with Creole seasoning on each side. Mix together honey and lime juice and set aside. Mix two flours and meal together and set aside. Dust trout with flour mixture and dredge in honey and lime juice. Return to flour a second time. Heat butter in skillet and over medium heat brown trout on both sides until done. Remove trout from pan and set on serving dish. Drain ½ butter from pan and return to heat. Add peppers and roasted pecans – sauté briefly. Add juice from lime and scrape pan bottom. Add crab meat, salt and pepper, tarragon and heat gently. Pour over trout and serve with starch and vegetable.

Serves 10.

THE TEAHOUSE

A casual 24-hour restaurant where you can get breakfast at any time of day or night. The Teahouse also serves other coast favorites and chef's special creations.

MARINATED GRILLED BREAST OF CHICKEN WITH A CURRANT GLAZE

½	cup rosemary oil	10	6-ounce boneless skinless breasts
⅛	cup double black soy sauce	¼	cup bourbon
⅛	cup pineapple juice	⅛	cup brown sugar
1	tablespoon minced ginger	2	tablespoons fresh minced herbs
		1	cup currant jelly

Mix together and pour over 10 6-ounce chicken breasts (allow to marinate).

Serves 10.

Recipe for Currant Glaze on following page.

CURRANT GLAZE

⅛ cup teriyaki sauce
¼ cup brown sugar
1 cup pineapple juice
1 cup strong chicken stock
⅛ cup minced yellow bell pepper
Salt and pepper to taste

¼ cup minced fresh pineapple
3 tablespoons arrowroot slurry
1 cup currant jelly
1 tablespoon minced fresh tarragon

Bring all to a boil and thicken with slurry.

Plating instructions: Grill chicken until done and slice thin on a bias. Fan out around the plate and top with currant glaze.

Serves 10.

SALSA'S MEXICAN RESTAURANT

Featuring Mexican & Southwestern Cuisine

BLACK BEAN CRAB CAKE WITH MOLE SAUCE

¼ cup minced habanero peppers
⅛ cup minced green onions
1 tablespoon minced jalapeño peppers
⅛ cup minced yellow bell peppers
2 cups cooked drained black beans
½ cup mayonnaise

2 each egg yolks
3 cups cooked flaked crab meat
1 tablespoon chili powder
½ teaspoon cumin
Salt and pepper to taste
1 teaspoon lime juice
3 tablespoons fresh cilantro

Mix all ingredients together and form into patties.

Breading procedure as follows:

Seasoned flour
Egg wash

Bread crumbs

Sauté until light brown on both sides. Serve over an underliner of the mole sauce.

MOLE SAUCE

4 cups roasted, peeled and diced habanero peppers
2 tablespoons chili powder
1 tablespoon cumin
Salt and pepper to taste
3 tablespoons cane syrup
2 tablespoons vinegar

1 quart vegetable oil
3 cups pinolas, roasted
2 cups almonds, roasted
2 cups roasted sesame seeds
1 tablespoon lime juice

Blend all ingredients in food processor except oil. Gradually add oil while mixing.

Yield: 12 cakes

*The Lighthouse
Biloxi, Mississippi*

THE MING TERRACE RESTAURANT

Featuring Mandarin & Cantonese Cuisine from the Far East

DUCKLING STIR FRY WITH CHINESE MUSHROOMS & MANDARIN ORANGES

¼ cup sesame oil
1 tablespoon minced ginger
1 cup bok choy, diced
4 cups boneless diced duckling
1 cup julienne red bell peppers
3 cups mandarin orange segments

⅛ cup double black soy sauce
¼ cup reduced strong duck stock
2 cups plum sauce
Salt and pepper to taste
2 cups Oriental mushroom of choice

Heat oil in wok or large sauté pan and add ginger and bok choy (toss briefly).

Add duckling and peppers and cook briefly. Add mushrooms, oranges, soy sauce, stock and plum sauce and simmer 2 minutes.

Serve over fried rice or Oriental noodles.

Yield: 10 portions

MORRELLI'S ITALIAN RESTAURANT

Featuring Italian casual dining from sandwiches to pizza to great pasta favorites.

PASTA CARBONARA WITH SUNDRIED TOMATOES & SHIITAKE MUSHROOMS

2 cups sliced fresh shiitake mushrooms
2 tablespoons whole butter
½ cup sundried tomatoes
½ tablespoon chopped garlic
2 teaspoons fresh chopped basil, oregano

10 portions cooked pasta of choice
¼ cup sherry
2 cups heavy cream
1 cup Romano cheese
½ cup strong chicken stock
1 cup julienne prosciutto ham
Salt and pepper to taste

In sauté pan add butter, mushrooms, ham and tomatoes. Sauté briefly. Add garlic, basil and deglaze pan with sherry. Add stock, heavy cream and bring to a simmer. Add cheese and reduce until it thickens. Fold in pasta and serve.

Yield: 10 portions

EMBERS' STEAK HOUSE

OYSTERS EMBERS

6	each large Gulf oysters	1	teaspoon shallots
1	tablespoon white wine	¼	teaspoon garlic

Sauté oysters gently until oysters' edges begin to curl and place in cleaned oyster shell or casserole dish.

SPINACH & PROSCIUTTO SAUCE

⅛	cup fresh spinach, minced	⅛	teaspoon garlic
1	tablespoon prosciutto ham strips	⅛	cup oyster juice
		¼	cup heavy cream
1	tablespoon sherry	1	teaspoon blond roux

Sauté ham, spinach and garlic briefly. Add sherry, oyster juice and cream. Bring to a simmer and thicken with the blond roux.

HOLLANDAISE SAUCE

2	egg yolks	½	tablespoon lemon juice
½	teaspoon wine		
1	drop hot pepper sauce	¼	cup clarified butter
1	drop Worcestershire sauce		

Place yolks, wine, pepper sauce, Worcestershire sauce and lemon juice in double boiler and whisk until thick. Once thickened, slowly whisk in butter.

Plating method: Place oysters in oyster shells or ramekin and top with cream sauce. Bake briefly and top with Hollandaise. Brown under salamander and serve.

Yield: 1 serving

IMPERIAL PALACE HOTEL & CASINO

870 Bayview
Biloxi, MS 39530

BREAD PUDDING

3	whole eggs	2	cups heavy cream
1½	cups sugar	½	cup raisins
1½	teaspoons vanilla extract	½	cup roasted, chopped pecans
1	teaspoon nutmeg	5	cups stale French bread, cubed
1½	teaspoons ground cinnamon		
¼	cup unsalted butter, melted	2	cups bourbon sauce (see below)

In a mixing bowl, beat the eggs until frothy. Add the sugar, vanilla, nutmeg, cinnamon and butter, beat in the heavy cream and stir in the raisins and pecans. Place the bread cubes in a lightly greased baking pan. Pour over the egg mixture and toss until the bread is soaked. Let sit about 30 minutes, occasionally turning bread to fully soak. Place in a 325 degree preheated oven and bake approximately 45 minutes, until pudding is cooked, puffy and browned.

Serve topped with bourbon sauce.

Yield: 8 servings

BOURBON SAUCE

½	pound butter	¼	cup bourbon whiskey
1	pound brown sugar		
1	cup heavy cream		

Melt butter, add brown sugar, blend well. Add heavy cream, bring to boil. Reduce heat, add whiskey and blend.

Yield: 3 cups

SEAFOOD GUMBO

2	cups onions, medium dice	1	tablespoon garlic, minced
1½	cups green peppers, medium dice	¼	cup vegetable oil
		2	dashes pepper sauce
1¼	cups celery, medium dice	1	tablespoon tomato paste
2	bay leaves	6	cups seafood stock
2	teaspoons salt	1⅔	cups dark roux
½	teaspoon white pepper	1	pound smoked sausage, sliced
½	teaspoon cayenne pepper	1	pound medium shrimp, peeled
½	teaspoon black pepper	1	pound crawfish tail meat with fat
½	teaspoon thyme leaves	½	pound crab meat, picked
¼	teaspoon oregano leaves	3	cups cooked white rice

In a large soup pot on a hot fire, briefly sauté the vegetables in the salad oil. Add all seasonings and cook until well sweated. Add tomato paste and cook briefly.

Add seafood stock and bring to boil. Reduce heat and simmer, skimming top if necessary, for 15 minutes.

Add roux, stir well and cook for 5 minutes.

Add sausage, return to simmer and cook for 15 minutes.

Add shrimp, crawfish and crab meat. Bring to boil, remove from heat.

Fry okra to seal, and add to gumbo.

Serve garnished with rice and chopped green onions.

Yield: 1 gallon

STUFFED CRABS

3	ounces butter	¼	teaspoon seafood seasoning
1	diced onion (each)		
¼	cup diced celery (each)	1	bay leaf (each)
		2	cups shrimp stock
1	diced bell pepper (each)	1	pound claw crab meat
1	teaspoon chopped garlic	2	cups bread crumbs
		10	crab shells (each) or glass baking dish
½	teaspoon basil		
½	teaspoon thyme		

In tilt skillet, melt butter and sauté onions, celery, bell pepper, bay leaves, basil, thyme and garlic. Add shrimp stock and seafood seasoning. Let simmer 15 to 20 minutes. Turn off heat. Add crab meat and bread crumbs. Fold in. Taste for seasoning and salt and pepper to taste. Place on sheet pans and put in cooler. Let cool. Stuff shells. Egg wash and bread crumb and deep fry.

KEPPNER'S GASTHAUS

1798 Beach Boulevard
Biloxi, MS 39531

Norbert Johann Keppner
Host & Owner

Michael Herrmann, Chef

The only authentic German restaurant
in Mississippi

HEISSE BIER SUPPE
(HOT BEER SOUP)

3	12-ounce bottles or cans of light beer	½	teaspoon cinnamon
½	cup sugar	¼	teaspoon salt
4	egg yolks		Fresh ground black pepper to taste
⅓	cup sour cream		

Pour beer and sugar into a heavy 4 to 5 quart saucepan. Bring to a boil over high heat, stirring constantly until the sugar is dissolved, then remove the pan from the heat. In a small bowl, beat the egg yolks with a wire whisk or fork to break them up. Beat in the sour cream a little at a time. Stir about ¼-cup of the last beer into the mixture, and then whisk into the beer. Add the cinnamon, salt and a few grindings of pepper. Return the pan to low heat and cook, stirring constantly until the soup thickens slightly. Do not let it boil or make it curdle. Taste for seasoning and serve at once from a heated tureen or in individual soup bowls.

Serves 6.

KARTOFFELSALAT
(GERMAN POTATO SALAD)

6	medium-sized boiling potatoes	2	tablespoons prepared Dusseldorf mustard
1	cup finely chopped onions	2	teaspoons salt
⅔	cup chicken stock	1	teaspoon ground black pepper
⅓	cup olive oil	1	tablespoon lemon juice
1	tablespoon white vinegar		

Drop the unpeeled potatoes into enough lightly salted boiling water to cover them completely. Boil them briskly until they show only the slightest resistance when pierced with the point of a fork or sharp knife. Be careful not t let them overcook or they will come apart when sliced. Drain the potatoes in a colander, then peel and cut them into ¼-inch slices. Set the potatoes aside in a bowl tightly covered with aluminum foil. In a heavy 2 to 3 quart saucepan, combine the chopped onions, stock, oil, vinegar, prepared mustard, salt and pepper. Bring to a boil over high heat, stirring occasionally. Remove the pan from the heat and stir in the lemon juice. Pour the sauce over the potato slices and serve.

Serves 7 to 8.

BEEFSTEAK TARTARE

½	pound lean boneless beef, preferably beef tenderloin	2	tablespoons capers
		2	tablespoons finely chopped onions
2	egg yolks	2	tablespoons fresh parsley
2	tablespoons salt	8	flat anchovy fillets
2	tablespoons fresh ground pepper		Dark bread
			Butter

Shape the beef into two patties and place them in the center of one serving plate. Make a well in the middle of the wounds and carefully drop an egg yolk in each. Serve the salt, black pepper, capers, chopped onions, parsley, anchovy fillets in small separate saucers.

Serve beefsteak tartare with dark bread and butter.

Serves 1.

CINNAMON PARFAIT

6	egg yolks	2	cups heavy cream
3	full eggs	2	teaspoons cinnamon
7½	ounces sugar		

Put the 6 egg yolks, the 3 full eggs and the sugar together in a bowl. Place the mixture over a water bath on the stove and stir it fast until it is hot and smooth. Stir it for 8 to 10 minutes. Add the heavy cream and cinnamon and stir it all carefully. Fill up small aluminum forms and put in the freezer for 10 hours.

Serves 7 to 8.

MARY MAHONEY'S CRABMEAT AU GRATIN

5	tablespoons butter	1	tablespoon Worcestershire sauce
3	tablespoons flour		
1	cup milk	1	teaspoon salt
1	cup chicken bouillon	¼	teaspoon black pepper
1	egg, well beaten	1	cup grated cheddar cheese
2	tablespoons sherry Dash pepper sauce	1	pound <u>lump</u> white crab meat

Make a white sauce of butter, flour, milk, bouillon and egg. Remove from heat, add wine, salt, pepper, pepper sauce and Worcestershire sauce. Add crab meat to white sauce and put in 1½-quart casserole or six individual ramekins. Sprinkle with cheese and bake at 350 degrees for 20 minutes or until bubbly brown.

Serves 6.

BREAD PUDDING

6	slices day old bread	2	tablespoons melted
2	tablespoons plus		butter
	½ cup sugar	½	cup seedless raisins
1	teaspoon cinnamon	1	teaspoon vanilla
4	eggs		extract
2	cups milk		

Break bread in small pieces in baking dish (about 1½ quart size).

Sprinkle cinnamon over bread and add raisins and melted butter.

Toast lightly bread mixture in oven about 350 degrees. Then add mixture of eggs, sugar, milk and vanilla extract, after mixing well. Bake about 30 minutes or until solid.

Serves about 8.

RUM SAUCE

2	cups milk	1	tablespoon vanilla
½	stick butter		extract
½	cup sugar		Rum to taste
1	tablespoon nutmeg		

Place milk, butter and sugar in saucepan. Let come to a boil, thicken with a roux made of 2 tablespoons flour and 1 tablespoon oil. Remove from fire, add nutmeg, vanilla and rum to taste. Serve over pudding.

SHRIMP ITALIENNE SALAD

(for 10)

8	eggs	2	cups vinegar (or to
1	stick celery		your taste)
1	small bunch green	1½	cups salad oil
	onions	½	cup Italian
1	46-ounce can		seasoning
	tomato juice	1	cup garlic purée
			(or to your taste)

Finely chop eggs, celery and onions. Add 2 pounds of very small shrimp (peeled). Mix all ingredients together.

OLD FRENCH HOUSE RESTAURANT SHRIMP DOLORES

STUFFING

1. Chop and sauté in 2 tablespoons oil or shortening: 1 large onion, 4 blades celery and 4 buttons garlic. Stir until slightly browned over low heat.
2. Soak ½ loaf stale bread in small amount of water. Squeeze out most of water. Squeeze out most of water and add bread to onion mix.
3. Add 1 pound crab meat, stirring in well (still over low heat).
4. Add small amount of chopped pimiento and salt and pepper to taste.
5. Break one raw egg over mixture and stir in.
6. Add Worcestershire sauce (2 tablespoons) and poultry seasoning (2 tablespoons).
7. Stir well and remove from heat.

STUFFING SHRIMP

1. Clean large (jumbo) raw shrimp, leaving tail section (about 30). Slit down center back almost through.
2. Prepare baking pan: Make base of 2 tablespoons melted butter and 2 tablespoons water.
3. Carefully place rounded portion of stuffing in slit.
4. Place shrimp, stuffing side up and close together in baking pan.
5. Bake in moderate oven about 15 to 20 minutes.

SAUCE

1. Mix into saucepan: 1 stick butter, juice of ½ lemon, 3 tablespoons Worcestershire sauce and ⅓ cup cooking sherry.
2. Simmer over very low heat, after butter melts, for about 8 minutes.
3. Pour over baked shrimp and serve.

Serves 6.

C. F. GOLLOTT & SON SEAFOOD, INC.

9357 Central Avenue
D'Iberville, MS 39532

GOLLOTT'S CAJUN BOILED SHRIMP

(These are for beer drinkers)

5	pounds Gollott's shrimp (in shell)	5	tablespoons salt
2	tablespoons liquid shrimp or crab boil	1	can beer (optional)
			Juice of 1 lemon
2	tablespoons ground red pepper (cayenne)	1	small onion
		1	tablespoon garlic powder

Bring all seasoning, except salt, to hard boil in enough water to cover shrimp in shell. Drop in shrimp. When shrimp come to a hard boil, add salt, stir well. Hard boil one minute. Turn off heat, cover pit and let stand 8 minutes. Drain shrimp. Serve hot or cold.

ARNY GOLLOTT'S QUICK & EASY ÉTOUFÉE

1	pound Gollott's gumbo peeled shrimp or crawfish meat	1	Cajun étoufée mix
		2	cups water
		5	tablespoons butter

Melt 5 tablespoons butter in saucepan, stir until light brown. Add étoufée mix, stir over low heat until mix has a medium brown color. Add 2 cups water and 1 pound boiled and peeled crawfish tails or 1 pound raw peeled shrimp. Cover and bring to a boil, stirring often. After mixture comes to a boil, reduce heat to low and cook 15 minutes. After 15 minutes of cooking, cover, turn heat off and let stand 15 minutes. Serve over hot cooked rice and enjoy.

SEAFOOD GUMBO – GOLLOTT STYLE

2	pounds Gollott's peeled shrimp		Cayenne pepper (optional)
1	pound Gollott's crab meat and/or dressed crabs	2	large onions (chopped)
2	heaping tablespoons bacon fat	2	tablespoons oil
		2	tablespoons all-purpose flour
1	can tomatoes	3	cups okra (cut in small pieces)
2	quarts water (boiling slow)	1	large sweet pepper (chopped)
3	pods garlic, cut (optional)		Salt to taste

Make a roux by heating 2 tablespoons of oil till hot, add flour and stir till dark brown. Take one cup of water (from the boiling 2 quarts of water), and add to flour mixture. When well blended, add back to boiling water. Heat 2 heaping tablespoons bacon fat, fry cut okra in fat till slime is removed. Add onions and sweet pepper to okra and cook until tender. Smash tomatoes and add tomatoes and garlic to okra, onion, pepper mixture. Fry about 5 minutes, add mixture to roux and water. Peel and wash shrimp. Pick through crab meat for any remaining shell. Add seafood to other ingredients. Salt and pepper to taste. Simmer gumbo for 1½ hours. Serve hot over cooked rice.

Shrimp Boats

GOLLOTT'S SHRIMP SALAD

6	tablespoons mayonnaise	5	diced hard-boiled eggs (set aside 1 egg for garnishment)
3	stalks celery (diced)		Salt and pepper to taste
5	pounds Gollott's small peeled shrimp (fresh or frozen)		Parsley for garnishment

Completely thaw shrimp. Place enough water in pan to cover shrimp. Bring water to a boil, add shrimp, bring to a boil, add 4 tablespoons salt. Cook shrimp in a rolling boil for 1 minute. Drain shrimp and spread out to cool to room temperature. Combine all ingredients and season to taste. Place on cracker and garnish with parsley and remaining egg.

BOILED SHRIMP & POTATOES

(Medium Seasoning)

5	pounds Gollott's shrimp (in shell)	5	tablespoons salt
1½	tablespoons liquid crab and shrimp boil	3	pounds potatoes (medium-size)
1	tablespoon garlic powder	1	small onion
		1	tablespoon red pepper (cayenne)
			Juice of 1 lemon

Bring crab boil, pepper, lemon juice, onion and garlic powder to hard boil in enough water to cover potatoes and shrimp. Drop in potatoes. Boil until not quite cooked. (Potatoes can be pierced with a fork and the center should be a little hard.) When potatoes reach this stage, drop in shrimp in shell. When shrimp and potatoes come back to a boil, add salt. Hard boil one minute. Turn off heat, cover pot and soak 8 to 10 minutes. Drain shrimp and potatoes. Serve hot or cold.

EASY MARINATED CRAB CLAWS

Splash with Italian dressing and salt, marinate at least 2 hours.

CRABMEAT STUFFING

(For Crab Burger, Stuffed Shrimp, Sweet Peppers, Stuffed Flounder or Stuffed Lobster))

1	pound Gollott's crab meat (white or claw)	1	egg
⅓	cup chopped celery	⅓	cup chopped parsley
⅓	cup chopped green pepper	⅓	cup melted butter or oil
1	cup chopped onion	1	loaf stale French bread
1	large pod garlic		

Grate stale French bread and soften with just enough ice water to make it stick together. Drain crab meat, remove any remaining shell. Sauté onion, celery, green pepper and garlic in fat until tender. Combine bread crumbs, egg, parsley, salt and pepper and add to cooked vegetables. Add crab meat to mixture and mix thoroughly.

GOLLOTT'S BRAND SHRIMP TEMPURA

2	small eggs (or 1 large)	2	teaspoons baking powder
1	cup milk	1	teaspoon sugar
1⅛	cups all-purpose flour	½	teaspoon paprika Oil
3	pounds Gollott brand peeled shrimp		

Beat eggs in small mixing bowl, stir in milk. Add flour, salt, sugar and paprika. Beat until well blended. Add baking powder and mix well. Dip shrimp in batter and fry in hot oil until golden brown, turning once.

Editor's Note: If the Gollott brand is not available in your area, any peeled and deveined shrimp will do.

GOLLOTT'S AU GRATIN

1	pound Gollott's crab meat	4	tablespoons butter
2	slices American cheese	4	tablespoons all-purpose flour
2	cups grated cheddar cheese	1	tablespoon salt
		2	cups milk

Melt butter over low heat, add flour and salt, stir until well blended. Remove from heat, gradually stir in milk and return to heat, cook, stirring constantly until thick and smooth. Pour over crab meat in a casserole dish. Top with grated cheddar cheese. Bake in 450 degree oven until cheese is melted.

Serves 4 to 6.

GOLLOTT'S SEAFOOD HINTS

* *To Freeze Shrimp – Freeze raw shrimp, head off, shell on, in rigid container. Cover shrimp completely in ice water, so that they freeze in a solid block of ice.*

* *To Remove Head of Shrimp – Hold shrimp at first joint behind head with thumb and index finger and squeeze.*

* *To Peel Shrimp (raw or cooked) – Start at legs under shrimp and peel shell around.*

* *To Devein Shrimp – Using sharp knife, cut the headed and peeled shrimp on top side, gently slide straight down back, wash out vein.*

* *To "Fantail" Shrimp – When peeling shrimp, leave last section of shell and tail intact.*

* *To "Butterfly" Shrimp – When deveining shrimp, cut almost through top side to beginning of last section of shrimp. This opens and flattens shrimp, giving a "butterfly" effect.*

* *Crab meat, in order to be picked from the shell, has to be cooked. This product can be eaten right from its container.*

* *Crab meat contains enough water to be frozen in its natural state. It should be drained and picked through for any remaining shell after thawing. Crab meat can be frozen in its own container as long as it is not glass and, of course, airtight.*

OYSTER, ASPARAGUS & CHAMPAGNE SOUP

3	pounds fresh asparagus	⅛	teaspoon salt
1	quart chicken stock	⅛	teaspoon white pepper
8	ounces diced onions	¼	teaspoon hot pepper sauce
½	ounce garlic	¼	teaspoon Worcestershire sauce
1	quart oyster liquor		
8	ounces champagne		
½	gallon oysters	4	ounces roux

Trim asparagus (saving the tips). Combine chicken stock, oyster liquor, asparagus bottoms, onions and garlic. Bring to a boil and simmer for 30 minutes or until asparagus is tender. Strain out the asparagus, onions and garlic, reserving liquid. Purée the asparagus, onions and garlic, then add it back into the liquid. Bring to a simmer, add champagne and simmer for 30 minutes. Strain the soup through a china cap and discard the pulp. Bring the soup back to a simmer, thicken with blonde roux. Once roux has cooked out, add oysters and asparagus tips, season with salt, white pepper, pepper sauce and Worcestershire sauce.

Serves 10.

RABBIT TENDERLOIN WITH APRICOT & PECAN STUFFED FIGS

3	cups fine chopped pecans	2	teaspoons salt and pepper
5	cups flour	10	each rabbit tenderloins
6	cups eggs		
½	gallon milk		

Combine 3 cups flour with 3 cups pecans. Combine milk and eggs to make egg wash. Season tenderloins with salt and pepper mix. Dredge through flour, dip into egg wash and dredge through pecan breading.

SAUCE

1	ounce clarified butter	2	tablespoons Creole mustard
5	fresh smoked jalapeños	2	ounces bourbon
1	cup pecans	½	cup heavy cream
2	tablespoons Worcestershire sauce	½	cup demi-glaze
		2	tablespoons whole butter

In clarified butter, sauté jalapeños and pecans. Deglaze with bourbon and add Worcestershire sauce, demi-glaze, heavy cream and Creole mustard. Reduce until it starts to thicken and mount with whole butter.

FRESH FIGS WITH APRICOT & PECAN CHUTNEY

3	tablespoons pecan pieces	2	teaspoons dry sherry
¾	cup chopped dried apricots	2	teaspoons orange zest
2	teaspoons cider vinegar	10	large fresh figs
5	tablespoons apple juice		

Toast pecans 10 to 12 minutes and allow to cool. Soak apricots in cider vinegar, apple juice and sherry until soft. Add pecans and orange zest. Sauté mixture over medium heat for 10 minutes.

Serves 10.

CASINO MAGIC
195 Beach Boulevard
Biloxi, MS 39530

Joseph St. Paul
Chef d'Cuisine

SEARED SCALLOPS WITH MANGO ROASTED RED PEPPER RELISH

| 16 | each scallops |

For Salsa (relish)

1	fresh mango	⅛	teaspoon chili powder
2	red peppers (roasted, peeled and diced)	4	tablespoons red onion, finely diced
1	teaspoon chopped cilantro		Salt and pepper to taste
4	drops pure vanilla extract	3	tablespoons fresh lime juice
⅛	teaspoon cumin		

Heat a heavy pan (cast iron). Use a few drops of oil in pan. Season scallops with salt and pepper. Sear scallops until edges brown. Transfer scallops to a warm oven and heat thoroughly.

For Salsa: Combine all in a stainless bowl and allow to sit for 2 hours to allow flavors to mix. Serve with scallops.

Serves 4.

CRAWFISH BISQUE

1	pound crawfish tails	1	tablespoon dry tarragon
3	ounces shallots, minced	4	bay leaves
2	ounces garlic, minced	1½	quarts seafood stock
½	cup brandy	½	quart heavy cream
1	ounce tomato paste		Roux
			Salt and pepper to taste

Sweat tails, shallots and garlic until soft. Add tomato paste and mix. Cook for 2 to 3 minutes. Add brandy and cook off alcohol (about 4 minutes). Add tarragon, bay leaves and stock. Simmer for 1 hour. Incorporate roux and allow to cook for 30 minutes. Add cream and season with salt and pepper.

Yield: 2 quarts

MIXED SUMMER LETTUCES WITH ORANGE & GRAPEFRUIT SEGMENTS WITH RASPBERRY VINAIGRETTE

	Lettuce mix	1	teaspoon Dijon mustard
24	orange segments		
24	grapefruit segments	3	tablespoons cider vinegar
1	cup raspberries, frozen	1	cup canola oil
¼	cup brown sugar		Salt and pepper to taste
1	teaspoon shallot, minced	2	tablespoons honey

Wash lettuce and set aside. Segment oranges and grapefruit and set aside.

For Vinaigrette: Place raspberries and sugar in sauce pot and cook to a syrup. Strain and cool. Combine raspberry syrup, shallot, mustard, vinegar and honey in a mixing bowl. Slowly add oil to form an emulsion. Season with salt and pepper.

Assembly: Arrange lettuce on plate. Randomly place orange and grapefruit segments over greens. Drizzle dressing over salad.

Serves 4.

ROASTED FILET OF BEEF STUFFED WITH ROASTED GARLIC & ANCHO CHILI/GRILLED CORN SAUCE

FILET

4	beef filets (10-ounces each)		Salt, coarse ground black pepper
24	cloves roasted garlic		Oil as needed

Method: Make a small hole in the side of each filet. Stuff with 6 cloves of garlic in each filet. Season with salt and pepper. Set aside in refrigerator.

To Cook: Sear top and bottom in hot pan. Transfer to hot oven to finish.

SAUCE

2	tablespoons garlic, minced	½	ounce ancho chilies, toasted in dry sauté pan (chopped fine)
4	ounces yellow onions, minced		
¼	cup cooking oil	3	cups fresh corn
1	cup bourbon	2	cups veal stock, reduced to a glaze
1	tablespoon Worcestershire sauce		Salt and black pepper to taste
¼	teaspoon cumin		

Method: Place corn on grill (or in oven) and cook for 10 to 15 minutes or until kernels are soft (remember to leave corn in husk). Cool and cut corn off cob and set aside for garnish. Scrape corn cobs with back of a knife and save pulp for sauce.

For Sauce: Sweat onions and garlic in oil until soft. Add ancho chilies and mix. Add bourbon and Worcestershire sauce. Simmer for 20 to 30 minutes. Season with salt, pepper and cumin. Strain through cheesecloth and hold warm. Stir in cut corn to finished sauce.

Serves 4.

GERMAINE'S FINE DINING

On Highway 90
1203 Bienville Boulevard
Ocean Springs, MS 39564

Jack & Jane Gottsche, Owners

THOUSAND ISLAND DRESSING

1	quart mayonnaise	½	cup parsley, chopped
4	cups ketchup		
1	cup onions, minced	1	cup pimiento, chopped
4	cups celery, minced	1	cup hard boiled eggs, mashed
1	cup bell pepper, chopped	1½	cups sweet pickle relish

Blend together all ingredients, put into sterile jars and refrigerate.

Yield 1½ gallons (1 ounce per serving)

CRABMEAT MORNAY

¾	stick butter	½	pound grated Swiss cheese
1	small bunch green onions, sliced	1	tablespoon sherry
½	cup finely chopped fresh parsley or ¼ cup dried parsley	½	teaspoon red pepper, or more to taste
3	tablespoons flour	½	teaspoon salt
2	cups heavy cream	1	pound crab meat

Melt butter and sauté onions and parsley. Blend in flour and cook several minutes. Add cream and cheese, cook until melted. Add seasonings, adjust to taste. Gently fold in crab meat. Serve warm with toasted French bread rounds.

Yield: 6 cups

SHRIMP CREOLE

CREOLE SAUCE (TOMATO SAUCE)

1	cup oil	1	tablespoon seafood base (optional)
1	cup flour		
4	cups diced celery	1	No. 10 can tomatoes and juice
2	green peppers, chopped	4	teaspoons thyme
4	large onions, chopped	10	bay leaves
12	cloves garlic, chopped	1	tablespoon salt
3	12-ounce cans tomato paste	2	tablespoons Worcestershire sauce
10	cups water, heated	4	teaspoons Creole seasoning

Yield: 2 gallons

40 to 50-count peeled shrimp, boiled and seasoned (normal serving – 8 shrimp per person)
Rice

Make roux of oil and flour and cook until peanut butter colored. Add celery and cook 15 minutes or until partially cooked. Add onions, peppers and garlic; cook till transparent (about 10 minutes), stirring frequently. Add tomato paste, then mix seafood base with the heated water and blend slowly into the vegetable mixture. Add tomatoes and their juice. Add seasonings and blend well. Cook, stirring occasionally to prevent scorching for one hour.

To serve: Add tomato sauce to boiled shrimp, and heat. Serve over rice.

TROUT BERNICE

SAUCE

¾ cup butter or margarine
1 13.75-ounce can quartered artichokes
¼ cup green onions
¼ cup wine (Germaine's uses Chardonnay)
2 teaspoons fresh basil (1 teaspoon dried)
¼ teaspoon Italian Blend whole peppercorns, ground (regular pepper may be used or a variation using ⅛ teaspoon cayenne pepper or mild, medium or hot pepper sauces)
¼ teaspoon salt
¾ cup fresh whipping cream

Melt butter in sauté pan. Cut artichoke hearts and sauté in the butter. Add sliced green onions, then sauté several more minutes. Add chopped basil and parsley, ground peppercorns (or above substitute), salt and the wine. Cook on a low temperature to reduce some liquid. Remove from heat.

The Fish: Poach the trout or substitute such as red snapper in a small amount of olive oil, wine and water. Cover the bottom of the pan with the oil, water and wine to keep the fish from sticking. Squeeze a small amount of lemon juice on the fish. Incorporate the whipping cream slowly into the butter and artichoke sauce. Heat on slow for several minutes until very hot. Pour sauce over the trout filet that has been carefully moved from the pan to a serving plate. We add some fresh ground Parmesan cheese to put a little extra Italian touch and garnish with basil. This dish can be served with fresh angel hair pasta and fresh steamed asparagus. It's also good with a broiled tomato.

VEAL ANGELA

SAUCE

2 tablespoons butter
1½ tablespoons flour
½ cup milk
⅓ cup water
⅓ teaspoon Creole mustard
1½ teaspoon dry port
¼ (scant) teaspoon salt
Dash white pepper
4 ounces lump crab meat (add later)

Melt butter in saucepan and add flour and cook 3 to 4 minutes. Warm milk and water in another saucepan. Slowly incorporate the milk mixture into the butter-flour blend. Cook over low heat adding the additional ingredients. Remove from heat when sauce thickens.

12 ounces veal (allow 2 to 3 ounces per person)

Melt 3 tablespoons butter in a sauté pan. Bring to high temperature and brown butter slightly. Quickly sauté the veal slices in the brown butter. Remove to warm plate. Add 4 ounces of lump crab meat to the sauce, heat until very warm. Place several spoonfuls of sauce onto the veal. Cover with freshly grated Parmesan cheese, then run under the broiler for several minutes until slightly brown. Sprinkle with chopped parsley. Serve with potato or pasta and green vegetable if desired.

Germaine's Veal Angela will serve 3 to 4 people.

GERMAINE'S RUM CREAM PIE

5 egg yolks
1 envelope unflavored gelatin
½ cup dark rum
¾ cup sugar
½ cup cold water
½ pint whipping cream

Fill one 10-inch pie plate with graham cracker crust and freeze. Do not bake. Beat egg yolks, add sugar gradually until creamy. Dissolve gelatin in cold water and bring to a boil. In a steady stream, pour slowly into egg-sugar mixture. Add rum. Chill until mixture mounds on spoon. Beat whipping cream, add chilled mixture and blend well. Pour into frozen pie shell and freeze at least 6 hours or until ready to serve. Top with shaved chocolate pieces.

Yield: 1 pie

ANTHONY'S UNDER THE OAKS

1217 Washington Avenue
Ocean Springs, MS 39564

Ronny Hamilton
General Manager
Hobson Cherry, Chef

1986 graduate of the Johnson & Wales Culinary School in Providence, Rhode Island

RASPBERRY VINAIGRETTE

1	cup raspberry vinegar	1	teaspoon salt
¼	cup dry white wine	1	shallot (minced)
1	teaspoon coarse black pepper	1	tablespoon fresh basil leaves, minced

Blend in bowl. Cover and refrigerate for 1 hour.

PEANUT BUTTER PIE

1	10-inch baked pie shell	8	ounces cream cheese, softened
1	cup peanut butter	1	pint whipping cream
1	cup sugar	1	teaspoon vanilla

Combine peanut butter, sugar and cream cheese. Whip whipping cream and vanilla until it forms stiff peaks. Take the two mixes and beat together for 5 to 8 minutes until light and fluffy. Pour into pie shell. Refrigerate at least 3 to 4 hours. Sprinkle with chocolate.

Yield: 1 pie

JOCELYN'S

Highway 90 East
Ocean Springs, MS 39564

Jocelyn Mayfield
Executive Chef/Owner

CORN CRAB SOUP

3	cups chicken stock	2	tablespoons cornstarch
½	stick butter	1	cup evaporated milk
	Small chopped onion	1	pound white crab meat
1	tablespoon chopped parsley		Salt and pepper to taste
1	16-ounce can kernel corn		
1	16-ounce can cream-style corn		

Sauté onion in butter. Add chicken stock. Reserve enough stock to blend into cornstarch. Add to hot broth and stir vigorously. When thickened, add both cans of corn and evaporated milk. Simmer over low heat. Add crab meat just before serving and sprinkle with chopped parsley.

Serves 8.

FROZEN FRUIT SALAD

1½	cups sour cream	1	20-ounce can pineapple, crushed
½	cup powdered sugar	1	can white grapes
	Pinch of salt	1	can apricots
2	tablespoons lemon juice	1	envelope plain gelatin
½	cup maraschino cherries, sliced	8	ounces whipped topping

Drain all fruits. Use one cup of juice from can of pineapples and apricots (½ cup from each). Use juice to dissolve gelatin. Mix all ingredients thoroughly. Pour mix into a pan sprayed with non-stick spray. Freeze.

Serves 16.

CRISPY CHICKEN CASSEROLE

2	cups cut, cooked chicken	1	tablespoon lemon juice
1	10-ounce can cream of mushroom soup	¼	cup chopped onion, lightly cooked
¾	cup mayonnaise	½	pound sliced mushrooms
1	cup diced celery, lightly cooked	½	cup sliced almonds, toasted
1	cup cooked long grain rice (cooked in chicken broth)		Buttery round snack crackers

Combine all ingredients. Pour into greased casserole dish. Melt ½ cup butter and crush one cup of crackers. Mix together and sprinkle on top of casserole. Bake for 30 minutes at 350 degrees.

Serves 6.

GLAZED CORNISH HENS

8	Cornish hens	½	cup bourbon
2	boxes long grain and wild rice	1	chicken bouillon cube
1	cup butter	8	tablespoons currant jelly
½	cup slivered almonds	1	pound sliced fresh mushrooms
1	teaspoon black pepper	2½	teaspoons salt

Prepare rice by sautéing in ½ cup butter along with almonds. Stir constantly. When brown, add package seasoning and follow cooking instructions on box. When done, add sliced mushrooms.

Prepare hens by seasoning with salt and pepper. Stuff cavity with rice dressing. Tie legs together with cooking string so that dressing is secure. Place hens in shallow baking pans. Use remaining butter (melted) with bourbon and chicken bouillon. Mix to baste hens. Bake about 1 hour at 425 degrees. Baste hens 3 or 4 times during baking process. Melt jelly and pour over hens during the last 20 minutes of baking.

Serves 8.

ASPARAGUS CASSEROLE

1	cup buttery round snack crackers	½	cup butter
2	14-ounce cans cut asparagus	1	egg, beaten
1	cup sharp grated cheese	½	cup milk
			Salt and pepper

Line casserole dish with layer of crushed crackers. Add asparagus and cheese. Mix egg, milk and melted butter with salt and pepper. Pour half the mixture over asparagus and use remaining crackers for top layer. Pour remaining sauce over top layer. Bake 1 hour at 350 degrees.

Serves 6.

CARROT RING SOUFFLÉ

1	dozen medium carrots, cooked and mashed	½	cup chopped onion
		2	eggs, beaten
1	tablespoon prepared horseradish	½	cup mayonnaise
		1	tablespoon Dijon mustard
			Salt and pepper

Lightly oil a ring mold. Place mold in pan of hot water. Mix all ingredients together. Pour into mold. Bake for 45 minutes at 350 degrees. When ready to serve, remove from mold and place on platter. Have prepared frozen green peas with sautéed mushrooms and tiny boiled onions, season with salt, pepper and butter. Fill center of mold with these vegetables. Serve immediately.

Serves 8.

FUDGY PECAN PIE

1	deep 9-inch unbaked pie shell	3	teaspoons vanilla
⅓	cup butter	1	cup light corn syrup
⅔	cup sugar	¼	teaspoon salt
⅓	cup cocoa	1½	cups chopped pecans
3	eggs		

In bowl, beat eggs. Add sugar, salt, cocoa, vanilla and melted butter. Mix well. Add syrup and beat. Add pecans. Pour into pastry shell. Bake 50 minutes at 375 degrees. Serve with whipped cream or whipped topping.

Yield: 1 pie

THE PORTER HOUSE

604 Porter Avenue
Ocean Springs, MS 39564

"Classical Cuisine, Sensational Service, Southern Charm"

Jake & Janet Jacobs
Owners

Relax in a century-old home setting. Rustic front and back porches perfect for cocktails, choose from our select wine list and full bar service. Peruse our menu filled with a variety of specialty recipes paired with classical French sauces. We feature wood burning grills & smokers with a focus on Southwestern, Creole and authentic Southern cooking. An exciting menu to meet all needs.

ROASTED POBLANO PEPPER SOUP

8	poblano peppers	½	gallon unsalted chicken stock
2	medium carrots (peeled)	3	cups Parmesan cheese
3	medium potatoes (peeled)	1	quart heavy cream
2	medium onions		

Roast peppers over burner or grilled until completely black. Place in paper bag and seal for 30 minutes. Wash peppers under running water removing skin and all seeds. Place peppers and remaining cleaned and chopped veggies in chicken stock and boil until tender. Purée mixture. Add cheese and cream. Salt and pepper to taste. Garnish with croutons and grated Parmesan.

Serves 10 to 15 people.

CULINARY TERMS FREQUENTLY USED BY MISSISSIPPI CHEFS

Aioli ~ A garlic mayonnaise from France usually served with seafood.

Ancho ~ A fairly mild red chili pepper.

Andouille (Fr) ~ A popular sausage served with red beans and rice.

Anise ~ An herb that tastes like licorice. It is often used in pastries, cheeses, etc.

Antipasto ~ An antipasto is an appetizer that is generally served before pasta.

Appareil (Fr) ~ A mixture of ingredients already prepared for use in a recipe.

Arborio rice ~ An Italian medium-grain rice that is used frequently for risotto.

Arugula ~ A leafy salad herb that has an aromatic peppery flavor.

Bain-marie ~ (Water bath) consists of a bowl placed over a bowl of boiling hot water to gently cook the sauce, etc. without over-cooking.

Balsamic vinegar ~ Balsamic vinegar is a very fine aged vinegar made in Modena, Italy. It is expensive but is the favorite vinegar of most Mississippi chefs because of its sweet, mellow flavor.

Basil ~ An aromatic herb widely used in Mediterranean cooking. It is used in pesto sauce, salads and cooking fish.

Basmati rice ~ A long-grain rice with a nutty flavor.

Bay ~ Dried bay leaves are used frequently in poultry, fish and meat dishes as well as stocks and soups.

Béarnaise ~ One of the classic French sauces. It is made with emulsified egg yolks, butter, fresh herbs and shallots. It is often served with poultry, grilled fish and meat.

Béchamel ~ It is also one of the basic French sauces. It is a sauce made from white roux, milk or cream, onions and seasonings.

Beignet ~ A French word for batter dipped fried fritters, usually sweet like a doughnut.

Beurre blanc ~ It is a white butter sauce made from shallots, white wine vinegar and white wine that has been reduced and thickened with heavy cream and unsalted butter. Salt and ground white pepper to taste.

Beurre manié ~ A paste of flour and butter used to thicken sauces.

Bisque ~ A thick seafood soup usually made from oysters, shrimp or lobster and thickened with cream.

Blanch ~ The purpose is to loosen the skin on a fruit or vegetable by placing it in hot water for a few minutes and then into cold water to stop the cooking process.

Braise ~ The slow cooking of food in a tight container with a flavoring liquid equal to about half the amount of the main ingredient.

Brie ~ A soft cows' milk cheese made in the French region of Brie.

Brûlé ~ A French word for "burnt" and refers to a caramelized coating of sugar, such as a topping for crème brûlée.

Cannelloni ~ Italian pasta tubes filled with ricotta cheese, chocolate, etc.

Caper ~ The pickled bud of a flowering caper plant. It is found on the Mediterranean coast. Capers are often used as a condiment in salads, used in making tartare sauce and as a seasoning in broiling fish.

Capon ~ A castrated male chicken.

Caramel ~ Sugar "caramelizes" when dissolved in water and boiled to a golden brown color.

CULINARY TERMS FREQUENTLY USED BY MISSISSIPPI CHEFS

Cardamom ~ A member of the ginger family. It has a spicy flavor and is used in Indian and Middle Eastern dishes.

Cayenne pepper ~ Red chili pepper that is dried and ground fine for home use.

Chaurice ~ A highly spiced sausage used in Cajun cooking.

Chervil ~ An herb belonging to the parsley family. It is best used fresh because of its delicate flavor.

Chiffonade ~ Leafy vegetables such as spinach and lettuce cut into thin strips.

Chipotle ~ A brownish-red chili pepper that has been dried and smoked and sometimes canned. This chili pepper has a smoky flavor and is very hot.

Chive ~ A member of the onion family used in flavoring foods.

Chutney ~ A sweet and/or sour seasoning that can be made from fruits and vegetables and flavored with many kinds of spices.

Cilantro ~ A fresh coriander leaf.

Clarified butter ~ Butter that has been heated to remove the impurities.

Clarify ~ To remove all impurities.

Condiment ~ Any seasoning, spice, sauce, relish, etc. used to enhance food at the table.

Consommé ~ A clear strained stock, usually clarified, made from poultry, fish, meat or game and flavored with vegetables.

Coriander ~ A member of the carrot family. Fresh coriander is also called cilantro. This herb is prized for its dried seeds and fresh leaves and is used in similar ways to parsley.

Coulis ~ A thick sauce or purée made from cooked vegetables, fruits, etc.

Couscous ~ Traditional couscous is generally made from coarsely ground semolina, a wheat flour used for pasta. It is popular in the Mediterranean areas of Morocco and Algeria. It is often served over vegetables or meats along with sauces.

Crème Brûlée ~ A custard made from eggs and covered with a "burnt" layer of sugar which has caramelized in the oven.

Crème fraîche ~ It is often made from unpasteurized cream with an additive such as yogurt which gives it a distinctive flavor.

Crevette ~ It is a French word for shrimp.

Cumin ~ A spice from the seeds of the cumin plant. It is often used in making pickles, chutneys and especially in curries.

Currant ~ A delicious fruit used to make jams and jellies. It is also used as a glaze for meats. The red variety is widely used.

Curry ~ A mixture of spices widely used in preparing and cooking meats and vegetables. It is often used in Indian cooking.

Daikon ~ A large radish.

Deglacer ~ A process of dissolving cooking juices left in a pan where meats or poultry have been cooked. This is achieved by adding liquids such as stock or wines to the sediment and then reducing it to half the volume. The sauce is then strained and seasoned.

Demi-glace ~ A brown sauce boiled and reduced by half.

Dente, al ~ Vegetables cooked until they are firm and crunchy.

Dijon mustard ~ Mustard made from a white wine base.

CULINARY TERMS FREQUENTLY USED BY MISSISSIPPI CHEFS

Dill ~ An herb used with vinegar to pickle cucumbers. It is also used to flavor foods.

Dredge ~ To coat food with a dry ingredient such as breadcrumbs, cornmeal or flour.

Dungeness crab ~ A large rock crab found in the Pacific Northwest.

Fagioli ~ The Italian word for beans.

Farfalle ~ "Butterfly"-shaped pasta.

Fennel ~ A vegetable bulb or herb with a spicy flavor. It is often used in soups and salads.

Feta cheese ~ A soft and crumbly goat's milk cheese often used in salads and Greek dishes.

Filé powder ~ Sassafras leaves that have been dried and used in the final stages to thicken gumbo. Okra can also be used to thicken gumbo instead of filé powder.

Filo (phyllo) A very thin dough that contains little fat and is used for strudel, baklava and other pastries.

Flan ~ An open custard tart made in a mold. Caramel cream custard is a popular flan dessert.

Foie gras ~ The enlarged liver of a fattened or force-fed goose.

Frais, fraîche ~ Fresh.

Fraise ~ Strawberry.

Fumet ~ Liquid that gives flavor and body to sauces and stocks. Fish fumet is used to poach fish fillets. It is made from dry white wine, fish stock, and bouquet garni.

Garde manger ~ Pantry area where a cold buffet can be prepared.

Garnish ~ A small amount of a flavorful, edible ingredient added as trimmings to compliment the main dish and enhance its appearance

Ginger ~ A spice from a rhizome of a plant native to China. It is used fresh in Chinese cooking, but can also be used dried or ground.

Glace ~ (Fr) ice cream; also used for cake icing.

Glaze ~ It is used as a coating to give a shiny appearance to roasts, poultry, custards, jams and jellies.

Glutinous rice ~ Sticky rice used by the Japanese to make sushi and rice cakes.

Gorgonzola ~ A strong Italian blue cheese.

Guava ~ A tropical fruit shrub. It makes delicious jellies.

Gumbo ~ A Cajun or Creole soup thickened with okra or filé powder. Gumbo is an African word for okra.

Habañero ~ An extremely hot chili pepper, oval-shaped and smaller than the jalapeno. The color changes from green to orange and red upon ripening. It is used in stews and sauces.

Haddock ~ It is closely related to a cod but smaller and thin-skinned. It is excellent broiled in butter.

Halibut ~ The largest member of the flounder family. It can be smoked, broiled or grilled.

Hoisin sauce ~ It is used in Chinese cooking to flavor sauces and marinades. It is a thick brown sauce made from soybeans, garlic, sugar and salt.

CULINARY TERMS FREQUENTLY USED BY MISSISSIPPI CHEFS

Hollandaise ~ It is one of the classic sauces in French cooking. It is made from an emulsion of hot clarified butter and eggs lightly heated until it begins to have the consistency of a smooth custard. It also contains lemons and shallots.

Haricot vert ~ Green string beans.

Infuse ~ To soak spices, herbs, or vegetables in a liquid to extract their flavor.

Jalapeño ~ A very hot green chili pepper generally used fresh, but also available canned.

Jambalaya ~ A Cajun dish of rice, shrimp, crawfish, sausage, chicken and beans, seasoned with Creole spices.

Julienne ~ Vegetables and meats cut into thin strips.

Kalamata ~ Kalamata are large black Greek olives.

Kale ~ A frilly, leafy vegetable of the cabbage family.

Leek ~ A member of the onion family. Leeks are used in soups, casseroles, etc.

Loganberry ~ Similar to a blackberry and raspberry. It can be served with cream as a dessert, a filling for tarts or as a cream pudding.

Mandoline ~ A tool use to cut vegetables evenly into thick or thin slices.

Mango ~ A delicious, sweet tropical fruit served as desserts and also used in cooking preserves and chutneys.

Marinade ~ A liquid, including seasonings, to flavor and tenderize fish, meat and poultry before cooking.

Marinara ~ A tomato sauce flavored with herbs and garlic, usually served with pasta.

Merlot ~ A red-wine grape that produces a fruity flavor.

Mesclun ~ A mixture of wild salad leaves and herbs. They are generally served with dressing containing walnut or olive oil and wine vinegar.

Mirepoix ~ A mixture of cut vegetables – usually carrot, onion, celery and sometimes ham or bacon – used to flavor sauces and as a bed on which to braise meat.

Mirin ~ A sweet and syrupy Japanese rice wine used for cooking.

Mornay ~ A classic French sauce; béchamel sauce to which egg yolks, cream and cheese are added.

Oregano ~ Oregano is an herb very similar to marjoram but more pungent. It is widely used in Greek and Italian cooking.

Orzo ~ Rice-shaped pasta.

Paprika ~ A variety of red bell pepper that has been dried and powdered and made into a cooking spice. It is used in making Hungarian goulash, etc.

Penne ~ tube-shaped pasta cut on the diagonal.

Peperonata ~ An Italian dish of bell peppers, tomatoes, onions and garlic cooked in olive oil. It can be served hot or cold.

Pepperoncini ~ A hot red chili pepper served fresh or dried.

Pepperoni ~ An Italian salami of pork and beef seasoned with hot red peppers.

Phyllo ~ See filo.

CULINARY TERMS FREQUENTLY USED BY MISSISSIPPI CHEFS

Picante Sauce ~ Hot spicy tomato-based sauce.

Piccata ~ Veal scallop.

Plantain ~ A tropical fruit similar to the banana.

Poisson ~ French for fish.

Poivre ~ French for pepper.

Pomodoro ~ Italian for tomato.

Porcino ~ Italian for a wild mushroom.

Portobello mushroom ~ A large cultivated field mushroom which has a firm texture and is ideal for grilling and as a meat substitute.

Prawn ~ A large shrimp.

Prosciutto ~ Italian ham cured by salting and air drying.

Purée ~ Food that is pounded, finely chopped, or processed through a blender or strained through a sieve to achieve a smooth consistency.

Quiche ~ A custard-filled tart with a savory flavor.

Radicchio ~ A reddish member of the chicory family used as a garnish or for salad.

Ratatouille ~ A mixture of tomatoes, eggplants, zucchini, bell peppers and onions cooked in olive oil. It can be served hot or cold.

Reduce ~ To boil down a liquid to thicken its consistency and concentrate its flavor.

Relleno ~ Stuffing.

Remoulade ~ One of the classic French sauces. It is made from mayonnaise seasoned with chopped eggs and gherkins, parsley, capers, tarragon and shallots. It is served with shellfish, vegetables and cold meats.

Rice wine ~ Distilled from fermented rice.

Ricotta ~ The word ricotta means "recooked" in Italian. It is a soft cheese made from whey. It has a slightly sweet taste.

Rigatoni ~ Italian macaroni.

Risotto ~ An Italian arborio rice dish simmered slowly.

Roghan josh ~ A spicy lamb dish from India, red in color and served with rice.

Rosemary ~ A shrub with aromatic needle-like leaves. It is used fresh or dried as an herb, especially with lamb, pork and veal.

Rouille ~ A spicy red pepper and garlic mayonnaise.

Roux (Fr) ~ A mixture of flour and fat (usually butter or shortening) cooked together slowly to form a thickening agent for sauces, gumbos, and other soups.

Sec ~ Means dry.

Shallot ~ A sweet member of the onion family. It has a more delicate flavor than regular onions. It is used extensively in French cooking.

Shiitake ~ It is a dark brown mushroom with a meaty flavor. It is available both fresh and dried. ~ It was originally from Japan but is now cultivated in both America and Europe.

Sommelier ~ (Fr) Wine Steward.

Sorrel ~ A leafy plant often used in salads, soups, omelets, purees and sauces. It has a distinct lemon taste.

CULINARY TERMS FREQUENTLY USED BY MISSISSIPPI CHEFS

Sweat ~ To sauté in a covered vessel until natural juices are exuded.

Tartare ~ Tartare sauce is made with mayonnaise, egg yolks, chopped onions, capers and chives. It is often served with fish, meat and poultry.

Tasso ~ A highly seasoned Cajun sausage made from pork or beef.

Thyme ~ A herb with a pungent smell that belongs to the same family as mint. It is used in soups, stocks, casseroles and stews.

Timbale ~ (Fr) Metal mold shaped like a drum.

Tofu ~ It is a white Japanese bean curd made from minced soy beans boiled in water then strained and coagulated with sea water. It is soft and easily digested.

Tomatillo ~ Mexican fruit related to the tomato. It is often used in salsa, salads, sauces, etc.

Toufflé ~ Similar to soufflé.

Tournedos ~ A trimmed cut of beef or veal fillet.

Veal ~ The meat of milk-fed baby beef.

Vermicelli ~ A thin Italian pasta.

Vinaigrette ~ A basic dressing of oil and vinegar with salt, pepper, herbs and sometimes mustard.

White sauce ~ Béchamel or velouté sauce, both made from roux.

Zabaglione ~ A rich Italian custard made of egg yolks beaten with Marsala wine and sugar until very thick.

Zest ~ The outer skin of citrus where the important oils have accumulated.

REGIONAL INDEX

Old Covered Bridge, Brookhaven, Mississippi

Pilgrimage Headquarters, Stanton Hall, Natchez, Mississippi

PLEASE SEND ME:

_____ copies of **Fine Dining Mississippi Style** @ $29.95 each $ _____

Tennessee residents add sales tax @ $ 2.62 each $ _____

Add shipping & handling @ $ 4.50 each $ _____

Total Enclosed $ _____

Mail cookbook(s) to:

Name _____

Address _____

City _____ State _____ Zip _____

Make checks payable to Starr★Toof.

Charge to ☐ Visa ☐ MasterCard Valid thru _____

Account Number _____ Signature _____

Mail to: Toof Cookbooks
Starr★Toof
670 South Cooper Street
Memphis, Tennessee 38104

PLEASE SEND ME:

_____ copies of **Fine Dining Mississippi Style** @ $29.95 each $ _____

Tennessee residents add sales tax @ $ 2.62 each $ _____

Add shipping & handling @ $ 4.50 each $ _____

Total Enclosed $ _____

Mail cookbook(s) to:

Name _____

Address _____

City _____ State _____ Zip _____

Make checks payable to Starr★Toof.

Charge to ☐ Visa ☐ MasterCard Valid thru _____

Account Number _____ Signature _____

Mail to: Toof Cookbooks
Starr★Toof
670 South Cooper Street
Memphis, Tennessee 38104